THE LITERACY COACH'S HANDBOOK

SOLVING PROBLEMS IN THE TEACHING OF LITERACY
Cathy Collins Block, Series Editor

RECENT VOLUMES

The Literacy Coach's

HANDBOOK

*A Guide to
Research-Based Practice*

Sharon Walpole
Michael C. McKenna

THE GUILFORD PRESS
New York   London

To the literacy coaches with whom we have worked

© 2004 The Guilford Press
A Division of Guilford Publications, Inc.
72 Spring Street, New York, NY 10012
www.guilford.com

Printed in the United States of America

This book is printed on acid-free paper.

Last digit is print number: 9 8 7 6 5 4 3

Library of Congress Cataloging-in-Publication Data

Walpole, Sharon.
   The literacy coach's handbook : a guide to research-based practice / Sharon Walpole, Michael C. McKenna.
      p. cm.—(Solving problems in the teaching of literacy)
   Includes bibliographical references and index.
   ISBN 1-59385-034-4 (pbk.: alk. paper)
   1. Reading (Elementary)—United States. 2. Literacy programs—United States—Administration. 3. Group work in education—United States. I. McKenna, Michael C. II. Title. III. Series.
   LB1573.W364 2004
   372.41—dc22
                                                                 2004003282

About the Authors

Sharon Walpole, PhD, is Assistant Professor in the School of Education at the University of Delaware, where she teaches graduate and undergraduate courses in literacy education. Upon graduation from the University of Virginia, she spent 3 years as a full-time school administrator working with elementary teachers to develop schoolwide reading programs. She has worked with literacy coaches in Iowa, Virginia, Georgia, and Delaware as part of the Reading Excellence Act and Reading First Reforms. She was a member of the Center for Improvement of Early Reading Achievement research team studying the characteristics of Beat the Odds schools. Her research interests include the design, implementation, and evaluation of schoolwide reading programs.

Michael C. McKenna, PhD, has been Professor of Reading at Georgia Southern University since 1989. For 12 years prior to that, he was Professor of Reading at Wichita State University. He has authored, coauthored, or edited 12 books and more than 80 articles, chapters, and technical reports on a range of literacy topics. He recently coedited the *Handbook of Literacy and Technology,* and was awarded both the National Reading Conference's Edward Fry Book Award and the American Library Association's Award for Outstanding Academic Books. His research interests include comprehension in content settings, reading attitudes, technology applications, and beginning reading.

Preface

The Literacy Coach's Handbook represents a best-evidence summary of a series of topics that we have found to be essential to address in school-based reforms. For literacy coaches, we hope it is an informed overview of important aspects of their work and also a resource to guide their continued professional development. It is also an initial effort to summarize the research that is most useful to our work, the wisdom of practice that we are gaining from and with literacy coaches, and the challenges we still face.

In Chapter 1, we begin with the story of one literacy coach as she moved from her university-based undergraduate training to the classroom, to important professional networks, and to her job as coach with its many challenges. We know many coaches have had similar developmental experiences and few have had the chance to reflect with others about those transitions. This chapter could be compared with rich descriptive studies of the experiences of other coaches in other settings.

In Chapter 2, we define a schoolwide reading program as something that cannot be bought from any vendor of literacy materials, however well constructed. We argue that a schoolwide program starts with an assessment system to identify the needs of the children to be served and then locates and allocates all available resources: time, groupings, and materials. The schoolwide program also addresses the needs of adults in the school by scheduling time and allocating resources to support their continued growth as professionals. This chapter could be compared with school-based case studies to examine the costs and benefits of different choices in allocating and coordinating resources.

In Chapter 3, we identify and summarize important sources of research-based advice about literacy development that are useful in schools. This advice, while necessary to the work of a literacy coach, will not be completely sufficient without expansion. In fact, we hope that the research summarized in this chapter will be quickly expanded with new findings, as researchers learn more about what makes a difference in the literacy lives of children and teachers. Therefore, we have also included strategies for locating information in handbooks, books, and journals.

Chapter 4 is a primer on assessment as it pertains to schoolwide initiatives. Assessment in schools is complex, and it is particularly so for the literacy coach. Viewed at the school and classroom levels, assessment data can establish goals for schoolwide programs, and it can provide access to appropriate instruction and intervention for all children. Assessment can also prove divisive. We (and, we hope, others) will continue to examine this issue and to write about assessment systems that provide essential information to answer important questions about achievement in schools and its impact on children and teachers.

In Chapter 5, we address the issue of instructional schedules. We consider both the scheduling of protected time for literacy instruction and intervention in whole-group and needs-based groups across grade levels and the content of that instruction. We provide some scheduling choices that we have personally used with success, and then we share sample schedules created by literacy coaches dealing with specific resources in specific schools. We know literacy coaches who identify the creation of an elegant school-level schedule as one of the most crucial steps toward establishing their reading programs. They (and we) would benefit from evaluations of the relationship between specific scheduling choices and growth in student achievement and additional case studies of scheduling successes and failures.

Chapter 6 discusses scheduling issues within grade levels and classrooms. We identify essential components of instruction in a comprehensive reading program, and then nest them within grouping configurations and within the precious minutes available for instruction. Our goal in this chapter is to provide a model that each literacy coach must revisit and refine time and time again, making it more and more specifically geared toward the resources in his or her reading program. This chapter is about choices; we know that it could be compared with alternative options, and we invite others to publish those options.

In Chapter 7, we take on one of the many obstacles in school reforms—the issue of materials selection. While we identify many sources that literacy coaches might consult for information about commercial materials for literacy instruction, we actually argue that true coaching demands knowledge not of the "ratings" of materials but of their actual day-to-day contents. We provide a template for close examination of literacy materials that we have used to help coaches make informed choices and also to better understand the choices that they have made. Like most of our colleagues, we want teachers to have materials consistent with research and with best practice; however, we know that *how* materials are used is more important than *what* they are. This chapter would benefit from comparisons with new research on the effects of particular instructional materials on various indices of literacy achievement.

Despite the best efforts of teachers and coaches, some children still require intervention in order to achieve and maintain adequate literacy skills and strategies. In

Chapter 8, we summarize the work of researchers who have helped us to conceptualize intervention and then we provide an overview of potential contexts for intervention during and after school. We also describe interventions that have been successful and provide sample intervention plans targeting specific areas of literacy achievement. This is an area in which new research is sorely needed, especially research on interventions for English language learners, special education students, and preschool children, and interventions that target vocabulary development.

In Chapter 9, we review research on professional development and present our own conception of the literacy coach as designer of a professional development system responsive to the needs of adults and children. Such a system combines work outside the classroom to build knowledge of literacy achievement, literacy development, and literacy instruction with work inside the classroom in modeling, observation, and feedback. We place this chapter close to the end of this volume because literacy coaches cannot actually craft coherent professional development systems until they have addressed the issues identified in previous chapters. This chapter, though, is the heart of the literacy coach's work—the part that is truly new and exciting to us. Unfortunately, compared to the other issues addressed in this book, this is the area about which research gives the least direction. It will take the combined efforts of many, many researchers and many, many literacy coaches to produce descriptive and empirical evidence of the effects of different professional development systems on the knowledge and skills of teachers and on the literacy achievement of children.

In our final chapter, Chapter 10, we introduce an issue which we have only just started to grapple with—the issue of levels of leadership and their interaction in the success and failure of school-based reforms. We know that the most successful coaches with whom we've worked have established their own leadership, but we also know that they have done it in decidedly different ways. Some have assumed administrative authority, some are partners with administrators, and some are simply knowledgeable, flexible instructional role models. Identifying some potential routes to successful leadership is the goal of this chapter. Once these routes are identified conceptually, we know that they could be investigated descriptively and empirically.

We are committed to learning more about extensive, supportive, and effective professional development efforts in schools—efforts that improve the work of teachers and the literacy opportunities of children. We maintain that literacy coaches can be change agents. However, we need to work harder to understand the roles that coaches might play, the choices that coaches might make, and the effects of those choices on schools, teachers, and children. We invite you to add your voice to the voices of coaches quoted in this book (all of whom are real but protected by pseudonyms) and to our voices, by tackling real problems in real schools and by writing about your successes and failures. That is the work that we have begun here.

Contents

CHAPTER 1

What Is a Literacy Coach?

> Once there was a peddler who sold caps.
> But he was not like an ordinary peddler,
> carrying his wares on his back.
> He carried them on top of his head.
> First he had on his own checked cap,
> then a bunch of gray caps,
> then a bunch of blue caps,
> and, on the very top,
> a bunch of red caps.
> —SLOBODKINA (1940, n.p.)

For a literacy coach, a stack of caps might be most appropriate. A literacy coach is not a principal, not an assistant principal, not a reading specialist, and not a teacher. On a given day, he or she probably dons each of these caps, but not for long. In fact, a literacy coach is fashioning a new cap—one that fits better than any of those, and one that is sensitive to the needs of the teachers in a particular school building. The purpose of this chapter is to provide an introduction to the many roles of the literacy coach through an overview of professional standards and also through the eyes of a literacy coach. The chapters that follow will provide more specific discussion of the knowledge and skills that literacy coaches must have in each of their roles.

Christy Harris (a pseudonym) is a literacy coach. Her job, funded by the Reading Excellence Act, is to direct a reform of the elementary reading program in a rural school. Her school is small, with 369 students in grades K–5, 20 classroom teachers, two special educators, and four Title I teachers. In January 2001, her school was in trouble. The information below comes from documents drafted at that time.

Mt. Pleasant Elementary (again, a pseudonym) is isolated geographically, and many of its families are struggling. There is no public transportation. There are no day care centers or licensed in-home day care providers in the community. Few children attend the free prekindergarten program offered at the school; the program is not full. Most parents are employed, but there are few jobs paying living wages. Twenty-two percent of Carsen (another pseudonym) County's children live in poverty; 55% qualify for free or reduced-price lunches. Forty-four percent of Carsen County residents aged 25 or older have not earned a high school diploma.

The school-based team at Mt. Pleasant identified many problems within the building. Curriculum was vague and implemented haphazardly within and across grade levels. Teachers had insufficient professional development. There were few materials for implementation of guided oral reading or fluency work, and the existing phonics program was not implemented with fidelity. There was no consistent work to develop vocabulary knowledge, even though children appeared to have weak vocabularies. Few teachers understood or taught comprehension strategies.

Test data supported this fairly bleak picture. Mt. Pleasant Elementary School was in the fourth year of Title I "needs improvement" status. Table 1.1 provides mean third-grade scores on the Stanford Achievement Test—Ninth Edition in 2000. The mean for Mt. Pleasant was far below the national norm in all areas of the curriculum. No classroom-based data were regularly collected at Mt. Pleasant to inform instruction for struggling children.

In the pages that follow, we will update you on progress at Mt. Pleasant. Christy Harris, Mt. Pleasant's literacy coach, is driving the reform in collaboration with an outstanding principal. Our intent is that you will be inspired by her story, and that you will learn with her and from her.

TABLE 1.1. Mean Percentile Scores on Stanford Achievement Test—Ninth Edition for Mt. Pleasant Third Graders, 2000

Subtest	Score
Reading	33
Language Arts	29
Mathematics	19
Science	30
Social Studies	32

LITERACY COACH AS LEARNER

Successful literacy coaches must make a substantial and permanent commitment to their own learning. That message is surely not new, but it is communicated more loudly, aggressively, and specifically now than ever before. Literacy coaches are responsible for understanding both what is known about the process of reading and the teaching of readers, and what is learned as that knowledge base expands. To illustrate, we will trace the evolution of language about phonics instruction through several widely distributed publications about the content knowledge required of literacy leaders in schools.

In 1996, the International Reading Association and the National Council for Teachers of English teamed to produce literacy standards for students in kindergarten through grade 12. These standards were broad and focused on meaning construction across texts; the goal was to establish standards for readers and writers that could be applied across ages and stages of reading development and across states. The third standard, quoted below, referred vaguely to the use of phonics:

> Students apply a wide range of strategies to comprehend, interpret, evaluate, and appreciate texts. They draw on their prior experience, their interactions with other readers and writers, their knowledge of word meanings and of other texts, their word identification strategies, and their understanding of textual features (e.g., sound–letter correspondences, sentence structure, context, graphics). (International Reading Association & National Council of Teachers of English, 1996, p. 25)

Clearly, phonics is one of many textual features that students can use to understand text; the standard's implication for teaching was that teachers should know about phonics as one of those systems that readers might use. What they should know about it, though, was not specified.

Later documents were much more specific about what teachers should know about phonics and be able to do with children. In 1998, the Professional Standards and Ethics Committee of the International Reading Association published specific skill-based competencies for reading specialists and reading coordinators. Some of those were more specific to phonics. In fact, these reading professionals needed comprehensive understanding of instruction in word identification, vocabulary, and spelling, defined below:

6.1 teach students to monitor their own word identification through the use of syntactic, semantic, and grapho-phonemic relations;
6.2 use phonics to teach students to use their knowledge of letter/sound correspondence to identify sounds in the construction of meaning;
6.3 teach students to use context to identify and define unfamiliar words;
6.4 guide students to refine their spelling knowledge through reading and writing;

6.5 teach students to recognize and use various spelling patterns in the English language as an aid to word identification; and

6.6 employ effective techniques and strategies for the ongoing development of independent vocabulary acquisition. (International Reading Association, Professional Standards and Ethics Committee, 1998, pp. 14–15)

Phonics, although targeted more specifically, was still only one language system—one that readers should be able to coordinate with syntax and semantics in word recognition. The mandate to reading specialists and coordinators was that they could teach children how to use these various language systems.

Teaching Reading Is Rocket Science (American Federation of Teachers, 1999) took a different approach. In that document, the entire language structure of English—with phonetics, phonology, morphology, orthography, semantics, and syntax and text structure—was clearly targeted, with specific knowledge and skills in each area. The document called for a whole-scale refocusing of teacher-training programs and professional development programs to expand this knowledge base. Specific teacher skills in the area of orthography, quoted below, provide a sample:

Choose examples of spelling correspondences, patterns, rules, and exceptions.
Recognize and sort predictable and unpredictable words.
Adopt and learn a systematic plan for teaching decoding and spelling.
Link decoding and spelling instruction.
Evaluate the design of instructional materials. (American Federation of Teachers, 1999, p. 19)

Semantics and syntax were likewise defined and described, but never as language systems readers would coordinate in word recognition. The emphasis was clearly on phonics.

The Learning First Alliance (1998) also abandoned this vague language about the role of phonics in word recognition: "The bottom line is that children have to learn to sound out words rather than relying on context and pictures as their primary strategies to determine meaning" (p. 12). The alliance targeted professional development for current teachers, recommending substantial commitment to teacher training at school, in an effort to coordinate standards, assessments, and curriculum. They identified models for that professional development with significant follow-up activities. And they specified the content for that professional development as separate categories of knowledge and skills, with potential professional development strategies for each category. That system of knowledge, skills, and professional development is presented in Table 1.2 for phonics and decoding.

By 2003, the International Reading Association again revised its *Standards for Reading Professionals* to focus more squarely on candidate performance. This time, rather than define word recognition processes in very specific cognitive language, the document referred directly to large-scale research syntheses in this area.

TABLE 1.2. Phonics and Decoding Competencies

Teacher knowledge	Teacher skills	Possible professional development exercises
Understand speech-to-print correspondence at the sound, syllable pattern, and morphological levels.	Choose examples of words that illustrate sound–symbol, syllable, and morpheme patterns.	Practice various active techniques including sound blending, structural word analysis, word building, and word sorting.
Identify and describe the developmental progression in which orthographic knowledge is generally acquired.	Select and deliver appropriate lessons according to students' levels of spelling, phonics, and word identification skills.	Identify, on the basis of student reading and writing, the appropriate level at which to instruct.
Understand and recognize how beginner texts are linguistically organized—by spelling pattern, word frequency, and language pattern.	Explicitly teach the sequential blending of individual sounds into a whole word.	Observe, demonstrate, and practice error correction strategies.
Recognize the differences among approaches to teaching word attack (implicit, explicit, analytic, synthetic, etc.).	Teach active exploration of word structure with a variety of techniques.	Search a text for examples of words that exemplify an orthographic concept; lead discussions about words.
Understand why instruction in word attack should be active and interactive.	Enable students to use word attack strategies as they read connected text.	Review beginner texts to discuss their varying uses in reading instruction.

Note. From Learning First Alliance (2000, p. 15). Copyright 2000 by Learning First Alliance. Reprinted by permission.

Table 1.3 provides a bibliography of those works in which this knowledge base is communicated. Taken together, they represent a history of reading research; in accord with these standards, a reading specialist or administrator would understand the current scientific basis for describing word recognition, and would also be able to describe the development of this scientific knowledge base over the past three decades.

This gradual movement—from a view of word recognition as a coordinated cueing system that teachers help children to orchestrate, to a focus on specific content and process knowledge for decoding—did have effects on the knowledge and training of teachers. Teachers were trained in specific years by teacher educators with specific access to, knowledge of, and biases about reading development. Few teachers had access to continued training as the knowledge base developed. Many

TABLE 1.3. References Informing the 2003 International Reading Association's Standards

Handbooks of reading research

Pearson, P. D., Barr, R., Kamil, M. L., & Mosenthal, P. (Eds.). (1984). *Handbook of reading research*. New York: Longman.

Barr, R., Kamil, M. L., Mosenthal, P. B., & Pearson, P. D. (Eds.). (1991). *Handbook of reading research* (Vol. 2). White Plains, NY: Longman.

Kamil, M. L., Mosenthal, P. B., Pearson, P. D., & Barr, R. (Eds.). (2000). *Handbook of reading research* (Vol. 3). Mahwah, NJ: Erlbaum.

Theoretical models and processes of reading

Singer, H., & Ruddell, R. B. (1976). *Theoretical models and processes of reading* (2nd ed.). Newark, DE: International Reading Association.

Singer, H., & Ruddell, R. B. (1985). *Theoretical models and processes of reading* (3rd ed.). Newark, DE: International Reading Association.

Ruddell, R. B., Ruddell, M. R., & Singer, H. (1994). *Theoretical models and processes of reading* (4th ed.). Newark, DE: International Reading Association.

Preventing reading difficulties in young children

Snow, C. E., Burns, M. S., & Griffin, P. (Eds.). (1998). *Preventing reading difficulties in young children*. Washington, DC: National Academy Press.

Report of the national reading panel

National Reading Panel (NRP). (2000). *Teaching children to read: An evidence-based assessment of the scientific research literature on reading and its implications for reading instruction*. (NIH Publication No. 00-4754). Washington, DC: U.S. Department of Health and Human Services.

Handbook of early literacy research

Neuman, S. B., & Dickinson, D. K. (Eds.). (2001). *Handbook of early literacy research*. New York: Guilford Press.

---

teachers learned to support student decoding by teaching them to rely on syntax and semantics; few developed comprehensive knowledge of the orthographic system. Christy Harris was no exception.

Christy had always been aggressive about her own learning. She graduated from a teachers' college in 1990 with a BS in elementary education and started her teaching career at Mt. Pleasant. Like all first-year teachers, she devoted much of her energy that year to just getting through the day. Falls turned quickly to summers, though, and Christy gained experience and confidence, building classroom learning communities with children in kindergarten, in first grade, and in second grade.

By 1992 Christy had more questions than answers. She started a master's degree in an extension program of a regional university. She attended classes part-time, taking two courses each semester and three each summer. In 1994, she earned her master's degree in elementary education. In terms of early reading development, Christy learned many of the basics of whole-language instruction, and she recognized the need for authentic children's literature, but she acquired little practical information about teaching reading. At the time Christy finished her master's program, only four of the nine works cited as the current knowledge base for reading professionals (see Table 1.3) had even been published.

Christy was still not satisfied. In the summer of 1999, she began to explore "balanced literacy" programs. A state department of education teacher trainer encouraged her to think about dividing her literacy time into "Four Blocks": Guided Reading, Self-Selected Reading, Writing, and Working with Words (Cunningham, Hall, & Sigmon, 1999). What really appealed to Christy about the Four Blocks approach was that it offered her a chance to both balance her time and to attend more to phonics instruction. She also appreciated the Self-Selected Reading component, which encouraged students to make better use of her classroom library. It was her first introduction to the teaching of writing; she had not taught writing at all. Four Blocks was an important steppingstone for Christy.

She quickly learned that there were teacher-friendly professional resources available to guide implementation of Four Blocks (e.g., Cunningham, Hall, & Heggie, 1994; Hall, Cunningham, & McIntyre, 2002), and also Web-based networks to support her (e.g., http://teachers.net; http://www.wfu.edu/~cunningh/fourblocks). Christy bought and read the books, participated actively in Web-based discussions, and forged connections with teachers and teacher trainers from various states. By the summer of 2000, she was making professional presentations at schools as they implemented Four Blocks programs.

Christy's own interpretation of the Four Blocks structure is presented in Figure 1.1. She set up a literacy environment in which she observed children in their own reading and writing, and taught short lessons to address needs that she noticed. As Christy became more comfortable with management of her own Four Blocks, she became less comfortable with the quality of the comprehension instruction she was providing. She again looked for new ideas. She found a professional book, *Mosaic of Thought* (Keene & Zimmerman, 1997), to inform her work. As she had done with Four Blocks, she had Web-based discussions with other teachers about using strategies from *Mosaic of Thought*, and she began to include comprehension strategy instruction in her Guided Reading block.

Although Christy had earned a master's degree, discovered a classroom-based curriculum on her own, entered a professional network, begun to work as a consultant, and amassed her own professional library—all evidence of a significant commitment to keeping her own learning up to date—her professional development was just beginning. In the fall of 2001, it switched into high gear. Chapter 3 will summarize much of what Christy learned. Beginning at that time, either directly or indirectly, she was introduced to the rest of the research listed in Table

Guided Reading	Self-Selected Reading
• Christy used a mini-lesson each day to focus on comprehension. • Children read from a basal plus trade books. • Children engaged in choral, echo, and partner reading.	• Children chose books from a rich, literature-oriented classroom library. • Children selected a bag of books to read each week. • Children used the five-finger rule (counting difficult words) to avoid books that were too difficult.
Writing	Working with Words
• Each day, Christy taught a mini-lesson that she found in a teacher's resource book. • Children selected their own topics and genres. • Children wrote freely in journals.	• Christy led word wall activities. • Christy taught mini-lessons on word families. • Children used game-like procedures to work with word families.

FIGURE 1.1. Christy's Four Blocks organization.

1.3. Christy began her literacy coach training. This training, as you will see, corresponded directly to the mandates the International Reading Association had set for reading professionals. Through a combination of learning and doing, Christy became the reading professional that she needed to be. In the following sections, we describe Christy's learning in relation to the International Reading Association's standards[1] available at that time.

LITERACY COACH AS GRANT WRITER

The reading professional will be able to
12.3 supervise, coordinate, and support all services associated with literacy programs (e.g., needs assessment, program development, budgeting and evaluation, and grant and proposal writing.

Frequently, school-level reform efforts require money—money for new curriculum materials, money for additional intervention personnel, money for professional development. State and federal moneys, once available through pro forma grant competitions, are increasingly competitive. They demand extensive research and writing, and they require a commitment to scientifically based practices.

---

[1]The standards at the beginning of each section below are from International Reading Association, Professional Standards and Ethics Committee (1998). Copyright 1998 by the International Reading Association. Reprinted by permission.

In the fall of 2001, Christy joined her school-based team in applying for a competitive grant to reform their reading program. There was little time between the announcement that the funds were available and the date the applications were due. In October 2001, Christy attended her first state-level technical assistance workshop. She left the workshop knowing that she had to start reading in earnest and that there was little choice in what she should read. She started with *Preventing Reading Difficulties in Young Children* (Snow, Burns, & Griffin, 1998). That text introduced Christy to the need for systematic instruction right from the start of school; she learned that parents and preschoolers needed support in language development; and she began to focus her attention both on early intervention and on prevention.

In December 2001, Christy attended a state-level best-practices institute along with two colleagues from her district office, her building principal, and eight teachers from her school. Together they attended research talks, attended information sessions about the grant-writing process, met with state department officials, and plotted. They carried more reading materials home with them: *Teaching Reading Is Rocket Science* (American Federation of Teachers, 1999) and the report of the National Reading Panel (NRP, 2000). When they got home from the conference, there was just over a month until the grant application was due.

Christy's principal realized that this was an enormous opportunity for his school, and that he needed Christy's work to get it finished. He hired a substitute for her classroom in those final weeks. Christy worked as part of a writing team, with the principal, the district curriculum director, a professional from the local community collaborative, and a Title I teacher. Together they wrote, and in the process of writing, they were able to craft a new vision for reading instruction for Mt. Pleasant Elementary.

The grant was submitted January 31, 2001. It contained a comprehensive description of the community, an analysis of 3 years' standardized test data, a survey of current curriculum and practice, and a plan. In a nutshell, the plan promised the following:

- The school would hire a literacy coach.
- The school would restructure its schedule to allow grade-level teams daily common planning periods.
- Teachers would assess student performance in phonemic awareness, phonics, fluency, vocabulary, and comprehension.
- Teachers would deliver phonemic awareness instruction that targeted blending and segmenting.
- Teachers would use a structured phonics program.
- The school would provide teachers with professional development in adapting the phonics program to the specific needs of the students.
- Teachers would use guided oral reading procedures for all students in mate-

rials at the appropriate level, including materials designed to practice phonics patterns in context.

- An intervention team would provide additional assessment and instruction
  to struggling students in small groups in the classroom.
- Teachers would directly explain, model, facilitate guided practice, and plan
  independent application of comprehension strategies.
- Teachers would read aloud daily to build vocabulary knowledge.
- The school would partner with community service providers to offer comprehensive family literacy services directed by a family literacy coordinator.

And then they waited.

By April 2002 (when awards were announced), Christy was already convinced that they had to make their plan a reality, regardless of whether they were
awarded the money. She was convinced that the children of Mt. Pleasant Elementary deserved better instruction. She was also convinced that she had not been using research-based practices in her own classroom. Finally, she was convinced that
she could work with the members of her staff to update their understanding of
reading research and instruction, and that together they could support increased
reading achievement at Mt. Pleasant.

Christy's team did win the support of federal dollars for the project. The
award, over $700,000 for 2 years, meant that the work could start in earnest. In
the chapters that follow, we will share much of the research background necessary
for winning these federal grants, and we will provide resources and models for
school-based teams to plan, write, and implement these grants.

In May, Christy was one of five candidates interviewing for the job of literacy
coach at Mt. Pleasant. She was not a shoo-in; in fact, there were candidates from
other states, and she had to compete for the job. She wanted the job, but she
would have gladly stepped aside for someone with better training. She had read
the federal reports, and she realized that the teachers needed to do different things,
but she was not certain that she knew what those things were. She was most concerned that the literacy coach understand and maintain the vision for change that
had been crafted in the grant application. When Christy was hired as literacy
coach, it was with the understanding that she would continue to be aggressive
about pursuing her own professional development.

That summer, state-level professional development for literacy coaches com-
menced. Their first professional development experience was a summer institute—
a series of eight back-to-back 3-hour sessions. The summer institute was a crash
course in reading research and school change. The sessions began with the story of
a year's work by a literacy coach in a federally funded school reform effort: creating a school-based assessment system; allocating instructional time for students;
creating professional development time for teachers; buying and organizing new

curriculum materials and a new text collection; reframing the curriculum for explicitness in phonemic awareness, decoding, fluency, vocabulary and comprehension; collecting, analyzing, and presenting school-level achievement data; conducting professional development sessions; and observing teachers and providing feedback. It was a lot to think about in 1 week.

At the end of that session, Christy read *Every Child Reading: A Professional Development Guide* (Learning First Alliance, 2000). She completed a survey designed as a response to that document and rated a series of possible professional development experiences as most beneficial to her, moderately beneficial to her, slightly beneficial to her, or unnecessary. In the area of phonemic awareness, she indicated that she needed to learn to critique instruction. For decoding, she wanted to extend her current knowledge to focus more on word-sorting techniques; she needed practice determining reading levels for individual children; she needed to learn about how to review texts for beginning readers for their utility in instruction; and she wanted to learn more about the use of spelling data to inform decoding instruction. For fluency, she really wanted to work on devising a system for collecting data and then interpreting assessment results to identify children for intervention. In the area of vocabulary, Christy wanted very much to learn how to choose words for instruction. For comprehension, Christy was confident in her own knowledge and skills.

LITERACY COACH AS SCHOOL-LEVEL PLANNER

The reading professional will be able to
12.6 plan and implement programs designed to help students improve their reading and writing including those supported by federal, state, and local funding.

Literacy coaches, especially those who work in school-level initiatives funded through state and federal grants, are site-based school reformers. They are charged with working in every classroom so that every teacher can have the support he or she needs to implement a specific, school-level program. They work with all teachers to understand and implement a *schoolwide reading program*—a concept we define in Chapter 2.

After returning from her summer literacy coach training, Christy worked with her building principal to create a school-level schedule conducive to teaching, learning, and professional development. Without any formal training in scheduling, they relied on some general guidance that Christy had gotten in the summer training, and they turned to a third-grade teacher who had a knack for it. Figure 1.2 shows Mt. Pleasant's original basic instructional schedule.

	Kindergarten	First grade	Second grade	Third grade	Fourth grade	Fifth Grade
8:30	Literacy instruction and intervention		Literacy instruction and intervention			Literacy instruction and intervention
9:00					Specials and professional development	
9:30						
10:00						Specials and professional development
10:30		Lunch				
11:00	Lunch					
11:30		Specials and professional development			Lunch	
12:00			Lunch			
12:30		Literacy instruction and intervention		Specials and professional development		Lunch
1:00					Literacy instruction and intervention	
1:30			Specials and professional development			
2:00						
2:30	Specials and professional development					
3:00						

FIGURE 1.2. Mt. Pleasant's instructional schedule.

Christy reframed the schedule for the four teachers who provided reading interventions at Mt. Pleasant. Her goal was to move those interventions into the classrooms. Again, this was no small feat. The planning process was iterative for Christy, and this was not always comfortable for teachers; changes had to be made along the way. There were many obstacles. The main ones were difficulties in meshing the schedule with the rules for intervention provided by the state. Children identified for state-level services had to be served outside of the language arts block and outside of mathematics instruction. That left little time to use. Christy held strongly to her commitment not to pull children out for reading intervention. Interventions were conducted within the language arts block, providing additional instruction for struggling children. The intervention schedule for one Title I teacher at Mt. Pleasant is presented in Figure 1.3.

Finally, Christy had to plan (and replan) her own schedule. She needed to schedule her time so that she could interpret data, observe teachers, and conduct professional development sessions. She realized that this sort of strict scheduling was essential:

Time	Place	Focus
8:45–9:30	First-grade classroom A	Special education intervention
9:30–10:15		Regular education remediation group
10:15–11:00	Kindergarten classroom A	Regular education remediation group
11:00–11:45	Lunch	
11:45–12:30	First-grade classroom B	Regular education remediation group
12:30–1:00		Special education intervention
1:00–1:45	First-grade classroom C	Regular education remediation group
1:45–2:15		Special education intervention
2:15–3:00	First-grade commons	Collaborative planning time
3:00–3:30	Reading room	Individual planning time

FIGURE 1.3. Schedule for K–1 Title I teacher.

"I need to set a schedule. It is so hard not to be crisis-driven. I come in with an agenda and end up in left field. If I set times during the day to do the things I need to do, it will help me (and the teachers) manage my time better."

Christy's dream schedule is presented in Figure 1.4. Even as Christy became more consistent in her use of time, she always had to be flexible and respond to the

Time	Place	Focus
8:15–12:00	Classrooms	Observing, modeling, and coaching in classrooms
12:00–12:45	Lunch	
12:45–2:00	Reading room	Planning for professional development Reading professional literature Selecting, ordering, and organizing curricular materials
2:00–2:45	Reading room	Providing professional development for tutors and intervention providers
2:45–4:30	Library	Monitoring tutors Scoring and interpreting assessments Providing professional development

FIGURE 1.4. Christy's dream schedule.

needs of administrators, teachers, and children. Her morning sessions were often interrupted by meetings with central office personnel and last-minute administrative paperwork. Her lunches were always spent discussing children and instruction with teachers. She learned over time that she could both set a general schedule and respond to individual needs. She compromised this way:

> "I usually have a 'to-do' list, which may or may not get done. If a crisis hits, forget it! One thing I have had to realize with this job is that I never complete anything. That is not necessarily a bad thing. I have had to realize that my job satisfaction must come from evaluating our progress over time, not completing tasks."

LITERACY COACH AS CURRICULUM EXPERT

The reading professional will be able to
12.4 select and evaluate instructional materials for literacy, including those that are technology-based.

Among the barriers to effective literacy instruction are inexplicit, uncoordinated instructional materials. Literacy coaches evaluate curricula currently in place against research-based standards, and help to locate and implement new curricula that are better matched to the research base and to the needs of children.

For Christy, curriculum selection was a high-stakes, expensive game. Her teachers needed the tools to teach children. She selected curriculum materials to correspond with the research that she was learning and with the needs of her teachers and children. We will summarize the research that she reviewed in Chapter 3, and we share the process she used in Chapter 7; Table 1.4 presents a preview.

Christy eventually directed $67,000 of the money in her grant to the purchase of new curriculum materials and leveled classroom libraries. She reviewed these materials on her own, page by page. She participated in two different materials fairs; in a 4-day meeting during the summer of 2002, where she worked as part of a team to examine core reading programs and intervention programs for their match to research; and then in a 2-day institute in January 2003. Christy found that many different publishers had materials consistent with research in specific dimensions. For her school, she chose the program that appeared best integrated in teaching and applying phonics knowledge, and whose comprehension strategy instruction resonated with her; she knew that the program would support her teachers as she built their knowledge of comprehension strategies instruction.

TABLE 1.4. Research That Informs Curriculum Selection

Curriculum area	Relevant findings
Phonemic awareness	• Blending and segmenting are the most important tasks. • Initial lessons should be oral, but later lessons should include manipulation of alphabet letters.
Phonics	• The curriculum must include a preset sequence for introduction of letter sounds. • Instruction in how letters map to sounds must be explicit.
Fluency	• Guided oral reading procedures improve fluency. • Timed repeated-reading procedures improve fluency.
Vocabulary	• New words should be taught before text reading. • Lessons that include definitions and context are most effective.
Comprehension	• Comprehension strategies should be directly explained with declarative, procedural, and conditional knowledge. • Comprehension strategies should be taught before, during, and after reading.

LITERACY COACH AS RESEARCHER

The reading professional will be able to

10.2 administer and use information from norm-referenced tests, criterion-referenced tests, formal and informal inventories, constructed response measures, portfolio-based assessments, student self-evaluations, work/performance samples, observations, anecdotal records, journals and other indicators of student progress to inform instruction and learning.

12.2 adapt instruction to meet the needs of different learners to accomplish different purposes.

12.5 use multiple indicators to determine effectiveness of the literacy curriculum.

14.2 conduct research with a range of methodologies (e.g., ethnographic, descriptive, experimental, or historical).

Literacy coaches are charged with answering questions few PhD-level researchers would be able to answer easily. They are also questions with high-stakes consequences for children.

1. To what extent are teachers able to implement the school's curriculum?
2. To what extent are student needs being addressed by the school's curriculum?
3. In what ways must the curriculum be supported and/or modified to promote both teacher implementation and student achievement?

Building research skills has been extremely challenging work for Christy. Although the model in the federal grant guidelines is clean and sensible, the reality of school-based data collection and analysis is messy. In the summer of 2002, Christy's summer institute experience included a framework for selecting appropriate assessments for phonemic awareness, decoding, fluency, and comprehension for each grade level. She also participated in a calendar-building exercise, where she first marked specific times during the year when data could be reported to various stakeholders (children, parents, teachers, administrators, central office staff, and the state); she then planned backward for the data to be analyzed, entered, and collected, as well as for the training of personnel doing the data collection. Clearly, all of these constraints on the data collection system meant that it was the number one priority.

Christy chose assessments for phonemic awareness, decoding, and fluency that summer. She investigated assessments that researchers had mentioned during the technical assistance workshops. She used the Internet to gain access to test materials and reviews. She contracted for staff training with trainers recommended by the test designers. Initial assessment training was scheduled for teacher workdays before school opened in 2002. Training sessions included both collection and interpretation of the assessment data.

Implementation of the assessment plan was an enormous challenge. Christy decided to use a schoolwide assessment team (SWAT) approach, which we discuss further in Chapter 2. The team members started by establishing interrater reliability. The five testers first worked together: One child was tested by one team member, with the other four observing and shadowing the scoring. They shared their scores and resolved discrepancies. Then they called another child. When they had reached agreement, they began to work as partners, still using one member to test and the other to shadow and score. Finally, they were ready to work alone. This procedure established reliability in the initial data set, and it also established trust and respect among the team members.

After the data were collected, Christy struggled with some of the nuts-and-bolts issues in data management. She struggled to organize her data efficiently on the computer. Some of the big issues were managing such a large data set and providing timely classroom reports to teachers. By the middle of the year, Christy was working with technology specialists in her district's central office to design a more user-friendly system that was geared directly to her needs.

Once the data were organized, Christy summarized the results and shared them with her teachers. The first wave of data was very powerful for the teachers. They saw that the children's performance was unacceptable, and they felt compelled to do something about it. As the year progressed, teachers realized that assessment-based instruction was very difficult. Christy commented:

"One of the biggest weaknesses I see across the board is the fact that most all of our teachers teach books and programs, not kids. There is very little informal assessment going on in classrooms. Teachers seem reluctant to evaluate kids' work to determine if their teaching is causing students to learn or not. And when they do evaluate, they seem unsure of how to plan for small groups or redesign lessons to teach students the skills they aren't getting with whole-class instruction. Breaking the barrier to show teachers how to teach small groups effectively will be a huge jump in the project. Getting them to use informal assessments will help our students gain by leaps and bounds. One teacher has discussed how difficult it is to do (and I realize this is so)—but I pointed out to her how much better it will be to know each step of the way how the students are doing, rather than teaching the book all year, coming down to the end, and suddenly realizing that several children don't know any of the material that they have covered all year."

This reluctance was gradually replaced with confidence. By the spring of year 1, teachers reported that the biggest change at the school was the use of data to drive instruction. Even though changing their instruction to meet student needs continued to be difficult, teachers were convinced that it was essential. Teachers began to ask for more data and to use these data to design balanced, heterogeneous classrooms for the coming year.

Data analysis led to constant changes in the plan. For example, at the beginning of October, Christy analyzed developmental spelling data (Ganske, 2000) and realized that first graders were not able to apply specific phonics features in spelling that they had already been taught in their phonics program. She purchased additional reading materials to allow children to have more practice with these features; she established a greater emphasis on spelling in the curriculum; and she worked with the first-grade team to build these changes into their instructional schedule and into the interventions.

Adjustments were made in other segments of the curriculum as well. Data drove adjustments, and teachers became partners with Christy in data collection and in data analysis:

"Once the initial fluency assessment was given, we determined that most of our kids were reading accurately, but with depressed rates. Using our core materials, as well as passages with the same phonic patterns, teachers now assess one child per day (they usually do more) and record their speed and accuracy. In addition, they do various interventions with students. They can choose between timed partner readings, repeated readings, and group timed readings. They turn in a chart to me and they have graphs to use with individual students. All teachers are sharing results and setting goals with students."

In her role as researcher, Christy had to learn to observe teachers in ways that were helpful to them. She had to negotiate her role as observer, and doing this was a roller-coaster ride. At first, she observed but was unwilling to provide any specific feedback. Later, she observed but was too critical. Gradually, she worked together with other literacy coaches and with her principal to build a metaphor for observation. In terms of observation, Christy was the "good cop." She would observe with these questions: "What can I learn about the curriculum today that can help me to understand its strengths and weaknesses?" and "What can I learn about individual teachers today that can make my professional development more effective?" She had to abandon the "bad cop" role, which included observations to answer this question: "Is this individual fulfilling his or her professional responsibilities?" In order to do that, her principal had to assume the role of bad cop. His observations of teachers became linked more closely to their instruction and to the instructional initiative at the school. Christy noted that, by December, the system was working:

"I think I have gotten bogged down, and I am now back on track. I realized that I have turned into the bad cop. I need to step back and realize that my job is not to enforce, but to model and offer professional development."

As Christy grew into her role as researcher, drawing upon her skills as planner and curriculum expert, she approached roadblocks in various places in the curriculum. She eventually realized that the data supported her work with teachers:

"If student learning becomes the focus, then I can use shared decision making to bring more teachers on board and cause 'buy-in' to what I am doing. For instance, I plan to share info about our fluency weaknesses and assessment data to get input from the team as to the direction of staff development. In addition, this can help pave the way for study groups and small-group staff development on a needs- and interests-based model. Many of the teachers are beginning to recognize areas in which they need more knowledge, which allows me to pull appropriate resources to meet these needs."

What Christy was learning was that the road to school change was long and winding, but that data she collected about teachers' instruction and children's learning provided her with a road map.

LITERACY COACH AS TEACHER

The reading professional will be able to
13.2 initiate, implement, and evaluate professional development programs.
13.3 provide professional development experiences that help emphasize the dynamic interaction among prior knowledge, experience, and the school context as well as among other aspects of reading development.
13.5 use multiple indicators to judge professional growth.

The No Child Left Behind Act of 2001 is bringing unprecedented funding for professional development to struggling schools. The legislation itself *requires* districts to provide professional development to K–3 teachers and special educators. The goal of the legislation is to provide sufficient support to develop the knowledge and skills of classroom teachers so that they can change student achievement. We will describe models for providing this type of site-based staff development in schools in Chapter 9.

Christy designed a professional support system for her teachers. First, she arranged for curriculum representatives to show teachers how to use new materials in their classrooms. The goal of these sessions was to support immediate changes in teacher practice. Christy was able to work with these representatives so that their presentations were targeted directly to the needs of the schools, and also to the demands of the grant to use scientifically based instructional methods.

Christy used study groups to provide professional development herself. These sessions were conducted initially after school every week. By January, Christy realized that she needed more time and that this time should be during the school day. She began to meet with each grade-level team weekly for 45 minutes. The goal of these sessions was to build teacher knowledge targeted specifically to the needs of each grade level.

Christy brought professional resources into the building. She purchased professional books consistent with the initiative, and she lent them to teachers. She also subscribed to *The Reading Teacher* for the school and joined the International Reading Association's Book Club.

Christy used her role as teacher to address things she was learning in her role as researcher. She was concerned that teachers were starting to recognize that students needed intervention, but they were unable to provide it. She saw that as a clear indication that she needed to provide professional development:

> "It is a management issue. I see the need for professional development in managing small groups. They have little experience (nor do I) in managing several groups. I would like some guidance here as to resources and ways to help them. They recognize the need, but it is a management nightmare for them. I can sympathize, and am trying to decide how to get the resources they need to be able to do this effectively."

Christy learned to manage her professional development sessions so that they were more interactive. She learned that teachers could work together productively, especially if they worked in groups to reflect on the implications of research in their classroom work. She also learned that she had to be very specific about how new ideas could be addressed within the framework of the curriculum and materials that they were using.

THE LITERACY COACH: A NEW ROLE

In 2000, the International Reading Association released a position statement on the roles of the reading specialist. This statement argued for a three-part role, with leadership skills, diagnosis and assessment skills, and instructional skills all serving the overall goal of improving student learning. In this book, we will argue that the role of the literacy coach is to fulfill that leadership role in very specific ways. We will argue that knowledge of diagnosis and assessment and knowledge of instruction are necessary but insufficient for literacy coaches. We will argue that a literacy coach is a learner, a grant writer, a planner, a researcher, and a teacher.

Literacy coaches are the people who are directing continual school improvement work at the state, district, and school levels. Through our work at the federal level with the Reading Excellence Act program and the Reading First program and through our collaboration with literacy coaches in Iowa, Virginia, Georgia, and Delaware, we have learned some important lessons about that work. We hope that this book will support professionals who wish to take on this role. Our caps are off to them already.

CHAPTER 2

What Is a Schoolwide Reading Program?

Despite what vendors of reading materials might argue, a schoolwide reading program is more than a set of commercial materials provided for every classroom. There is a lot of jargon to sort out. A *comprehensive reading program* is a set of commercial materials addressing instruction and intervention for all learners at all grade levels. A *core program* is a set of commercial materials used by all learners at a grade level. We see a schoolwide program as more than curriculum and materials, however. A *schoolwide reading program* is a plan for using personnel, time, curriculum materials, and assessments designed specifically to meet the needs of the children it serves. In this chapter, we introduce some variables that literacy coaches and other building-level leaders must consider in crafting and supporting a schoolwide reading program. We rely on the experiences of literacy coaches in working to design schoolwide programs.

SCHOOLWIDE RESEARCH

Research on schoolwide reading initiatives must weigh the effects of different factors, each of which can be targeted for reform: leadership and organization for instruction, curriculum materials, curriculum implementation, and teacher knowledge. Researchers who consider all these things at once have much to say about the characteristics of effective reform initiatives. Others have also located especially effective schools for study. These real-life models should guide building-level leaders in the creation of their schoolwide programs.

Effective Schools

Johnson (2002) summarized nine case studies of high-performing, high-poverty urban elementary schools. These schools had impressive standardized test scores, including (but not limited to) high reading achievement scores. Johnson identified several trends that were apparent across the sites:

- They targeted a visible, attainable goal that could be tracked across the school year. For example, they focused on improving attendance or increasing the number of books read.
- They focused energy on providing services to children, rather than on resolving personal or professional conflicts between adults.
- They set high, clear standards for children's behavior, so that the environment was conducive to teaching and learning.
- They created a collective (rather than personal) sense of responsibility for increasing achievement.
- They enhanced building-level instructional leadership, either through redesigning the role of the principal or by creating new curriculum support positions.
- They aligned their instruction with state and federal standards and with assessments.
- By investigating needs across the school year, they supported teachers with the materials and training that they needed to be successful.
- They allocated time for teachers to collaborate, to plan, and to learn together during the school day.
- They reached out to parents.
- They created additional time for instruction.

These characteristics of generally successful schools have also been found in schools especially successful in supporting literacy achievement.

Researchers at the Center for the Improvement of Early Reading Achievement undertook a large-scale study of effective schools (Taylor, Pearson, Clark, & Walpole, 2000). They selected 14 schools in four different states with impressive literacy achievement—specifically, schools with both better standardized test scores and a larger proportion of children qualifying for free and reduced-price lunches than their district neighbors (i.e., "beat the odds" schools). Surveys, interviews, observations, time logs, and both researcher-collected and state-level achievement tests were analyzed for two target classrooms at each level (kindergarten through third grade). In that group of potentially very successful schools, three schools emerged as most successful. They shared some important characteristics that separated them from the other schools in the study:

- They had strong links to parents (e.g., site councils, meetings, phone calls, surveys, letters, newsletters, and work folders).
- They had collaborative models for specialists to support classroom teachers.
- They had better building-level communication about children's achievement and about curriculum implementation, both within and between grade levels.
- They had a systematic procedure for evaluation of student progress, including a regular assessment schedule, a system for sharing and reporting data, and a system for using data in instructional decision making.
- They spent more time in small-group instruction, with those groups formed and reformed on the basis of achievement.
- They had small-group early reading interventions, including both national reform models and locally developed models across the elementary grades.
- They offered integrated, ongoing professional development programs for teachers.

These schoolwide findings can surely be used to direct reform efforts. Other researchers, working at virtually the same time in other settings, have reported almost identical characteristics of especially successful schoolwide literacy programs (e.g., Mosenthal, Lipson, Sortino, Russ, & Mekkelsen, 2002; Taylor, Pressley, & Pearson, 2002; Duffy & Hoffman, 2002).

Effective Reforms

Admiring the work of successful sites does not solve many problems for struggling schools. For them, it is the process that matters first. How does a school move toward the characteristics of effective schools identified above? Edward Kame'enui, Deborah Simmons, and their colleagues (e.g., Simmons, Kuykehdall, King, Cornachione, & Kame'enui, 2000) have provided a common-sense model of reform that they call the *schoolwide reading improvement model*. They propose five stages for this model:

1. Describe the context thoroughly, including attention to curriculum, instruction, assessment, and interventions.
2. Form instructional groups, using the data.
3. Design coordinated instruction for all groups, adopting new curriculum materials if necessary.
4. Set goals that can be evaluated through data collection during the year, and adjust grouping and pacing plans accordingly.
5. Evaluate the success of the program for children at the end of the year, and adjust instruction and intervention programs accordingly.

As we have worked inside schools to promote the creation of schoolwide efforts, we have been informed by the work of our colleagues who are studying effective schools and effective change processes. You will see their influence below. The topics that follow here represent our own efforts to bring this research into practice—to work with schools to become exemplary sites through building-level reform initiatives. The remainder of this chapter provides specific guidance for those efforts, along with reports from literacy coaches as they have grappled with these issues. In this chapter, we rely primarily on the experiences of Maya Burton (a pseudonym), another first-year literacy coach.

ASSESSMENT

Given the evidence above that effective schools document progress at the building level, we start with assessment. Assessment informs the design of a schoolwide program in many ways; it documents the immediate instructional needs of children and measures the success of the program in the long term. We will deal with designing an assessment system in Chapter 4. Here we discuss broader issues in the management of assessments.

Scheduling Assessments

School-level assessments should not be surprises to teachers. A well-designed reading program has a clear schedule for conducting assessments. This schedule is created before the school year begins and provided for teachers to use to plan their work. Table 2.1 provides such a calendar. This calendar was presented to teachers by Maya during preplanning and was then used with grade-level teams to schedule the specific testing days and times for year two of the reform.

Maya learned about scheduling assessments the hard way. In her first year, she started with an assessment calendar, but she didn't share it with teachers during preplanning, because it seemed too new and overwhelming. Later she realized that this was not an effective strategy. As she rolled assessments out gradually, she realized that teachers were not able to see the big picture; they felt that the assessments were being added on top of one another, rather than working together to form a school-level data set. The purpose of the assessments was also unclear. Some of the teachers suspected that Maya and her principal were "winging it," thinking up new assessments somewhat impulsively as the year progressed.

Conducting Assessments

At the start of a schoolwide reform effort, a literacy coach faces a particularly difficult conundrum: Assessments are best conducted by the classroom teachers who

TABLE 2.1. Initial Calendar for Schoolwide Assessments

	Kindergarten	Grade 1	Grades 2 and 3
September	Letter names Letter sounds	Letter names Letter sounds Spelling	Word recognition Oral reading fluency Spelling
October	Phonemic awareness	Phonemic awareness Word recognition	Oral reading fluency
November		Oral reading fluency	Oral reading fluency
December	Letter sounds	Letter sounds Spelling	Comprehension
January	Spelling	Oral reading fluency	Spelling Oral reading fluency
February	Letter sounds	Oral reading fluency	Oral reading fluency
March			Oral reading fluency
April		Word recognition Oral reading fluency	
May	Phonemic awareness	Oral reading fluency	Oral reading fluency Comprehension
June	Spelling	Oral reading fluency Spelling list	Comprehension

will be using the data to drive their instruction, but assessment training takes time. One thing is certain: Conducting schoolwide assessments without training to ensure that all testers can administer the tests reliably is a waste of teaching and learning time.

One possibility for dealing with testing is a model based on gradual release of responsibility; the literacy coach takes much of the testing responsibility at first, and then scaffolds the responsibility onto the teachers. In the first phase, the literacy coach works with a small schoolwide assessment team (SWAT) to test all children. This team begins by simulating and practicing the testing with adults, moves to group testing of individual children with reliability checks, and finally proceeds to testing throughout the school. Classroom teachers can watch some of the testing of their own students and start to familiarize themselves with the procedures.

In the next stage of testing, the SWAT members provide training to all of the classroom teachers, and the teachers function as members of the team in their own classrooms. In that way, the teachers can learn to administer the test and also collect some of the data for their own students. Other members of the team are still participating, to help the teachers to get the data collected with the least possible time taken away from instruction.

Finally, responsibility can be released to the teachers to collect their own assessment data. Using the assessment calendar, a whole staff of teachers can learn to collect data that can be used to fine-tune their own instruction and look at issues of overall program success. In order to do that, the literacy coach must first provide an overview of the testing dates (as in Table 2.1), then schedule the actual testing dates, then plan backward to schedule the training that teachers will need to be ready to administer the tests.

Maya used the SWAT approach for two reasons: She didn't have enough time to train the teachers in the new assessments during preplanning, and she feared that the assessments would take too much time away from classroom instruction. She used her Title I and intervention teachers (six in all) as testers, because that made a smaller number to train, and those staff members already had more experience with assessment. She was able to collect the data she needed at the beginning of the year very quickly. The disadvantage of that SWAT decision was that when the data were shared with the classroom teachers, the teachers struggled to interpret it. They needed to know what the assessments were and how they were administered before they could use them to inform their work. Gradually, then, Maya shifted responsibility for assessments to the teachers in concert with the SWAT approach.

Summarizing Assessment Data

We have worked with many schools that have collected extensive assessment data, none of which is used for instructional decision making. The barrier is summarization; no staff member is actually charged with making sense of the data. This is surely a process on which a literacy coach must focus attention. Sometimes it is simply "math fear" that prevents building-level leaders from summarizing school-level data. Actually, very little mathematical knowledge is necessary; certainly statistical testing is unnecessary. Literacy coaches would be well served by a computer spreadsheet program that allows calculation of four figures—total number (N), percentage (%), mean or average (M), and standard deviation (SD)—and by a coding system for disaggregating data to show the performance of specific groups of children (e.g., by grade level, by teacher, by socioeconomic status, by gender, by ethnicity).

Table 2.2 provides an illustration. It is a summary sheet from a staff meeting that a literacy coach conducted in 1999. The data are simple: the total number of letter names and letter sounds each kindergarten child could produce, given a sheet of random letters. The data are summarized for two separate groups. The 9 at-risk children began the year with a mean score of 1.5 letter names and a standard deviation of 1.8. The small standard deviation score means that the individual data points were close to the mean score. By January the mean had risen to

TABLE 2.2. Kindergarten Letter Name and Letter Sound Data, 1999

Letter names, Sept.	Letter names, Jan.	Letter sounds, Sept.	Letter sounds, Jan.
At risk (N = 9)			
M = 1.5	M = 5.6	M = 1.4	M = 5.1
(SD = 1.8)	(SD = 5.2)	(SD = 1.6)	(SD = 3.0)
Progressing (N = 48)			
M = 17.1	M = 22.9	M = 6.7	M = 17.0
(SD = 7.0)	(SD = 3.7)	(SD = 5.4)	(SD = 4.0)

5.6, but the standard deviation was much larger. There was low achievement over-all, but the individual children varied more in their scores than they had in September. The at-risk children were responding to instruction at vastly different rates. The pattern was the same for the letter sounds.

The cohort of 48 students who were on track (progressing) exhibited a different pattern. They entered school with a larger mean score for letter names (17.1) and a large standard deviation (7.0), but by January they had progressed to a mean score of almost 23 letter names with a smaller standard deviation (3.7). Regardless of their initial status, the progressing students were responding to instruction in fairly similar ways, and they were close to mastery. The same pattern was true for these children with respect to letter sounds.

Table 2.3 provides another example from the same school. This time, the data were instructional reading levels (a broad concept that combines measures of decoding, fluency, and comprehension). A schoolwide assessment system allowed teachers to collect that data, and then it was summarized to help in program planning. Data here are reported as percentages of the whole cohort of second graders. Almost half the children had instructional reading levels below grade placement after the first two marking periods. At the end of the third marking period, however, there was a significant change: 86% of the students were reading on or above grade level. The use of percentages here allowed the teachers to see the magnitude of the change.

TABLE 2.3. Second-Grade Instructional Reading Level Data, 1999

End of first 9 weeks	End of second 9 weeks	End of third 9 weeks
42% below grade level	43% below grade level	14% below grade level
58% on or above grade level	57% on or above grade level	86% on or above grade level

Communicating Assessments

If a literacy coach has scheduled building-level assessments, set up a system for collecting the data reliably, and summarized the data, there is one step remaining: Those data must be made public to all of the school's stakeholders. There are two internal sets of stakeholders (the entire staff and the individual classroom teachers) and two external sets (the district office/school board and the parents). All of these stakeholders deserve to know about student achievement.

One set of stakeholders is the full staff—all professionals and paraprofessionals who work with children in any capacity. In order to develop a shared sense of responsibility for the achievement of all children, all adults should be well informed about the strengths and weaknesses of the instructional program that are identified in the data. Summary data, as described above, can be presented to teachers in a "State of the School" Address. The purposes of such an address are to share insights into the current achievement of children, and to take leadership in using those insights to respond immediately to student needs.

Figure 2.1 is an excerpt from a handout shared with teachers during the 2000–2001 school year. The data presented are for first grade, although the format was exactly the same for all grades. The literacy coach presented data in this form for all grades during one of four scheduled after-school State of the School meetings—meetings the staff came to anticipate as essential in establishing new goals during the course of the school year. All four State of the School addresses began the same way. For each grade level, the literacy coach reviewed the goals for that grade level in curriculum-specific language: text reading levels, text reading rates, and reading and spelling words in isolation. Next, she reviewed basic initiatives in classroom instruction. In this case, the school was using a new basal reading series to coordinate instruction in phonics, sight words, and text reading. Finally, she defined current intervention programs. A daily intervention served those children identified through the schoolwide screening, and a tutoring program served those children plus the 17 next weakest-performing children in twice-weekly sessions.

The next section of the handout, the "New data" section, told the whole staff that the two interventions mentioned above were insufficient for all children to meet the grade-level expectations. In fact, to translate instructional reading levels into time, 15% of the children were months behind and 22% were several weeks behind. For those children, then, an additional intervention was necessary. The data drove the literacy coach to implement one right away; these children were invited to an after-school program two afternoons each week.

Creation and delivery of a State of the School address legitimize a schoolwide reading program. Initially, it is one of the most difficult tasks of the literacy coach; eventually, however, it is the cement that binds the teachers' collective instructional efforts to the evidence of student progress. It also holds building-level leaders

Literacy goals in first grade

Increased vocabulary knowledge
Accurate reading through end of first-grade materials
Spelling through end of letter name stage
Reading and spelling first-grade high-frequency words
Reading rate of 60 words per minute

Instructional program initiatives in first grade

New basal materials: Coordination of phonics instruction, sight word learning,
and text reading

Interventions

Daily small-group intervention with reading specialists for 13 identified children
Biweekly tutoring for 30 weakest-performing children

New data

Current instructional reading level goal = starting third preprimer in basal

Below goal

15% of children starting second preprimer
22% of children ending second preprimer

At or above goal

63% of children

New plan

All students below current benchmark invited to after-school program twice
each week to review and preview daily lessons

FIGURE 2.1. Outline of first-grade State of the School address, 2000–2001.

accountable to the schoolwide plan by forcing the whole staff to consider the data
and to contemplate additional efforts and programs in response to the data.

Another important set of stakeholders in the school consists of the individual
classroom teachers who are delivering instruction. Summaries of assessment data
across the grade levels should be communicated in public; analysis of particular
classroom variables should be communicated in private. At a basic level, individual teachers should compare the data from their children to the data across their
grade level to see whether their own classes are contributing positively or nega-
tively to the overall mean, and to identify those individual children whose achievement is especially low. As we see it, one job of the literacy coach is to help teachers
interpret their own data and to reflect on their own practices in relation to those
data in an environment safe from teacher evaluation. At times, classroom formation skews classroom performance (e.g., when all struggling children are clustered

into specific classrooms). However, the goal of schoolwide improvement should be that all children receive the type and amount of instruction they need to achieve at grade level, regardless of where they start.

The State of the School address and the classroom teachers' individual data constitute the internal data communication variable; the same data should be reported externally to the district office and to the school board. You will notice in Tables 2.1 and 2.2 and in Figure 2.1 that no individuals (teachers or students) are named. Personal information is shared only with the classroom teachers. We will address this issue in Chapter 4. In sharing assessment data externally, this assurance of privacy is essential. The State of the School address should be communicated to district leaders and to the school board to keep them informed about the progress of the initiative. In an individual building, a literacy coach and a principal might choose to invite these external stakeholders to the schoolwide meeting or to host individual sessions for them.

These very same data should be used to communicate student achievement to parents. It is the responsibility of the literacy coach to ensure that parents are informed about their children's progress in the school's reading program. This may mean that report cards must be reformatted at the district level. At the very least, though, parents must know what the school's goals are and where their children are performing in relation to those goals; we are concerned when children are evaluated only for their effort and attitude on their report cards, rather than for their achievement.

Maya's approach to sharing data developed gradually. In the first year of her initiative, she shared data separately with each grade-level team, because she was unable to assemble the entire staff. At her first session, she shared the data that had been collected through the SWAT approach, but the discussion was side-tracked into a description of the assessments and procedures rather than the implications of the data. By the second session, though, she had planned for a different discussion. She provided each teacher with a summary sheet to direct his or her thinking. It directed the teachers to note the strengths and weaknesses in each curriculum area. Then it included a section for teachers to form needs-based groups in their own classrooms based on the data.

At the end of the year, Maya shared the school-level data with each team. At that time, her focus was on showing the very positive growth in the kindergarten and first grades, and the need for additional changes in second and third grades. The data showed her and the teachers that all children had made progress, but that the school's approach was insufficient to narrow the achievement gap between the highest- and lowest-achieving groups of children. The teachers needed to see the data across all grade levels in order to see this trend. Maya also shared this data with the district language arts coordinator. Unfortunately, though, the district representative did not seem interested in Maya's analysis; she congratulated Maya, but offered no constructive criticism and asked no questions of any kind. Involvement of the external stakeholders at the district level thus became Maya's goal for year 2!

When Maya tried to use her data to inform parents of their children's progress, she had to start working with the district very closely. At first, she found that the district's grading policies overreported achievement; students reading far below grade level were getting high grades in reading. In her own school, Maya had to send addenda to the report cards to explain to parents that, beginning immediately, grades would reflect grade-level achievement rather than effort. She then volunteered to redo the district-level assessment and grading system, to prevent her building-level reform from being sidetracked by procedures not informed by research. For instance, the district had mandated a set of teacher-designed assessments of individual competencies from the state standards—assessments not subjected to any validity or reliability tests. These needed to be replaced, and Maya volunteered to work on that project. This collaborative district-level work offered her an "in" for working toward involving the district in data-based decision making.

In the summer after her second year as literacy coach, Maya used the data to direct her own reflections. She realized that in order to narrow the achievement gap, she would have to substantially alter the content of the school's intervention programs. She worked with her principal to consider possibilities in that area.

Planning Assessment

To sum up, a literacy coach must consider the establishment of a unified, building-level assessment program. There are several essential steps:

1. Select assessments that address key components of reading development.
2. Create a calendar for assessment.
3. Train teachers to conduct the assessments.
4. Share assessment results with school stakeholders: the whole staff, the individual teachers, the district/school board, and parents.
5. Use data to continually evaluate the success of the program and to make adjustments.

GROUPING

Assessing student needs is the first step toward addressing these needs. A schoolwide reading program builds in structures to take assessment information and use it to form and reform instructional groups. Broadly defined, *grouping* is any system through which children are assigned to different instructional settings in order to better address their needs. A schoolwide reading program will take a schoolwide stance on how, when, and why students are grouped for instruction.

Grouping practices have long been a source of controversy. The essence of the controversy is this: One-size-fits-all instruction will not accommodate the range of needs in a classroom, *and* grouping children for instruction by their achievement is not necessarily the answer. Like others in the field, we advocate neither whole-group nor achievement-based groups, but rather a planful mixture (e.g., Caldwell & Ford, 2002; Reutzel, 1999)—with heterogeneous classrooms engaged in whole-group instruction, and also regrouped for specific times during the day into flexible achievement- or needs-based groups. Flexibility is the key here; we define *flexible* groups as groups formed and reformed at regular intervals on the basis of new student achievement data. We also label the choices below as *regrouping* rather than *grouping* options, to emphasize that they are all ways to meet the individual needs of children who are first grouped into heterogeneous classroom groups and then regrouped for a specific portion of time for specific reasons, and that these decisions are periodically evaluated.

Some major approaches to grouping for reading instruction (including costs and benefits) are the following:

- *Flexible within-class regrouping.* In this plan, children are assigned and re-assigned to one of a small number of groups in their own classroom based on achievement. They then receive instruction geared directly to their needs. The potential benefits of this grouping plan are that group membership can easily be adjusted without altering schedules, and that only one adult is re-sponsible for the bulk of instruction for an individual child and for commu-nicating progress with parents. The potential costs are that the number of actual groups in a classroom may be prohibitive, and that teachers must prepare to teach multiple lessons each day based on the needs of each group.

- *Flexible same-grade regrouping.* Under this plan, students are assigned to heterogeneous homeroom classes for most of the day, but are regrouped ac-cording to achievement level for a portion of their reading block. All teach-ers are potential reading teachers for all students at the grade level. A poten-tial cost of this plan is that many children will not receive reading instruction from their homeroom teacher, and thus clear systems for com-munication must be established. Valuable instructional time can also be lost as children make their way from one room to another. A potential benefit of this plan is that each teacher need only plan instruction to meet the needs of one specific group (in addition to the grade-level group) each day.

- *Flexible across-grade regrouping.* This plan dates to the late 1950s, when it was introduced in Joplin, Missouri, by Cecil Floyd. As in same-grade re-grouping, students are assigned to heterogeneous classes for most of the day, but move to homogeneous rooms for reading. Unlike same-grade grouping, the Joplin plan involves regrouping children of different grade levels together for reading instruction. Advanced second graders might join average-achieving third graders, for example. The potential benefits of this plan are especially apparent for the strongest- and weakest-performing readers: The instructional needs of these children in several grade levels might be very similar, and their small numbers at each grade level or in each heterogeneous classroom might prevent them from receiving the instruction they need. The potential costs of this plan are mainly in the constraints it places on the master schedule (e.g., all teachers at all grade levels must have their uninterrupted reading block at the same time) and in "selling" the plan to teachers who might question the wisdom of mixing children by age. As with flexible same-grade regrouping, the inevitable loss of instructional time is also a factor.

A schoolwide program must address the issue of grouping in a systematic way. Unfortunately, research has not pointed the way to any one ideal grouping plan. Each school must carefully consider a host of factors in order to reach a decision. Once a decision is made about how to group children, there are natural planning correlates, and they are cumulative. If flexible within-class grouping is chosen, then the logistics of that grouping and regrouping must be established (when, how, and by whom). If flexible same-grade regrouping is chosen, then to the logistics above is added the need to schedule a consistent protected time for instruction within each grade level. If flexible across-grade regrouping is chosen, that scheduling demand for protected time is extended to more teachers.

SELECTION OF CURRICULUM RESOURCES

A schoolwide program is driven by assessment data and addresses student needs with curriculum resources aligned with research and with the needs of children. In a broad sense, strong building-level leaders become wise consumers of the commercial products available for reading instruction; rather than viewing these products themselves as reading programs, effective leaders view them as supporting reading programs that are much more than curriculum and materials. In Chapter 7, we will discuss selection of curriculum resources in depth. Here, then, we focus on the role of curriculum resources in a schoolwide reading program. We challenge literacy coaches to consider a systematic approach to the selection of curriculum resources. In fact, we challenge them to make choices that could be summarized in the template in Table 2.4. In a schoolwide program, that template should be used for planning at each grade level. It may be that particular commercial products are listed in more than one category at more that one grade level, but it is important to question whether and how these programs correspond to research in each curricular area. You can use the procedures presented in Chapter 7 to consider programs in this way.

TABLE 2.4. Curriculum Resources in a Schoolwide Reading Program

	Whole-group instruction	Small-group instruction	Individual practice	Intervention
Vocabulary	All grades		All grades	All ESL students Grade 2 Grade 3
Phonemic awareness	Kindergarten Grade 1			Kindergarten Grade 1 Grade 2
Decoding	All grades	Kindergarten Grade 1 Grade 2	Kindergarten Grade 1	Grade 3
Fluency	All grades	All grades	All grades	All grades
Comprehension	All grades	Grade 2 Grade 3	All grades	All ESL students Grade 2 Grade 3

Note. ESL, English as a second language.

To choose curriculum resources wisely, the literacy coach must consider the potential benefits of whole-group instruction, small-group instruction, individual practice, and intervention. For us, *whole-group instruction* is undifferentiated, grade-level instruction. The goals of whole-group instruction are to provide all children with basic access to grade-level concepts and vocabulary, and to develop literacy skills and strategies according to an explicit, systematic, grade-level-appropriate scope and sequence for instruction. Although this portion of the instructional day is necessary, it is also insufficient. For some children, this grade-level instruction will be so far above their level of performance that they will be unable to use it to acquire flexible literacy skills and strategies.

The "small" in *small-group* is a designation of the differences in needs. In forming these groups, needs are more important than numbers; members of these groups have only "small" differences in their needs. By *small-group instruction,* we mean instruction within the regular reading block provided by the classroom teacher (or the designated teacher for within-grade regrouping or across-grade regrouping), with materials selected to match the needs of particular children.

Some of the characteristics of needs-based groups can be predicted from a knowledge of reading development. We see needs-based group instruction in phonemic awareness and decoding as essential in kindergarten, first grade, and second grade. We see needs-based group work in fluency as essential in all grades. Finally, we see needs-based group work in comprehension as essential in second and third grades. In Chapter 6, when we discuss reading development across ages and stages, we will explain this concept further.

We consider individual practice as an essential part of a reading program. For vocabulary and comprehension development, individual practice comes as children read widely or listen to literature that is appropriate for them. Texts for vocabulary and comprehension practice include authentic children's literature, content-related trade books, and high-interest books. For decoding, this individual practice should focus on wide reading and rereading of materials that beginning readers can actually use to practice their decoding skills in context. Decoding practice usually uses little books specifically designed to highlight phonics patterns. For fluency, individual practice includes wide reading of texts that are easy for children to read; the characteristics of "easy" texts shift as children proceed through stages of reading development.

Intervention, the focus of Chapter 8, is always needs-based and either small-group or individual; it occurs in addition to the regular reading block (before school, after school, in the summer, and sometimes in place of science and social studies instruction). We define *intervention* as extremely targeted, aggressively paced, explicit instruction delivered by personnel with specialized training. Children identified for intervention need specialized curriculum resources and extended time, compared to their grade-level peers.

Potentially, then, selection of instructional materials includes three tiers: materials for grade-level instruction, for needs-based instruction, and for intervention. Maya started her reform of curriculum resources by identifying a new core program for grade-level instruction. She also purchased separate new curriculum resources for needs-based instruction and tackled the prevailing preference of the teachers to teach on a whole-group basis all day. Once whole-group instruction and needs-based instruction were in place, she moved to materials selection for the intervention program. She worked to define the intervention programs more explicitly, purchasing a new phonemic awareness program for kindergarten and first grade, and a fluency-building program for third grade. Her curriculum decisions depended on her analysis of the data and her ability to introduce new curriculum resources in an organized way. In the end, she chose resources that worked together, and she removed old layers of curriculum.

Planning for Curriculum Selection

1. Start with your materials for whole-group instruction and practice.
2. Carefully consider the results of your assessments.
3. Move to your materials for needs-based instruction.
4. Carefully consider the results of your assessments.
5. Move to your materials for intervention.
6. Carefully consider the results of your assessments.

ALLOCATION OF TIME

With an effective assessment system, a regrouping philosophy, and curriculum resources that are consistent with research and the needs of children, the challenge is still in the details. Time for instruction is key to a schoolwide effort; effective schools allocate and reallocate time thoughtfully. In this section, we focus on choices that literacy coaches have regarding time: for instruction, for intervention, for planning, and for professional development. As in a schoolwide assessment system, the keys to organizing time effectively are to start with goals, to formulate a plan that supports those goals, and to monitor implementation of that plan, making necessary adjustments.

Time for Learning

One thing is certain: All schools can benefit from an analysis of the ways they use time. Allington and Cunningham (2002) conceptualize time as minutes, hours, days, weeks, and years, which can be either organized to support children or wasted. How many minutes can be lost in noninstructional activities (e.g., packing up, lining up, gearing up)? How many hours can be wasted in haphazard or poorly planned activities? How many days can be wasted in noninstructional programs? How many weeks can be wasted in redundant layers of assessment? Good leadership in a schoolwide program will address these issues of time.

Another way to think about using time well is to consider ways to extend time. It makes sense that children with greater needs may need more time to achieve the same goals. The traditional route to extending time—retention in grade—is clearly ineffective (Allington & McGill-Franzen, 1995). There are other ways, though. Additional hours of instruction can be provided during extended-day programs with clear curricular goals and specific materials. Additional weeks of instruction can be provided during extended-year programs, again with clear goals and materials. And additional years of instruction can be provided with preschool programs. All of these units of time are potentially malleable within a schoolwide reading program.

Time for Teaching

Regardless of how the structural decisions about time described above are made, extended, uninterrupted time for literacy instruction every day is essential. In one state-level initiative where we have worked, the state mandated 180 minutes of instructional time for literacy (defined as reading and writing). This block of time could be interrupted just once, for lunch or a "special" (see below), and it had to occur every day. We will provide some models for planning this time that are related to each of the grouping decisions above.

Figure 2.2 provides a framework if a schoolwide plan relies on flexible within-class regroupings. We assume that in most elementary school classrooms there are 20–26 children of varying achievement levels working with one teacher. For that group, then, it is useful to begin with a time allocation plan that includes whole-group, grade-level reading instruction; small-group, needs-based instruction; individual or paired practice time; and whole-group, grade-level writing instruction. In this model, then, with 180 minutes, 60 minutes could be devoted to the whole-group reading time; 20 minutes to needs-based work in each of three stations (teacher, vocabulary/comprehension practice, decoding/fluency practice); and 60 minutes to grade-level, whole-group writing time.

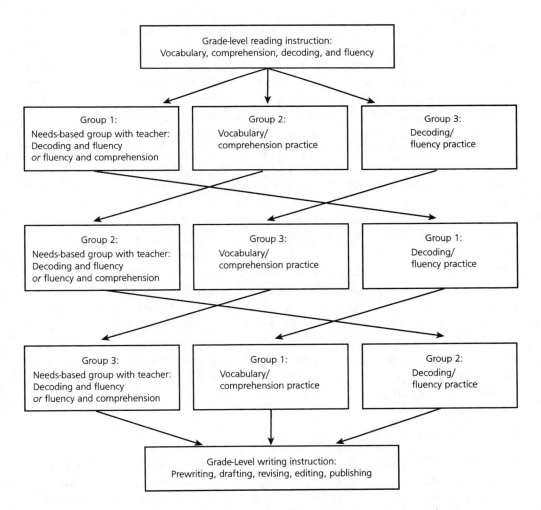

FIGURE 2.2. Conceptual organization of time by grouping plan.

One general framework where children move from whole-group reading to a mix of small-group reading and reading practice to whole-group writing can be easily adjusted to account for the total amount of time allocated in the instructional schedule and the needs of the children. For example, at the start of a reform, it is entirely possible that very few children will be starting the year reading on grade level. In that case, more time should be allocated for the needs-based portion of the literacy block. As children's literacy skills increase, the staff could increase the time spent in grade-level instruction.

School-level planning for this uninterrupted time involves consideration of when children move to "specials" (physical education, art, music, computer lab, library) and when they go to lunch. That scheduling problem (and many others) is virtually solved by dividing the school into two halves and alternating their literacy blocks. For example, in a K–3 building, the kindergarten and first grade could have their literacy block first thing in the morning, go to lunch, go to specials, have math instruction, and end the day with either science or social studies. The second and third grades could start the day with specials, move to math instruction and to science or social studies, begin their literacy block with their grade-level lesson, move to lunch, and end the day with their small-group time and their writing instruction. We will provide specific model schedules in Chapter 5.

Finding time to address the entire curriculum is daunting. Social studies, science, and math educators will undoubtedly question this emphasis on time for literacy, though the inclusion of thoughtfully selected nonfiction during the literacy block may help persuade them. The choice to group children within classrooms has time implications; in order for each group to meet with the teacher each day, time has to be allocated for each group. The alternative grouping decisions provide more constraints on the school-level schedule, but relieve some of the pressure on time.

Figure 2.3 merges a decision to use flexible same- or across-grade grouping plans with the general framework of grade-level reading instruction, needs-based instruction, and grade-level writing instruction. From a curriculum perspective, time here is saved for other curricular areas, because children can have their needs met and do their practice more quickly when they are supervised. If you compare Figure 2.3 with Figure 2.2, then you can probably shave 30 minutes (a lot of instructional time) from the literacy block, because all three needs-based groups meet at the same time.

Time for Intervention

Intervention, which we have defined above as something different from the needs-based time that we have already scheduled, is also important to plan in a schoolwide program. It is naïve to think that intervention can be scheduled during the school day without sacrificing another part of the curriculum; in fact, if it can,

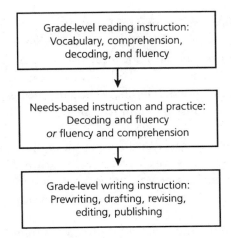

FIGURE 2.3. Time for literacy with flexible same-grade regrouping.

then the schoolwide planning for time use has not been effective. Children who need intervention are those children for whom grade-level achievement is not predicted within the structure of grade-level and needs-based instruction already provided. Supporting their literacy achievement is an emergency, and emergency measures must be taken. The best possible plan for providing intervention includes extending time—by extending the school day or year.

For interventions during the regular school day to work, they have to be as efficient as possible and connected directly to the schoolwide schedule. For efficiency's sake, interventions should be "push-in." This means that adults, rather than children, move—and therefore that children lose no instructional time in transitions to and from intervention. One possible way to schedule push-in intervention during the school day is for it to occur during reading practice time (one of the two stations in Figure 2.2). Another possibility is to have push-in intervention take place during part of the whole-class writing lesson, as children in need of intervention may have tremendous difficulty during that time. Finally, as a last resort, consider interventions that actually replace science or social studies instruction.

Time for Professional Development

Drafting a great assessment plan, carefully selecting instructional materials, and designing an efficient and effective school schedule will be a waste of time without a plan for professional development for the entire staff. We will discuss the "whats" and "hows" of professional development in Chapter 9. Right now, we concentrate on the "whos" and the "whens."

The "whos" are easy. Schoolwide reform efforts need to involve every adult who works with children in any capacity, many of whom are not regular classroom teachers: counselors, special education teachers, paraprofessionals, librarians, art teachers, music teachers, and physical education teachers. We are not suggesting that all of these individuals share the same needs for professional development. Nevertheless, all must be embraced in the overall professional development plan.

The "whens" are not as easy. Professional development sessions after a long school day are not always conducive to learning, but it is difficult to envision a reform effort that will not include at least some after-school time. Here are some lessons we've learned about scheduling professional development:

- Consider scheduling (and funding) more preplanning days. A paid, required summer institute of 3 days prior to the start of the new school year provides a much better start to a reform effort.
- Establish a weekly after-school professional development day, rotating among four meeting formats: professional development for all, professional development for the K–1 team, professional development for the 2–3 team, and faculty meeting for all.
- Establish common grade-level planning time during the school day, and schedule professional development with the literacy coach during that time 1 day each week, starting the first week of school.
- Be proactive with the district about schedules for building-level days. Often those days are interrupted by committee meetings, and whole-staff work is impossible. Instead, propose that all committee meetings be scheduled in the afternoons, and that mornings be reserved for professional development with the entire staff.

Time-Saving Tips

Time is of the essence in a schoolwide reading program. We have yet to interact with a literacy coach who has not struggled with issues of time, both conceptually ("How will we use time in this building?") and personally ("How will I find time to get all of this done?"). We offer a few suggestions that may help a coach contend with these issues systematically:

1. Select a regrouping philosophy.
2. Select a professional development time.
3. Create a schoolwide schedule for literacy blocks, specials, math, social studies and science.
4. Evaluate other interruptions to time and weigh their value in the school's mission.

Simmons et al. (2000) subtitled their article on schoolwide reform "No One Ever Told Us It Would Be This Hard!" They must not have asked any literacy coaches. Every one we've ever met reports the same thing: The process of designing and maintaining a schoolwide reading program is very hard work. Consider yourself warned. Also consider yourself invited. If you start to attend to these issues up front (assessment, grouping, instructional materials, and time), and if you make a long-haul commitment to the adults and children at your site, there is no more rewarding job than that of a literacy coach leading a schoolwide reading program. Consider Table 2.5, which documents the goals and activities of a literacy coach over 2 years.

TABLE 2.5. Calendar of Activities for 2-Year Schoolwide Reform Initiative

Time	Activities	Persons responsible
Spring, year 1	• Collect data and describe student achievement and curriculum implementation. • Identify strengths and weaknesses. • Set goals for coming year. • Meet with faculty and staff to set guidelines for coming year; allow for staff transfer. • Order new curriculum materials.	Literacy coach Principal Assistant principal
Summer, year 1	• Establish assessment calendar and assessment manual for teachers. • Revise instructional schedule to allow for whole- and small-group instruction. • Prepare staff directory and materials to introduce reading program to families.	Literacy coach Principal Assistant principal
Summer, year 1	• Attend summer professional development institute on explicit decoding instruction and expert comprehension instruction. • Prepare grade-level curriculum benchmarks for teachers and parents.	Whole-school team
Summer, year 1	• Consolidate and organize text sets for use in reading instruction and intervention.	Reading team
Fall, year 1 through spring, year 2	• Invite preschool and day care providers to attend professional development sessions. • Conduct whole-school, after-school professional development session 1 hour each month. • Conduct small-group, after-school professional development sessions 2 days each month. • Conduct two in-school professional development sessions each month for each grade-level team. • Conduct six formative observations of instruction for each teacher. • Establish professional development library.	Literacy coach Principal Assistant principal
Fall, year 1 through spring, year 2	• Implement comprehension strategies instruction across the grade levels and across the curriculum, including multiple daily read-alouds for all children.	Whole-school team
Fall, year 1	• Conduct one evening parent-and-child session for each grade level, including a focus on home literacy activities and local library offerings. • Schedule local library field trips for second, third, and fourth graders.	Principal Assistant principal Grade-level teams

(continued)

TABLE 2.5. *(continued)*

Time	Activities	Persons responsible
Fall, year 1 through spring, year 2	• Structure kindergarten schedules for large- and small-group instruction. • Train paraprofessionals in interactive read-aloud techniques. • Implement explicit phonemic awareness curriculum in classrooms. • Implement explicit phonemic awareness curriculum in kindergarten intervention groups. • Draft weekly newsletter to inform parents of progression in letter sounds. • Make kindergarten literacy kits to support parents.	Literacy coach Kindergarten team Title I teachers
Fall, year 1 through spring, year 2	• Structure first-grade schedule for small-group instruction. • Implement new basal series. • Link intervention program plan to scope and sequence of basal series. • Establish communication system between intervention providers and classroom teachers.	Literacy coach First-grade team Title I teachers
Fall, year 1 through spring, year 2	• Establish small-group, homogeneous, within-grade-level grouping plan for 1 hour each day in second, third, and fourth grades for phonics, spelling, and fluency. • Establish instructional procedures for phonics practice, rereadings for fluency, and writing for comprehension within heterogeneous classrooms.	Second-grade team Third-grade team Fourth-grade team Title I teachers
Fall, year 1 through spring, year 2	• Establish content area intervention for struggling second- and third-grade readers. • Establish after-school tutorial program for second and third graders.	Literacy coach Title I teachers
Spring, year 2	• Host community-based family literacy program.	Principal Assistant principal Local staff
Summer, year 2	• Analyze achievement data, year 1.	Literacy coach
Summer, year 2	• Manage kindergarten transition summer school.	Principal Assistant principal
Fall, year 2	• Arrange site-based graduate course in literacy development.	University professor Whole-school team

(continued)

TABLE 2.5. *(continued)*

Time	Activities	Persons responsible
Fall, year 2	• Conduct one evening parent-and-child session for each grade level, including a focus on home literacy activities and local library offerings. • Schedule library field trips for second, third, and fourth graders.	Principal Assistant principal Grade-level teams
Fall, year 2	• Schedule evening parenting classes.	Local Even Start program staff
Spring, year 2	• Host "Motheread/Fatheread."	Principal Assistant principal Local library staff
Summer, year 2	• Analyze achievement data, year 2	Literacy coach

CHAPTER 3

Reading Research

Some educators, such as the late Madeline Hunter, have argued that there are both an art and a science of teaching. The art of teaching involves somewhat intangible attributes, such as our emotional involvement in, and passion for, our craft and our ties to students as human beings. The science of instruction, on the other hand, involves which methods and materials we use and whether they can be expected to have the effects we desire. It is the job of researchers to undertake investigations that will help practitioners plan and conduct instruction leading to optimal learning. This is not to minimize the role of so-called "action research," which involves informal and often impromptu studies conducted by classroom teachers. However, we look to the community of reading researchers for findings that are likely to be useful across classrooms. In this chapter, we summarize some important research findings, and also suggest strategies coaches can use to keep up with research.

It is important that a literacy coach become a prudent *consumer* of research, rather than a *producer*. Being a research consumer means knowing something about the issues involved in research. For example, not all published studies are of equal merit, and some are actually rather shoddy. In addition, the research methodology varies considerably from study to study, depending on the questions an investigator chooses to pursue. In this chapter, we provide some guidance that will be useful to literacy coaches as consumers of educational research.

We start with research design. An important distinction in methodology is whether the researcher has chosen a qualitative or a quantitative approach. Qualitative methods are useful for describing processes and interactions that are difficult to reduce to a set of numbers. Interchanges during class discussions, for instance, are perhaps best studied through qualitative procedures. In contrast, studies of whether or not a particular teaching technique is more effective than an alternative technique are best grounded in quantitative measures. In recent years, quantitative research has dominated policy, particularly at the federal level. There is an increasing insistence that teachers responsible for reading employ teaching methods grounded in *scientifically based reading research* (SBRR). This policy is controversial and has been attacked by those who claim that it reduces the true complexity of learning to read. But let's examine the issue briefly, and you can decide for yourself.

WHAT IS SBRR, AND HOW CAN YOU GET SOME?

Few researchers would dispute that the most powerful design possible is the *true experiment*. In such a study, children are randomly assigned to two or more treatment groups, and valid and reliable measures of each treatment's impact are obtained. Rigorous statistical procedures are employed to analyze the data collected and to arrive at defensible conclusions. Variables that might contribute to (or detract from) the impact of a treatment are carefully controlled. For example, researchers may check to see how faithful teachers have been to implementing the treatment.

Needless to say, the true experiment sets a very high standard—one that very few studies can achieve. A frequent shortcoming is the random assignment of students to treatments. Random assignment is difficult to achieve, because educators in schools have their own ideas about which students are to be placed in which classes. Researchers often have to make do with preexisting, nonrandom assignments. The result is called a *quasi-experiment*—a design that can still have remarkable rigor even though it is a cut below the standard of the true experiment.

Studies designed in this way are based on *Bacon's law*. Sir Francis Bacon, founder of the scientific method, was the first to contend that a cause-and-effect relationship could not be proven unless a control group was available for which all conditions were the same except the factor being studied. (Today, these are sometimes called *contrast* or *comparison* groups.) Studies grounded in this logic are the mainstay of medical research, but they are far less common in education. In the report of the National Reading Panel (NRP, 2000), fewer than 1 in 1,000 studies represented a rigorously conducted experiment or quasi-experiment. This depressing fact is perhaps the result of the pressure on researchers to publish many pieces, as well as the large number of education journals.

It is unrealistic for a literacy coach, working alone, to be able to synthesize and summarize the existing scientifically based evidence related to reading instruction one study at a time. Recently, researchers have done some of that work and have presented their findings. Particularly powerful syntheses have been published by Marilyn Adams (1990), by Snow, Burns, and Griffin (1998), by the NRP

(2000), and by the Rand Reading Study Group (Snow, 2002). Taken together, these documents summarize many years' work for many researchers. They constitute a history of SBRR. We believe that it is the job of a literacy coach to understand the findings of these research reviews as they relate to instruction, and to develop strategies to keep up with new findings.

We will use the NRP's report to give a brief summary of some findings that simply cannot be ignored by literacy coaches. The NRP was commissioned by the U.S. Congress in 1997 to "assess the status of research-based knowledge, including the effectiveness of various approaches to teaching children to read" (NRP, 2000, p. 1-1). Its final report, released in 2000, has drawn both praise and criticism. Critics, however, have expressed concern mainly for the rigorous standards by which the panel's members excluded many available studies. Had they been less demanding, however, flawed studies might well have skewed the conclusions they ultimately reached.

Fortunately, the NRP found enough hard evidence to arrive at many useful conclusions about the nature of effective instructional approaches in the teaching of reading. At a large, programmatic level, the panel identified several components of a sound reading program in an elementary school. Key among these components are phonemic awareness, phonics, fluency, vocabulary, and comprehension. Naturally, the emphasis on each of these components varies according to grade level. In kindergarten, for example, the emphasis on phonemic awareness and phonics should be higher than it is in later years (other than for students who need additional instruction). The entire report of the NRP is available online (http://www.nationalreadingpanel.org), but we have based the discussion below on the NRP's summary, in which some of the instructional practices that meet the test of SBRR are described. Another online source is the University of Oregon's Big Ideas in Beginning Reading, drawn from the same body of research evidence (http://reading.uoregon.edu).

PHONEMIC AWARENESS

Phonemic awareness is the ability to segment oral speech into its component speech sounds, or phonemes. Phonemic awareness can be tricky business. SBRR suggests that not all students become phonemically aware without explicit instruction. Findings of note include these facts:

1. Phonemic awareness instruction must become a formal part of the reading program.
2. It is a prerequisite for effective phonics instruction.
3. The lack of it has been repeatedly tied to later reading failure.
4. It can be taught successfully to young children.

Evidence also documents the development of phonological awareness over five stages:

1. Rhyme recognition.
2. Sentence segmentation.
3. Syllable segmentation and blending.
4. Onset–rime blending and segmentation.
5. Blending and segmenting individual phonemes.

Instructional activities should be ordered along these lines from the simplest to the most sophisticated, and the five levels of awareness can serve as a useful guide in sequencing instruction.

NRP's Conclusions about Phonemic Awareness Instruction

Overall, the findings reviewed by the NRP showed that teaching children to manipulate phonemes in words was highly effective under a variety of teaching conditions with a variety of learners across a range of grade and age levels, and that teaching phonemic awareness to children significantly improved their reading more than instruction that lacked any attention to phonemic awareness.

Specifically, the results of the experimental studies led the NRP to conclude that phonemic awareness training was the cause of improvement in students' phonemic awareness, reading, and spelling following training. The findings were replicated repeatedly across multiple experiments, and thus they provide converging evidence for causal claims. Although phonemic awareness training exerted strong and significant effects on reading and spelling development, it did not have an impact on children's performance on math tests. This indicates that *halo* or *Hawthorne* (novelty) effects did not explain the findings, and that indeed the training effects were directly connected with and limited to the targeted domain under study. Importantly, the effects of phonemic awareness instruction on reading lasted well beyond the end of training. Children of varying abilities improved their phonemic awareness and their reading skills as a function of phonemic awareness training.

Phonemic awareness instruction also helped normally achieving children learn to spell, and the effects lasted well beyond the end of training. However, the instruction was not effective for improving spelling in disabled readers. This is consistent with other research showing that disabled readers have difficulty learning how to spell.

Programs in all of the studies provided explicit instruction in phonemic awareness. Specifically, the characteristics of phonemic awareness training found to be most effective in enhancing phonemic awareness, reading, and spelling skills included explicitly and systematically teaching children to manipulate phonemes with letters, focusing the instruction on one or two types of phoneme manipulations rather than multiple types, and teaching children in small groups. You will see these findings influence our plan for instructional tasks and procedures in Chapter 5, and our review of reading materials in Chapter 6.

Phonemic awareness instruction is ready for implementation in the classroom, but teachers should keep in mind several cautions. First, phonemic awareness training does not constitute a complete reading program. Rather, it provides children with essential foundational knowledge in the alphabetic system. It is one necessary instructional component within a complete and integrated reading program. Children learning to read and write must acquire several other competencies as well. Second, there are many ways to teach phonemic awareness effectively. In implementing phonemic awareness instruction, teachers need to evaluate the methods they use against measured success in their own students. Third, the motivation of both students and their teachers is a critical ingredient of success. Research has not specifically focused on this.

PHONICS

No one disputes the importance of phonics, given that we are all readers of an alphabetic language (one that uses letters to represent phonemes). However, the debate continues over how and how much phonics should be taught. In Jeanne Chall's (1967, 1996) classic book *Learning to Read: The Great Debate,* she produced the first systematic study of SBRR as it related to the question of phonics instruction. Chall's chief conclusion was that research clearly favors a systematic approach employing direct instruction—instruction in which teachers teach letter sounds directly. More recent studies, elegantly summarized in Marilyn Adams's (1990) *Beginning to Read: Thinking and Learning about Print,* have reinforced Chall's initial conclusion. An excellent (and far shorter) overview is that of Stahl, Duffy-Hester, and Stahl (1998).

The NRP examined five different approaches to phonics instruction. Its classification is a useful one. The approaches are as follows:

- *Analogy-based phonics*—Teaching students unfamiliar words by analogy to known words (e.g., recognizing that the rime segment of an unfamiliar word is identical to that of a familiar word, and then blending the known rime with the new word onset, such as reading *brick* by recognizing that *-ick* is contained in the known word *kick,* or reading *stump* by analogy to *jump*).
- *Analytic phonics*—Teaching students to analyze letter–sound relations in previously learned words to avoid pronouncing sounds in isolation. For example, children might first be taught words like *red, run,* and *rat* as whole

words. The teacher would then call the children's attention to the initial sound of all of these words without actually trying to pronounce the sound in isolation.

- *Embedded phonics*—Teaching students phonics skills by embedding phonics instruction in text reading. This is a more implicit approach that relies to some extent on incidental learning. In embedded phonics instruction, a teacher might use the shared book experience to present a big book to a small group or to the entire class. The text in the big book might then be used to teach phonics skills. The teacher might focus on rhyming words, for example.
- *Phonics through spelling*—Teaching students to segment words into phonemes and to select letters for those phonemes (i.e., teaching students to spell words phonemically).
- *Synthetic phonics*—Teaching students explicitly to convert letters into sounds (phonemes) and then to blend the sounds to form recognizable words. In a synthetic approach, children might first learn the sound represented by the letters *r, a* (its short sound), and *t*. They would then be taught to blend these sounds from left to right to make (synthesize) the word *rat*.

NRP's Conclusions about Phonics Instruction

The NRP produced many useful conclusions about phonics instruction. Systematic phonics instruction—instruction with a clear set of instructional procedures and a clear and sequential set of lessons—produced significant benefits for students in kindergarten through sixth grade and for children having difficulty learning to read. The ability to read and spell words was enhanced in kindergartners who received systematic beginning phonics instruction. First graders who were taught phonics systematically were better able to decode and spell, and they showed significant improvement in their ability to comprehend text. Older children receiving phonics instruction were better able to decode and spell words and to read text orally, but their comprehension of text was not significantly improved.

Systematic synthetic phonics instruction had a positive and significant effect on disabled readers' reading skills. These children improved substantially in their ability to read words, and they showed significant (albeit small) gains in their ability to process text as a result of systematic synthetic phonics instruction. This type of phonics instruction benefited both students with learning disabilities and low-achieving students who were not disabled. Moreover, systematic synthetic phonics instruction was significantly more effective in improving alphabetic knowledge and word-reading skills for children of low socioeconomic status (SES) than instructional approaches that were less focused on these initial reading skills.

Across all grade levels, systematic phonics instruction improved the ability of good readers to spell. The impact was strongest for kindergartners and decreased for children in later grades. For poor readers, the impact of phonics instruction on spelling was small, perhaps reflecting the consistent finding that disabled readers have trouble learning to spell.

Although conventional wisdom has suggested that kindergarten students might not be ready for phonics instruction, this assumption was not supported by the data. The effects of systematic early phonics instruction were significant and substantial in kindergarten and first grade, indicating that systematic phonics programs should be implemented at those age and grade levels.

The NRP's analysis indicated that systematic phonics instruction is ready for implementation in the classroom. The findings of the NRP regarding the effectiveness of explicit, systematic phonics instruction were derived from studies conducted in many classrooms with typical classroom teachers and typical American or English-speaking students from a variety of backgrounds and SES levels. Thus the results of the analysis are indicative of what can be accomplished when explicit, systematic phonics programs are implemented in today's classrooms. Systematic phonics instruction has been used widely over a long period of time with positive results, and a variety of systematic phonics programs have proven effective with children of different ages, abilities, and SES backgrounds.

These facts and findings provide converging evidence that explicit, systematic phonics instruction is a valuable and essential part of a successful classroom reading program. However, there is a need to be cautious about giving a blanket endorsement of all kinds of phonics instruction.

It is important to recognize that the goals of phonics instruction are to provide children with key knowledge and skills, and to ensure that they know how to apply that knowledge in their reading and writing. In other words, phonics teaching is a means to an end. To be able to make use of letter–sound information, children need phonemic awareness. That is, they need to be able to blend sounds together to decode words, and they need to break spoken words into their constituent sounds to write words. Programs that focus too much on the teaching of letter–sound relations and not enough on putting them to use are unlikely to be very effective in the long run. In implementing systematic phonics instruction, educators must keep the end in mind: They must ensure that children understand the purpose of learning letter sounds, and that they are able to apply these skills accurately and fluently in their daily reading and writing activities.

Of additional concern is the often-heard call for "intensive, systematic phonics instruction." Usually the term *intensive* is not defined. How much is required to be considered intensive? This is not a question that we can answer from research. In addition, it is not clear how many months or years a phonics program should continue. If phonics has been systematically taught in kindergarten and first grade, should it continue to be emphasized in second grade and beyond? How long should single instructional sessions last? How much ground should be covered in a program? Specifically, how many letter–sound relationships should be taught, and how many different ways of using these relations to read and write words should be practiced for the benefits of phonics to be maximized? These questions remain for future research.

Another important area is the role of the teacher. Some phonics programs showing large effect sizes require teachers to follow a set of specific instructions provided by the publisher; although this may standardize the instructional sequence, it also may reduce teacher interest and motivation. Thus one concern is how to maintain consistency of instruction while still encouraging the unique contributions of teachers. Other programs require a sophisticated knowledge of spelling, structural linguistics, or word etymology. In view of the evidence showing the effectiveness of systematic phonics instruction, it is important to ensure that the issue of how best to prepare and support teachers to carry out this teaching effectively and creatively is given high priority.

Knowing that all phonics programs are not the same brings with it the implication that teachers must themselves be educated about how to evaluate different programs, so that they can determine which ones are based on strong evidence and how to use these programs most effectively in their own classrooms. It is therefore important that teachers be provided with evidence-based preservice training and ongoing inservice training to select and implement the most appropriate phonics instruction effectively.

A common question with any instructional program is whether "one size fits all." Teachers may be able to use a particular program in the classroom, but may find that it suits some students better than others. At all grade levels, but particularly in kindergarten and the early grades, children vary greatly in the skills they bring to school. Some children will already know letter–sound correspondences, and some will even be able to decode words, while others will have little or no letter knowledge. Teachers should be able to assess the needs of the individual students and tailor instruction to meet specific needs. However, it is more common for phonics programs to present a fixed sequence of lessons scheduled from the beginning to the end of the school year. In light of this, teachers need to be flexible in their phonics instruction in order to adapt it to individual students' needs.

Children who have already developed phonics skills and can apply them appropriately in the reading process do not require the same level and intensity of phonics instruction provided to children at the initial phases of reading acquisition. Thus it will also be critical to determine objectively the ways in which systematic phonics instruction can be optimally incorporated and integrated into schoolwide reading programs. Part of this effort should be directed at preservice and inservice education to provide teachers with decision-making frameworks to guide their selection, integration, and implementation of phonics instruction within a schoolwide reading program.

Teachers must understand that systematic phonics instruction, like phonemic awareness, is only one component (though a necessary component) of a total reading program; systematic phonics instruction should be integrated with other reading instruction in phonemic awareness, fluency, and comprehension strategies to create a complete reading program. Although most teachers and educational decision makers recognize this, there may be a tendency in some classrooms, particularly in first grade, to allow phonics to become the dominant component—not only in the time devoted to it, but also in the significance attached to it. It is important not to judge children's reading competence solely on the basis of their phonics skills, and not to devalue or discourage their interest in books because they cannot decode with accuracy. It is also critical for teachers to understand that systematic phonics instruction can be provided in an entertaining, vibrant, and creative manner.

Systematic phonics instruction is designed to increase accuracy in decoding and word recognition skills, which in turn facilitate comprehension. However, it is again important to note that fluent and automatic application of phonics skills to text is another critical skill that must be taught and learned to maximize oral reading and reading comprehension. This issue again underscores the need for teachers to understand that although phonics skills are necessary in order to learn to read, they are not sufficient in their own right. Phonics skills must be integrated with the development of phonemic awareness, oral reading fluency, and reading comprehension skills.

FLUENCY

Fluency entails word recognition that is, except in rare instances, unconscious and automatic. The fluent reader reads aloud with proper phrasing, intonation, and expression (characteristics that are often called *prosody*). Until a reader achieves fluency (usually in second or third grade), comprehension is apt to suffer, because too much conscious attention must be directed at word identification and too little attention can be paid to comprehending what is read.

An issue of usage has arisen that may cause some confusion. The term *fluency* can refer to any process in which an individual has achieved a high level of proficiency. A child might be described as fluent in the naming of letters, for example. For our purposes, the word *fluency* refers to oral reading fluency, unless otherwise noted.

NRP's Conclusions about Fluency Instruction

On the basis of a detailed analysis of the available research that met the NRP's methodological criteria, the panel concluded that guided repeated oral reading procedures (i.e., procedures that included guidance from teachers, peers, or parents) had a significant and positive impact on word recognition, fluency, and comprehension across a range of grade levels. These studies were conducted in a variety of classrooms in both regular and special education settings with teachers using widely available instructional materials. This suggests the classroom usefulness of guided oral reading and repeated reading procedures. These results also applied to all students—good readers, as well as those experiencing reading difficulties. Nevertheless, there were important gaps in the research. In particular, the NRP could find no multiyear studies providing information on the relationship between guided oral reading and the emergence of fluency.

There has been widespread agreement in the literature that encouraging students to engage in wide, independent, silent reading increases reading achievement. Literally hundreds of correlational studies have found that the best readers read the most and that poor readers read the least. These correlational studies suggest that the more children read, the better their fluency, vocabulary, and comprehension will be. However, these findings are correlational in nature, and correlation does not imply causation. No doubt, it could be that the more that children read, the more their reading skills improve—but it is also possible that better readers simply choose to read more.

In order to address this issue of causation, the NRP examined the specific impact of encouraging students to read more on fluency, vocabulary development, and reading comprehension. The studies that were identified as addressing this issue were characterized by three major features. First, the studies emphasized silent reading procedures in which students read on their own with little or no specific feedback. Second, the studies did not directly assess fluency or the actual increase in the amount of reading due to the instructional procedures. Rather, only changes in vocabulary and/or comprehension were typically measured as outcomes, rather than increases in fluency that could be expected from the increased reading practice. Third, very few studies that examined the effect of independent silent reading on reading achievement could meet the NRP research review methodology criteria ($n = 14$), and these studies varied widely in their methodological quality and the reading outcome variables measured. Thus a meta-analysis could not be conducted. Rather, the 14 studies were examined individually and in detail to identify converging trends and findings in the data.

With regard to the efficacy of having students engage in independent silent reading with minimal guidance or feedback, the NRP was unable to find a positive relationship between programs and instruction that encouraged large amounts of independent reading and improvements in reading achievement, including fluency. In other words, even though encouraging students to read more is intuitively appealing, there is still not sufficient research evidence obtained from studies of high methodological quality to support the idea that such efforts reliably increase how much students read, or that such programs result in improved reading skills. Given the extensive use of these techniques, it is important that such research be conducted.

These findings do not negate the positive influence that independent silent reading may have on reading fluency; nor do the findings negate the possibility that wide independent reading significantly influences vocabulary development and reading comprehension. Rather, there are simply not sufficient data from well-designed studies capable of testing questions of causation to substantiate causal claims. The available data do suggest that independent silent reading is not an effective practice when used as the only type of reading instruction to develop fluency and other reading skills, particularly with students who have not yet developed critical alphabetic and word-reading skills. In sum, methodologically rigorous research designed to assess the specific influences that independent silent reading practices have on reading fluency and other reading skills and the motivation to read has not yet been conducted.

VOCABULARY

Vocabulary development represents one of the single greatest challenges to American educators. There is clearly a "vocabulary divide" that separates proficient and struggling readers and that grows larger over time. Hart and Risley (1995) have documented this trend in arresting terms. They teach us that those children whose vocabularies are richest when they start school also expand their vocabularies more quickly. Unfortunately, research has done more to reveal the problem than to solve it. The conclusions of the NRP summarize how SBRR has illuminated this area of reading instruction. Note that the NRP deftly avoids a long-standing (though friendly) debate about whether vocabulary should be taught *directly*, through planned lessons, or *incidentally*, through ensuring that students are exposed to words in many contexts. Both are important.

NRP's Conclusions about Vocabulary Instruction

The studies reviewed by the NRP suggest that vocabulary instruction does lead to gains in comprehension, but that methods must be appropriate to the age and ability of the reader. The use of computers in vocabulary instruction was found to be more effective than some traditional methods in a few studies. Computer-based instruction is clearly emerging as a potentially valuable aid to classroom teachers in the area of vocabulary instruction. Vocabulary can also be learned incidentally in the context of storybook reading or of listening to others. Learning words before reading a text is helpful, too. Techniques such as task restructuring and repeated exposure (including having the student encounter words in various contexts) appear to enhance vocabulary development. In addition, substituting easy words for more difficult words can assist low-achieving students.

The findings on vocabulary yielded several specific implications for teaching reading. First, vocabulary should be taught both directly and indirectly. Repetition and multiple exposures to vocabulary items are important. Learning in rich contexts, incidental learning, and use of computer technology all enhance the acquisition of vocabulary. Direct instruction should include task restructuring as necessary and should actively engage the student. Finally, dependence on a single instructional method will not result in optimal learning.

Although much is known about the importance of vocabulary to success in reading, there is little research on the best methods or combinations of methods of vocabulary instruction, or on the measurement of vocabulary growth and its relation to instructional methods.

COMPREHENSION

Reading comprehension is a vast area, complicated from the outset by differences in definition and perspective. When we look for research on effective instructional techniques, for example, do we mean *effective* in the sense of helping students comprehend a specific selection, or *effective* in the sense of making students better comprehenders in general? And when we look at how studies measure comprehension, are we content with questions that have only one correct answer, or do we adopt the constructivist view that such questions dangerously oversimplify the process of bringing meaning to text? Such questions are important to literacy coaches as they enter the morass of findings on comprehension instruction. We define *comprehension* as creation of a personal mental representation of the meaning of text. How to measure it and teach it is another matter—one open to intense debate. A good starting place is the NRP report. The conclusions of the NRP address the matters of how comprehension ability develops and the evidence underlying specific instructional approaches well.

NRP's Conclusions about Comprehension Instruction

Comprehension is enhanced when readers actively relate the ideas represented in print to their own knowledge and experiences, and when they construct mental representations of these ideas in memory.

The rationale for the explicit teaching of comprehension strategies is that comprehension can be improved by teaching students to use specific cognitive procedures or to reason strategically when they encounter barriers to understanding what they are reading. Readers acquire these strategies informally to some extent, but explicit or formal instruction in the application of comprehension strategies has been shown to be highly effective in enhancing understanding. The teacher generally demonstrates such strategies for students until the students are able to carry them out independently.

In its review, the NRP identified 16 categories of text comprehension instruction, of which 7 appear to have a solid scientific basis for conclusions that they improve comprehension in nonimpaired readers. Some of these types of instruction are helpful when used alone, but many are more effective when used as part of a multiple-strategy method. The types of instruction are as follows:

1. Comprehension monitoring, where readers learn how to be aware of their understanding of the material.
2. Cooperative learning, where students learn reading strategies together.
3. Use of graphic and semantic organizers (including story maps), where readers make graphic representations of the material to assist comprehension.
4. Question answering, where readers answer questions posed by the teacher and receive immediate feedback.
5. Question generation, where readers ask themselves questions about various aspects of the story.
6. Story structure instruction, where students are taught to use the structure of the story as a means of helping them recall story content, in order to answer questions about what they have read.
7. Summarization, where readers are taught to integrate ideas and generalize from the text information.

In general, the evidence suggests that teaching a combination of reading comprehension techniques is the most effective. When students use them appropriately, they assist in recall, question answering, question generation, and summarization of texts. When used in combination, these techniques can improve results in standardized comprehension tests.

Nevertheless, some questions remain unanswered. More information is needed on ways to teach teachers how to use such proven comprehension strategies. The literature also suggests that teaching comprehension in the context of specific academic areas—for example, social studies and science—can be effective. If this is true of other subject areas, then it might be efficient to teach comprehension as a skill in content areas.

Questions also remain as to which strategies are most effective for which age groups. Moreover, further research is necessary to determine whether the techniques apply to all types of text genres (including narrative and expository texts), and whether the level of difficulty of the texts has an impact on the effectiveness of the strategies. Finally, it is critically important to know what teacher characteristics influence successful instruction of reading comprehension.

Teaching reading comprehension strategies to students at all grade levels is complex. Teachers not only must have a firm grasp of the content presented in text, but also must have substantial knowledge of the strategies themselves, of which strategies are most effective for different students and types of content, and of how best to teach and model strategy use.

Research on comprehension strategies has evolved dramatically over the last two decades. Initially, investigators focused on teaching one strategy at a time; later studies examined the effectiveness of teaching several strategies in combination. However, implementation of this promising combined approach has been problematic. Teachers must be skillful in their instruction and be able to respond flexibly and opportunistically to students' needs for instructive feedback as they read.

The initial NRP search for studies relevant to the preparation of teachers for comprehension strategy instruction provided 635 citations. Of these, only 4 studies met the NRP research methodology criteria. Hence the number of studies eligible for further analysis precluded meta-analysis of the data derived from these investigations. However, because there were only 4 studies, the NRP was able to review them in detail. The studies investigate two major approaches: *direct explanation* and *transactional strategy instruction*.

The direct explanation approach focuses on the teacher's ability to explain explicitly the reasoning and mental processes involved in successful reading comprehension. Rather than teach specific strategies, teachers help students (1) to view reading as a problem-solving task that necessitates the use of strategic thinking, and (2) to learn to think strategically about solving comprehension problems. For example, teachers are taught that they can teach students the skill of finding the main idea by casting it as a problem-solving task and reasoning about it strategically.

Transactional strategy instruction also emphasizes a teacher's ability to provide explicit explanations of thinking processes. Furthermore, it emphasizes the ability of teachers to facilitate student discussions in which students collaborate to form joint interpretations of text and acquire a deeper understanding of the mental and cognitive processes involved in comprehension.

The four studies (two studies for each approach) demonstrated that teachers could be instructed in these methods. Teachers required instruction in explaining what they were teaching, modeling their thinking processes, encouraging student inquiry, and keeping students engaged. Data from all four studies indicated clearly that in order for teachers to use strategies effectively, extensive formal instruction in reading comprehension is necessary, preferably beginning as early as preservice training.

More research is needed to address the following questions. Which components of teacher preparation are most effective? Can reading comprehension strategies be successfully incorporated into content area instruction? How can the effectiveness of strategies be measured in an optimal manner? Can strategies be taught as early as grades 1 and 2, when children also are trying to master phonics, word recognition, and fluency? How can teachers be taught to provide the most optimal instruction?

FINDING ANSWERS

For the literacy coach, reading research has one primary function—to inform instructional decision making. Probably the best-known example of SBRR, the report of the NRP, has been useful for this purpose. This report has two major limitations, however. First, it was published in 2000 and is steadily becoming outdated. New findings continue to inform what we know about effective reading instruction, making it essential to keep up with the current literature.

Its second limitation is that it simply does not address all of the questions a coach is likely to face. Consequently, the effective literacy coach must look elsewhere for research summaries. Of course, such summaries have their own problems. They almost always include studies that do not meet the rigorous standards of SBRR. They are often vague or equivocal. And, unhappily, they are frequently written with other researchers in mind; thus they are likely to be laden with jargon and "inconsiderate text."

Nevertheless, research summaries can be instrumental in wrestling with the issues affecting school reform. They can be tackled by an individual coach, by a collegial group of coaches, or by teacher study groups guided by a coach.

We offer a few sources of research summaries. Although we have no wish to discourage a coach from going straight to the primary sources, such a strategy is in most cases unrealistic and sometimes even counterproductive. Summaries are designed for educators who wish to be rapidly apprised of the state of knowledge related to a particular topic. The literacy coach is such an educator.

Handbooks

A *handbook* is a somewhat encyclopedic volume that can double as a doorstop when not in use. A handbook consists of chapters devoted to specific subjects and authored by experts in those subjects. Each chapter contains an extensive review of research, and often ends with an overview of where the research community stands and what remains to be learned. Like an actual encyclopedia, a handbook is not intended to be read from cover to cover, but to be used topically as the occasion warrants.

Major handbooks include the following:

Handbook of Reading Research (Vol. 1), 1984, edited by Pearson et al.
Handbook of Reading Research (Vol. 2), 1991, edited by Barr et al.
Handbook of Reading Research (Vol. 3), 2000, edited by Kamil et al.
Handbook of Research on Teaching the English Language Arts (2nd ed.), 2003, edited by Flood et al.
Handbook of Early Childhood Literacy, 2003, edited by Hall et al. (British).
Handbook of Early Literacy Research, 2001, edited by Neuman and Dickinson.

Handbook of Literacy and Technology (Vol. 1), 1998, edited by Reinking et al.

Handbook of Literacy and Technology (Vol. 2), in press, edited by McKenna et al.

Handbook of Research on Teaching (4th ed.), 2001, edited by Richardson.

Handbook of Research on Multicultural Education (2nd ed.), 2002, edited by Banks and McGee Banks.

Literacy in America: An Encyclopedia of History, Theory, and Practice (2 vols.), 2002, edited by Guzzetti.

(Complete bibliographical information appears in the References list at the end of this book.)

ERIC Digests

A portion of the vast Educational Resources Information Center (ERIC) database includes brief summaries of available research. These are rarely very detailed, but can provide a quick overview of the topic. The ERIC digests are certainly not limited to reading, and can be useful in examining some of the related issues such as grouping and scheduling. The digests are free and are available online. A convenient way to access them is through a U.S. Department of Education Web site (http://www.ericfacility.net/databases/ERIC_Digests/index).

Journal Articles

Reading research journals sometimes publish articles that summarize the research on a topic, especially those topics that are multifaceted or involve major controversies. Some journals, such as the *Review of Educational Research,* publish nothing but research reviews. Of course, the opening portion of any research report published in the journal contains a review of the literature, but this is likely to be highly focused on the question being investigated in that particular study. We heartily recommend the following journal articles, which present summaries that are both rigorous and readable:

Ehri et al., "Systematic Phonics Instruction Helps Students Learn to Read," 2001.

Gersten et al., "Teaching Reading Comprehension Strategies to Students with Learning Disabilities," 2001.

Lou et al., "Within-Class Grouping," 1996.

Slavin, "Ability Grouping and Student Achievement in Elementary Schools," 1987.

Stahl et al., "Everything You Wanted to Know about Phonics (but Were Afraid to Ask)," 1998.

(Again, complete bibliographical information appears in the References list.)

Books

In a few cases, entire books have been devoted to sifting through the entire research on a broad topic, summarizing the results, and arriving at recommendations regarding instructional planning and practice. Such books usually make excellent selections for teacher study groups, and they are a must in the personal library of any literacy coach. Opinions will differ on which books to include in a "short list," but this has not stopped us from developing our own:

> Baker et al., *Engaging Young Readers,* 2000.
> Marzano et al., *Classroom Instruction That Works,* 2001.
> Pressley and Block, *Comprehension Instruction,* 2001.
> Snow, *Reading for Understanding,* 2002.
> Verhoeven and Snow, *Literacy and Motivation,* 2001.
> Stahl, *Vocabulary Development,* 1999.
> U.S. Department of Education, *Start Early, Finish Strong,* 1999.

(Once more, complete bibliographical information appears in the References list.)

Sharing the Burden

The sources we have listed here may seem overwhelming. A literacy coach can only do so much to keep up with current research and still meet other job expectations. In Chapter 9, we will discuss the idea of creating study groups among teachers to examine the research available in a particular area. Danielson (2002) recommends that teachers choose specific sources for which they are responsible—perhaps journals to which they subscribe or in which they have an interest. When these sources are straightforward, such as journal articles, this is probably a feasible plan. It may be harder to convince your colleagues to read a voluminous handbook chapter, however, let alone an entire hefty book. On the other hand, all of these sources should be read selectively and strategically, with specific questions in mind. This mindset makes a remarkable difference.

What If There Are No Answers?

Is it possible, given the thousands of research reports currently available, that there remain instructional issues that have not been put to rest? Unfortunately, such issues abound. In a sense, of course, even questions that are very well settled may still be issues for a particular teacher, school, and instructional setting. For example, the effectiveness of graphic organizers as an instructional tool has been established through many studies, but does this mean that they will be likely to work well for teacher X in school Y? Even the most rigorous of research studies cannot answer this question definitively, and yet previous findings can give us a road map that will allow a literacy coach to give teacher X informed advice.

Unfortunately, there are also a host of issues that are poorly informed by previous research. Should a first-grade needs-based reading group ideally consist of four members? Six? Eight? What is the optimal number of teacher read-alouds for third grade? Is parallel block scheduling the best way to accommodate individual reading levels? Is it worthwhile to provide an uninterrupted block of time for silent reading each day? Should incentive programs be instituted that reward children for the number of books they read? These questions (and many others like them) either are poorly addressed or have produced conflicting results in the research literature. When literacy coaches come to the planning table, they may well be asked to give informed opinions on such issues. Such an experience is likely to be outside their comfort zone, especially since they may feel obligated, in the words of one, to "know just about everything."

Our advice is simple. The most important thing to remember is that when an issue has not been resolved by research, other research findings can sometimes be useful. For example, a vast body of research supports the fact that learning is related to the amount of time spent on task. It is a short jump to conclude that activities that engage children for longer periods of time are likely to be more effective than those that allow or invite off-task behavior. Like us, literacy coaches will have to learn to say, "I don't know of research that answers that question directly. Maybe we can look at a related area." Other important things are to answer SBRR questions with SBRR answers, to recognize (and admit) that many questions have no SBRR answer, and to develop strategies to keep up with new evidence.

Research on Commercial Products

Literacy coaches are often asked about the likely effectiveness of particular commercial products. Can this question be researched? The answer is "It depends." It is rare to find an effectiveness study related to a particular product and conducted by researchers that are independent of the company. A company often makes available its own effectiveness studies, ostensibly conducted by outside experts, but research that is sponsored by a company in order to document the effectiveness of its own product must be viewed with a certain amount of skepticism. Studies like these may be completely unbiased and ethical, of course, but one never knows. We know of one company that rejected an investigation conducted by an outside expert with whom the company had contracted. The company simply did not like the results of the report and had no interest in disseminating it. It is a sure bet that any research report provided by a company, either in print form or online, will be supportive of the product in question.

Finding a research study that is completely independent of a company that has produced a product may not be easy. Professional journals have long discouraged *Consumer Reports* studies of this kind, though the attitudes of some editors may be changing. Doctoral dissertations sometimes address such issues, and it may be worthwhile to consult *Dissertation Abstracts International*, a source that is not indexed by ERIC.

A more frequent approach to evaluating the effectiveness of a commercial product is to conduct a component analysis. That is, the activities and methods embodied in the product are evaluated one by one, using a rubric that is based on SBRR. For example, we know that certain teaching methods tend to be effective in developing phonemic awareness, and we would expect to see those methods embraced within a commercial product designed to develop such awareness. In Chapter 7 (see Table 7.2), we have discussed one such rubric, "A Consumer's Guide to Evaluating a Core Reading Program Grades K–3." Although intended to be comprehensive across all of the major dimensions of reading, this rubric can also be used to evaluate products that target only one of the essential elements of a comprehensive reading program. Our own "Consumer's Guide," designed to evaluate reading software, is another case in point. It also appears in Chapter 7 (see Figure 7.2).

It may also be useful to keep one finger on the pulse of the experiences of similar schools. What are the opinions of teachers there who have actually implemented a particular commercial product? What benefits and pitfalls have they encountered? Does snooping of this kind count as research? Of course it does. It may or may not be iron-clad, and it certainly does not count as SBRR, but such inquiries may result in better-informed decisions.

Hidden Treasures

Wouldn't it be nice if there were people you could approach who are truly "up" on the latest research into a particular literacy-related topic? People who have spent countless hours poring over primary sources and distilling their lessons? People who wouldn't charge an arm and a leg for their expertise? People who would actually enjoy bending your ear about the effectiveness of a particular approach or program? People as yet relatively anonymous who might actually feel thrilled by your acknowledging their expertise?

Well, such people do exist. They're called doctoral students. Universities with major graduate programs in literacy generally have a number of individuals meeting this description. It will not take long to discover who they are and to make contact with them. They are not all cut from the same cloth, of course, but some brief inquiries should point you in their direction. Start by e-mailing some of the senior professors in literacy around the country and asking for recommendations. (You can ask *them* your questions, of course, but they may not answer.) Next, locate the institutional affiliation of a professor you have in mind—perhaps the author of a key book or article. Visit the institution's Web site and conduct a quick search for that individual. The e-mail address is generally easily accessible through a faculty directory. Ask this professor whether he or she would be willing to forward your question to a doctoral student.

Literacy coaches must learn to provide answers to questions already answered in research, as well as resources to answer more complex questions. Doing this demands habits of mind and also strategies for keeping abreast of new research findings. Research is not something you know; it is something you are always learning.

CHAPTER 4

Reading Assessment

Reading assessment serves a variety of purposes, and the literacy coach is connect- ed to all of them. We begin this chapter with a description of the major kinds of tests and the role that each plays in a comprehensive reading program. A working knowledge of these kinds of assessments and their different functions is essential to prudent decision making. A literacy coach is likely to be charged with selecting some or all of the assessments to be used in the building, with training teachers to give the assessments, with interpreting and summarizing the assessment data, and with planning programmatic changes based on trends in the assessments.

TYPES OF TESTS

Tests can be categorized in various ways. We often speak of the differences be- tween formal and informal tests, norm-referenced and criterion-referenced tests, and so forth. We focus here on the uses that are made of tests. From this perspec- tive, it is useful to categorize tests in four ways.

Screening Tests

Screening tests are quick assessments designed to alert teachers to the presence of a problem in a specific area. Good examples are the subtests in the Dynamic Indica- tors of Basic Early Literacy Skills (DIBELS) battery. Each DIBELS subtest requires only about a minute to give, but can provide a valuable "heads-up" about a stu- dent's progress in a particular area of reading development. We mention the DIBELS subtests as popular examples, but many other available assessments can be used for screening purposes. Screening tests are like colanders: They are designed to separate a group of children who need additional testing from the rest of the cohort, so that schools and teachers can focus their additional assessment time and resources on the children who need them.

Diagnostic Tests

A *diagnostic test* is one that is administered after a problem has been identified. Such measures are almost always individually administered, and they are designed to identify specific instructional needs. As a matter of best practice, a screening measure would first identify the presence of a problem, and the diagnostic test would then provide detailed information needed for effective planning to address the problem. For example, the Nonsense Word Fluency subtest of the DIBELS battery might signal a problem in the general area of phonics. An individually administered inventory of phonic skills would then be needed before a teacher could plan appropriate instruction.

Progress-Monitoring Tests

Once a screening measure has identified a deficit area, and measures are taken to accelerate the student's growth in that area, it is a good idea to monitor the student's progress from time to time in order to determine whether instruction is having the desired effect. *Progress-monitoring tests* are quick measures designed to be given periodically with little disruption of classroom practice. The DIBELS measures, for example, can serve both as screening and as progress-monitoring tests. Progress can also be monitored informally (through running records, anecdotal notes, etc.), but a school-level assessment plan provides systematic procedures and tools for gathering this information. Considered together, the system of screening, diagnostic, and progress-monitoring tests operates to ensure that instruction targets children's needs. In this system, instructional planning is sometimes described as "data-driven."

Outcome Tests

The type of test that is likely to have the least direct utility for a classroom teacher is an *outcome test*. Such measures are indicators of long-term growth and include the high-stakes tests that have been the source of so much scrutiny. Outcome measures are not always high-profile assessments, however. For example, a DIBELS subtest used for screening purposes might also be used to gauge trends from fall to spring. More often, outcome measures include nationally normed group achievement tests and state-developed competency tests aligned with the state curriculum.

If outcome measures have any real purpose for practitioners, it lies in their potential use as screening measures. A student's standardized test scores from the previous spring, for example, might be used to make tentative judgments about the student's proficiency in the fall. Such a use has two major problems, however. First, group measures of this kind are not designed for this purpose. The measurement error associated with them tends to be prohibitive, though it also tends to "wash out" when the scores of large numbers of students are averaged. A second problem lies in the fact that some students do not take such tests seriously. They may be frustrated by reading to begin with, and may tacitly refuse to expend much effort in a group setting where their noncompliance will not be recognized for months to come. A third problem is the shelf life of group achievement tests. A test taken in March or April can hardly be expected to have high predictive value in August or September, even if the first two problems do not apply. In short, group achievement measures are no substitutes for individually administered screening tests, and their frequent use for placing children in homerooms is highly questionable.

AN ASSESSMENT STRATEGY

Tests are useful tools for delivering appropriate instruction and for determining its effectiveness. However, like all tools, they must be used strategically, with a sense of purpose. Reading is a highly complex process, and without an overall strategy for conducting an assessment, it is often difficult to determine the best way to proceed. McKenna and Stahl (2003) have proposed a model of reading assessment that is driven by a sequence of strategic questions. These questions correspond to Figure 4.1. They encourage the coach to work backward, beginning with the most basic issue of whether a reading problem actually exists. The questions progress from general to specific:

1. Is the child able to read texts at the child's grade placement with automatic word recognition and adequate expression?
   - Does the child make use of previous text to monitor his or her decoding accuracy?
   - Does the child read at an adequate rate?
   - Does the child have adequate sight word knowledge?
   - Does the child have adequate knowledge of decoding strategies?
   - Does the child have adequate phonemic awareness?
2. Is the child able to comprehend the language of the text?
   - Does the child have an adequate vocabulary for his or her age and grade?
   - Does the child have the background knowledge necessary to understand the particular passage that he or she is reading?
   - Is the child able to use common text structures to aid in comprehension?

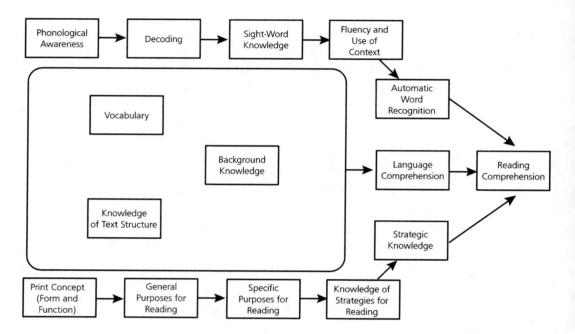

FIGURE 4.1. Component skills and their relationships. Adapted from McKenna and Stahl (2003, p. 22). Copyright 2003 by The Guilford Press. Adapted by permission.

3. Does the child have adequate knowledge of the purposes for reading and possess strategies available to achieve those purposes?
   - Does the child have a set of strategies that can be used to achieve different purposes in reading?
   - What does the child view as the goal of reading in general?
   - What concepts about print does the child have?

If the answer to any of the three broad questions is yes, the questions related to it may be skipped. If the answer to any of them is no, the related questions may help to pinpoint a problem area. These questions are deceptively simple. They provide a useful framework for thinking diagnostically, but they require dependable data to answer. The results of screening and diagnostic tests can provide such data, as can less formal classroom measures.

INTERPRETING GROUP ASSESSMENT SCORES

Morristown Elementary, like all of the other schools in the state, is required to administer a nationally normed group achievement test. Let's assume that this test must be given in grades 3 and 5, but that the district has opted to give it in the off years as well, as a matter of self-defense. (Through off-year testing, the administration hopes to prepare the students as much as possible for the highly publicized testing at grades 3 and 5. This policy may exacerbate the test anxieties so prevalent nowadays, but the pressures to do well make it understandable. Off-year testing also permits pre–post comparisons, which we'll discuss in a moment.)

When spring scores are released, typically in late summer, you may see them in the local newspaper. The stark numbers reported in Table 4.1 may elicit unpleasant memories. Indeed, the teachers at Morristown may wince when they see these disappointing results, particularly when displayed alongside those of Harmony and other higher-performing schools. Then their attention turns to a more fine-grained comparison—Morristown's progress (or lack of it) from last year to this year. The apparent achievement drop from the 45th to the 41st percentile rank will be especially disappointing. It may also raise eyebrows at the central office and on the school board, and pressures to do better can be expected from the top down. But comparing scores in this way, though commonplace in the popular media, can be very misleading. This is because two different groups of students have been assessed. (To a lesser extent, different groups of educators may have been involved as well.)

A more telling way to gauge progress over the year is to compare this year's third-grade results with last year's second-grade results. A cohort approach like this is designed to overcome preexisting differences between consecutive grade groups. You yourself may have experienced years during which the children in a grade level were unlike their predecessors. Their performance may be higher or lower for no apparent reason, and they move from grade to grade as a group anomaly. When such a group outperforms those that come before and after, their movement through the grades resembles that of a rat passing through a python (see Figure 4.2). (This analogy is not very appetizing, but we promise you'll remember it!) Think what happens when a high-performing group is followed by an average group. A same-grade comparison would signal a "drop" in achievement, even though the two groups started at very different points. Tracking cohorts can help to avoid this error.

TABLE 4.1. Reading Comprehension Percentiles for Grade 3

School	Last year	This year	Difference
Morristown	45	41	−4
Harmony	57	62	+5
District	49	51	+2
State	48	50	+2

FIGURE 4.2. When an unusual cohort passes from grade to grade, misleading conclusions about a school's achievement gains can be reached.

When student mobility is high, even a cohort approach can be problematic. Comparing this year's third graders with last year's second graders only makes sense when they are indeed the same children. The soundest comparison is limited to children who have spent the entire year enrolled at your school and for whom both pre- and posttest scores are available. In some schools, this may result in surprisingly small numbers of children. One of the large inner-city K–5 schools with which we work serves three housing projects and two shelters for homeless persons. We once tracked the children who began attending this school as kindergartners and who were still enrolled at the end of fifth grade. There were only five! Nevertheless, there will always be enough children to make a 1-year cohort comparison worthwhile, provided that scores are available every year.

Let's assume that you locate the previous year's scores for Morristown's third graders and discover that in grade 2 they scored at the 39th percentile rank as a group. You might try to publicize a statement like the one in Figure 4.3. We wish you luck! Such reasoning is well founded, but it requires a thoughtful perspective. Nonetheless, you may be able to persuade an editor to report the yearly results a little more fully. Even a letter to the editor or an op-ed piece can be helpful. You may wish to further arm yourself first by consulting important sources on high-stakes testing, such as Jim Popham's (2001) *The Truth about Testing* and the International Reading Association's position statement (http://www.ira.org/positions/high_stakes.html).

This year's Morristown Elementary School third graders scored at the 41st percentile rank, compared with the 45th percentile rank for last year's third graders. However, this year's group scored at the 39th percentile rank at the end of second grade. What appears to be a decline is caused by comparing two different groups of children. When the scores for this year's third graders are compared with their own scores as second graders, a net increase can be seen.

FIGURE 4.3. Sample "press release" promoting a valid interpretation of test results.

Test Scores and Auto Racing

What do you do when all of your careful analysis reveals no change from one year to the next? Let's assume that this year's third graders scored at the 41st percentile rank, and that they also scored at the 41st percentile rank as second graders. Does this mean that they made no progress during third grade? Of course not. It means that they did not change their position in relation to their age peers across the nation. Imagine an auto race in which all of the cars drive a full lap without any car passing any other car. The fifth-place car is still in fifth place, but this does not mean that it hasn't moved—just that its position in relation to the other cars has not changed. Naturally, our goal is to bring low-performing children into the average range, but the myth of no progress needs to be confronted and dispelled.

Sometimes test scores can take an unexpected turn. Let's assume you discover that this year's third graders have fallen from the 43rd percentile rank in second grade to the 41st at present. Let's further assume that last year's third graders scored at the 39th percentile rank. The newspaper has predictably reported what appears to be an increase. Are you ethically required to contact the editor and say, "We'd just like you to know that our kids actually did worse than you think"? We'll leave that question to you. Chances are that the difference is not statistically significant, but such an argument would probably fall on deaf ears. Even those who understand it might view it as a nimble attempt to evade accountability.

There are times, however, when the fault is not in the statistics. Group achievement tests, as much as we love to hate them, do provide an indicator of what children know and can do. They allow us to make broad comparisons over time. As Marie Clay (1990) put it, such tests are "elegantly designed for the comparison task" (p. 292). When careful comparisons suggest that declines in children's scores are real with respect to those of their age peers, it is time to entertain the idea that your race car has been passed.

Test Scores and Football

The widespread practice of reporting changes in percentile ranks is frowned on by statisticians. This is because percentile ranks are not arranged on a linear scale. The effort it takes to advance from the 3rd to the 6th percentile rank is greater than the effort required to move from the 53rd to the 56th percentile rank. The difference in each case is 3 percentile ranks, but that fact is misleading.

The problem can be compared with football. Anyone who has seen a game or two understands that it is much easier to move the football around the midfield than to move it in the vicinity of the end zone. The same rule applies to changes in percentile ranks. This is why reporting changes in this way is so misleading. The media (and, for that matter, school districts and state departments of education) should be discouraged from presenting the plus and minus changes shown in Table 4.1.

Statisticians prefer the normal curve equivalent (NCE), which is computed to be statistically equivalent at all points along the scale. NCEs can be added, subtracted, averaged, and compared. Percentile ranks cannot be. NCEs are conceptually harder to grasp, however, and we seldom see them in the morning paper.

It is important that literacy coaches be aware of the percentile rank problem. They must never add, subtract, or average percentiles. They must never make the mistake of judging changes in percentile ranks to be similar at different points on the 0-to-99 scale, and they must try to educate teachers and administrators about the potential for misinterpretation.

If percentile ranks cannot be averaged, you may ask, how can the average percentile rank for a class be computed? Such "averages" are routinely reported when a school's results are received. In truth, however, these are not averages. The scores for the children in a given class are first averaged using measures for which averaging is permitted, such as NCEs, scale scores, or raw scores. This average is then converted into the corresponding percentile rank. Technically, it's not proper to speak of an average percentile rank. It's better to refer to "the percentile rank corresponding to the class average."

Group Tests and Individual Teachers

Ms. Ellis is a second-grade teacher at Morristown Elementary. Her class average on a group achievement test of reading comprehension corresponds to the 35th percentile rank. Last year, her class average corresponded to the 42nd percentile rank. Has Ms. Ellis slipped? All of the reasons we have discussed for interpreting results for an entire grade level also apply to individual teachers. A fairer way to judge the changes in Ms. Ellis's class would be to contrast them with the same children's comprehension scores at the end of first grade, if available.

But would such a comparison be worth the effort? We suspect it wouldn't be. The fact that her class may have lost ground in relation to their national peers would not give a literacy coach anything specific to recommend that Ms. Ellis do differently. It could, of course, highlight a possible problem, but the presence of one was probably known beforehand.

In the case of a criterion-referenced state competency battery, a better case can be made for singling out Ms. Ellis. Such tests are usually organized around curricular objectives (or clusters of objectives). If so, it can be instructive to learn that most of Ms. Ellis's children did well in area A but poorly in area B. Feedback of this kind can be useful in reexamining a teacher's (or, for that matter, a school's) instructional focus.

MULTIPLE ASSESSMENT HATS OF THE LITERACY COACH

An effective literacy coach may be called upon to serve in a variety of assessment capacities. Official job descriptions will differ, of course, but we describe here the typical expectations related to assessment.

Coach as Tester

Depending on the available demands at the beginning of school, the literacy coach may be called upon to conduct screening assessments in order to identify deficits and place children in graded materials. Such tasks are arguably in the domain of the classroom teacher, but the coach may have to jump-start the process or lend a hand during time crunches. The coach may also be in a position to select assessments, or at least to have a major say in which assessments will be used. All literacy coaches should be familiar with the reading instruments that have been determined by the National Reading First Assessment Committee to possess adequate reliability and validity. A list of such instruments, categorized by how they are to be used (screening, diagnostic, progress monitoring, and outcome), is available online (http://idea.uoregon.edu/assessment/). The committee has been quick to point out that this list is far from comprehensive; many other commercial tests possess acceptable psychometric properties. An additional source to consult is the assessment section of the Florida Center for Reading Research (http://www.fcrr.org/assessment/PDFfiles/DiagnosticTools.pdf). Literacy coaches need to learn how to find information on the validity and reliability of assessment instruments and on their utility for screening, diagnosis, progress monitoring, and evaluation. For literacy coaches, there are also contextual factors to consider in selecting an instrument:

- How much time does it take to administer?
- How much and what kind of information does it provide?
- How much does it cost?
- What sort of training will be needed to administer it effectively?

Coach as Interpreter

It may well fall to a literacy coach to help interpret group achievement test results when they arrive. The knowledgeable coach will conduct a cohort analysis, contrasting last year's scores with the present year's, as we have discussed. Assistance may be available in the form of consultants to the school. For example, state-funded regional service agencies may have the expertise needed to help with test score analysis. In addition, Title I schools with schoolwide plans are required to have a Title I consultant. This individual may also be able to help with the analysis. University professors may be called upon as well, and teachers who are enrolled in graduate coursework in the area of research and measurement may be able to glean advice by asking professors to inspect group achievement results.

Arriving at a reasonable interpretation of testing results is a necessary first step. It is also a good idea to help with public relations. A letter to parents can be drafted; a press release can be sent (particularly when explanations are called for); and presentations can be made to parent groups.

Coach as Profiler

One of the most important tasks confronting the literacy coach is ensuring that instruction in the school is informed by data. Results of screening and progress-monitoring measures should be profiled for classroom teachers. One way of doing so is to provide each teacher with a class roster on which results of screening measures are briefly presented. Updates of this profile can be shared periodically during conferences. Such conferences can be held with individual teachers or with all of the teachers at a particular grade level. In the latter case, a grade-level profile will be needed in order to apprise the teachers of general areas where more intense instructional focus is called for.

The coach can also be instrumental in using screening results and other information to identify children who need diagnostic assessments. Whether or not this identification is actually carried out by the coach, the coach should share the results with the teachers responsible for these children. In the case of struggling readers, for whom diagnostic assessments have been administered, communication with teachers must center around instructional techniques. That is, it is not enough to identify areas of weakness. This information needs to be translated into instructional strategies that will help accelerate the progress of a particular child.

The actual means of preparing class profiles typically involve simple computer applications. For example, an Excel file can be created for each teacher in such a way that grade-level reports can also be generated. If the school administers DIBELS, then class rosters are automatically sent from the University of Oregon and can be downloaded as needed. These results can supplement a homemade Excel file, or they can be incorporated into it. We urge literacy coaches to create and maintain a data set at the school, so that they can incorporate all data available into one file that can be sorted and analyzed.

A sample class profile for Ms. Ellis, our fictional second-grade teacher, appears in Figure 4.4. It is especially helpful if the information in the profile can be tracked over time, so that the growth (or lack of it) of a particular child in a given area can be monitored. When a student's ID number is included, an Excel report can be generated across a span of years, displaying the child's progress. Notice also that the profile of the next second-grade teacher's class follows immediately

	A	B	C	D	E	F	G	H	I
1	Student name	Student ID no.	Teacher	Grade	Stanine comprehension last spring	State CRT comprehension last spring	August DIBELS ORF level	August DIBELS ORF WC/minute	August DRA level
2	Beck, Joe	66578	Ellis	3	4	Failed	Low risk	52	18
3	Chase, Fred	33412	Ellis	3	3	Failed	Some risk	36	16
4	Chatham, Sue	87609	Ellis	3	5	Competent	Low risk	48	20
5	Dodd, Kareem	45239	Ellis	3	3	Failed	Some risk	30	16
6	Flood, Lakesha	54890	Ellis	3	1	Failed	At risk	15	4
7	Good, Johnny B.	45124	Ellis	3	6	Proficient	Low risk	67	30
8	Hall, Monte	65409	Ellis	3	5	Competent	Low risk	60	20
9	James, Nancy	67845	Ellis	3	2	Failed	At risk	22	12
10	Keeshan, Jack	67567	Ellis	3	3	Competent	Some risk	28	16
11	Louis, Joe	87098	Ellis	3	3	Competent	Low risk	45	16
12	Newman, Fred	67121	Ellis	3	5	Competent	Low risk	55	20
13	Perez, Juan	43567	Ellis	3	1	Failed	At risk	8	3
14	Power, Tyrone	67543	Ellis	3	7	Proficient	Low risk	80	40
15	Rogers, Fred	87692	Ellis	3	5	Competent	Low risk	61	20
16	Rudd, Sarah	67545	Ellis	3	2	Failed	At risk	19	12
17	Smith, Raneesha	56780	Ellis	3	3	Failed	At risk	17	16
18	Tuttle, Wylie	90045	Ellis	3	3	Failed	Some risk	39	16
19	Vincent, Jim	56749	Ellis	3	5	Competent	Low risk	54	20
20	Wade, Trey	87496	Ellis	3	5	Competent	Low risk	59	20
21	Wilson, William	45671	Ellis	3	4	Competent	Low risk	47	18
22	Yopp, Hallie	34518	Ellis	3	4	Competent	Low risk	45	18
23	Young, Robert	87947	Ellis	3	5	Competent	Low risk	56	20
24	Avery, Steve	74859	Jones	3	5	Competent	Low risk	62	20
25	Baker, Joe	49824	Jones	3	2	Failed	At risk	15	12

FIGURE 4.4. Sample Excel profile for a second-grade classroom, around September.

CRT, criterion-referenced test; DIBELS, Dynamic Indicators of Basic Early Literacy Skills; ORF, Oral Reading Fluency; WC, words correct per minute; DRA, Diagnostic Reading Assessment after that of Ms. Ellis (see lines 24 and 25). This arrangement makes it easy to generate grade-level profiles.

A further advantage of using Excel is that columns can be added where needed, even for individual children. For example, in the case of Sarah Rudd, a poor score on the DIBELS Oral Reading Fluency (ORF) subtest warrants administering progress-monitoring ORF tests on a weekly or biweekly basis. These scores could be built into the database for Sarah and others being monitored (though they could be tracked in other ways as well). It is possible to include progress-monitoring columns for every child, even those not assessed; however, many of the cells would remain blank, and the grid would soon become unwieldy.

Finally, adding formulas permits automatic calculations of averages and other descriptive statistics. The time required to enter data into an Excel file is often offset by the time saved in computation. Without a doubt, a literacy coach with expertise in Excel is in a position to create many useful applications.

You'll notice in Figure 4.4 that we have avoided the thorny issues related to percentile ranks by using the stanine instead. The *stanine* (short for "standard nine") expresses a test result as a whole number on a scale from 1 to 9. The difference between any two consecutive stanines is statistically equivalent, so that it presumably takes the same effort to move from, say, the 3rd to the 4th stanine as it takes to progress from the 8th to the 9th. Stanines are easier to interpret than percentile ranks, and McKenna and Stahl (2003) recommend this simple guide:

Below average:	Stanines 1–3
Borderline:	Stanine 4
Average:	Stanine 5
Borderline:	Stanine 6
Above average:	Stanines 7–9

Like percentile ranks, stanines cannot be averaged. On the other hand, they have one useful feature that percentile ranks lack; this is called the *two-stanine rule*. When the difference in two scores for a child is two stanines or greater, the difference is likely to be real. When the difference is one stanine, the difference may be the result of chance. For example, if Sarah Rudd scores at the 3rd stanine next spring, it would be dangerous to conclude that she has made up ground. If she scores at the 4th stanine, she probably has in fact advanced with respect to other second graders. The two-stanine rule can also be used to compare a child's scores on two subtests. If Sarah scores at the 2nd stanine in comprehension and at the 4th in vocabulary, for instance, there is probably a real difference in her ability in these two areas.

Coach as Cheerleader

Good literacy coaches look for the positive aspects of assessment results. This is not to say that they should ignore bad news, but it must be presented in perspective. There is often a silver lining in an ominous cloud. For example, in one of our schools, a cohort analysis indicated that the percentage of children at risk in the area of oral reading fluency at the beginning of second grade had risen slightly by the beginning of third grade. This was certainly not good news for the second-grade teachers. On the other hand, they were happy to learn that the average number of words correctly read per minute had risen considerably during the year. Of course, it had not risen sufficiently to bring the worrisome children out of danger, but the teachers' initial reaction was that no growth had occurred whatsoever. The assessment data led them to understand that their efforts had facilitated some improvement, but not enough; they knew they would have to increase attention to this area of the curriculum.

A literacy coach is in a unique position to stimulate achievement by working with individual teachers and groups. Depending on the circumstances, the coach will be in a position to encourage, energize, reassure, counsel, and console.

Coach as Booster

The literacy coach may be called upon to lead efforts to improve scores on high-profile, high-stakes tests. This is serious business because of the demands related to adequate yearly progress. Not surprisingly, many schools have developed creative and sometimes ingenious approaches to improving achievement scores. In the next section, we present several of the strategies commonly used to accomplish this goal. We want literacy coaches to consider these suggestions with a grain of salt; none of them will matter at all unless systematic, explicit instruction has supported children's literacy growth so that they can read the test.

IMPROVING GROUP ACHIEVEMENT SCORES

Standardized testing is a burden most teachers bear resentfully. Such testing often has an undue influence on planning. It is a source of anxiety and frustration for teachers and administrators alike. Its validity is suspect, and its results can occasionally provoke unjustified criticism. For all of their shortcomings, however, standardized group achievement tests are not likely to be scrapped any time soon.

The suggestions offered here are made with this reality in mind. Most have been collected through interviews with practicing educators. Others come from the research literature. Together, they constitute what might be called a "survivor's guide" to norm-referenced testing. Although there is no magic bullet we can use to raise scores to the levels we'd like, there are nevertheless actions we can take to help ensure that scores reflect what students are capable of doing. The literacy coach can be instrumental in facilitating these actions.

Steps for Curriculum Alignment

If children are tested over knowledge and skills they have not been taught, the validity of the test is low, and scores will suffer accordingly. Making certain that the test reflects what actually happens in the classroom is the surest way to improve scores. This process of comparing the objectives covered by the test with those targeted by teachers is called *curriculum alignment.*

Fenwick English (1992), a long-time authority on how schools can narrow the gap between what is tested and what is taught, suggests that not one but three curricula are present in any school. The first is the *written curriculum,* the official set of objectives approved by authorities such as the district administration, the school board, or the state department. The second is the *taught curriculum,* those objectives actually targeted by teachers as they plan their instruction. The third is the *tested curriculum,* the objectives reflected in the group achievement test that students will eventually take.

The three-way Venn diagram presented in Figure 4.5 illustrates how these three curricula can dramatically diverge. When this occurs, the results will be depressed test scores—that is, scores that are lower than the true achievement levels

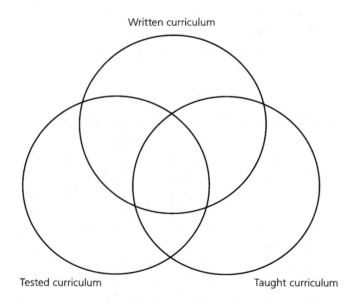

Written curriculum

Tested curriculum   Taught curriculum

FIGURE 4.5. The three curricula to be aligned.

of the students. To put this another way, their scores would have been higher had they been assessed with a properly aligned test. The properly aligned curriculum will focus teacher effort and energy into the shared portion of the diagram.

Evaluating the Curriculum

Effective curriculum alignment is a two-step process. First, the written and tested curricula must be painstakingly contrasted. Objectives that are tested and yet have no counterparts in the official curriculum must be identified. At the same time, objectives that are embraced by a district but that are not tested must be rethought, at least in terms of the emphasis teachers are encouraged to place upon them. There is a danger in this process that the test will, in effect, "drive" instructional decision making. Of course it will. This is a reality with which educators have lived for years. Our purpose here is not to debate the wisdom of this reality, but to offer ways of coming to terms with it. Bringing the written curriculum and the tested curriculum into alignment by identifying where the two do not overlap is the initial action we must take in doing so.

It is important to note that in the case of a test created by a state department of education—such as Florida's Comprehensive Assessment Test, Georgia's Criterion Referenced Competency Test, or Virginia's Standards of Learning test—this step is unnecessary. This is because those authorities who establish the written curriculum have also constructed the assessment instrument. In the case of a commercial achievement test, however—such as the Stanford Achievement Test—Tenth Edition, the Iowa Tests of Basic Skills, the TerraNova, or the Comprehensive Tests of Basic Skills—the differences between the official curriculum and the one embodied in the test can be sizeable.

The second step in curriculum alignment is to contrast the tested curriculum with the taught curriculum. This is done by making a long-term commitment to ensure that what is tested at the end of the year is what was taught during the year. The suggestions that follow will help to accomplish this goal.

Creating Curriculum Maps

A *curriculum map* is a chart that begins with an objective to be tested, includes activities that might be incorporated into lessons, and suggests how the objective might be assessed by a classroom teacher. Perhaps no single teacher can create a comprehensive curriculum map for his or her own subject or grade level, but teams of teachers working together can construct such maps. The literacy coach can lead or facilitate these teams.

We caution, however, that it is not enough to create a curriculum map. If it languishes on the shelf, the entire exercise will have been in vain. Teachers must use such maps in writing daily lesson plans, and the maps must be periodically reviewed and revised. They must become living, organic documents that actually inform instruction. If they are not, then the process is ineffectual and pointless—a waste of precious time that could have been put to better use.

Checking Curriculum Maps

A literacy coach should encourage teachers to acquire the habit of using the curriculum map to plan daily lessons. Each teacher should indicate the objective(s) to be targeted and should consider the activities and instructional techniques suggested by the map makers. Planning instruction, like planning a trip, is generally more successful when we use a map. Otherwise, we might not reach our destination.

Inspecting Item Formats

See whether you can locate item descriptions, published by the test maker, to see how the items are presented. If you can't, encourage teachers to consider the items carefully while they administer the test. (Doing so will at least help for next year.) For each unit taught, a teacher should include on the unit test at least one multiple-choice question similar in format to those on the achievement test the kids will eventually take.

Watching the Calendar

As the test date approaches, remind teachers to take stock of the objectives that have yet to be addressed in class. Since testing is usually done in March or April, there may be a number of tested objectives that will not be taught in time. Every teacher should make a "hurry-up" plan to touch on these objectives, even if they cannot be taught to mastery.

Steps for Making Sure Students Are "Test-Wise"

Reading All the Options

Encourage students to read all multiple-choice options before responding. Many distractors are chosen because they have a misleading appeal. Reading all of the options helps avoid this trap.

Skipping Harder Items

Encourage students to skip harder items and return to them later. Give each student an index card in advance, and show students how to use it to keep their place on the answer form. Tell them to write on the card the numbers of any test items they might wish to revisit.

Process of Elimination

Encourage students to use the process of elimination in responding to difficult multiple-choice items. A useful motto is "Narrow your choices, then make your best guess."

Time Management

Stress the importance of time management. Students should note the time regularly and adjust their pace as needed.

The First-Impression Myth

Encourage students to change their answers on reconsideration whenever closer inspection suggests a change. The widespread notion that one's first impression is best is a myth that runs counter to a large and consistent body of research.

Other Worthless Advice

Avoid making other "conventional wisdom" suggestions that simply don't work on standardized group achievement tests. Among these are the following:

> "If you're not at all sure, guess one of the inside options (those placed in the b or c positions), because test makers like to avoid 'exposing' a correct choice in the a or d position."

This may be true for some classroom tests, but it does not apply to commercial tests, in which answer placement is randomized.

> "Look for grammatical disagreement between the stem and an option. You can eliminate that option."

Again, this will be true of classroom tests on occasion, but commercial tests are carefully edited to prevent such unintended prompts. It's a waste of time even looking for them.

Reviewing Testing Terms

As a literacy coach, you should stress the importance of using the *language of testing* (terms and phrases used on standardized tests) from the beginning of the year in all classroom tests. Examine the subtests carefully to determine the terminology the test maker expects students to know. If a reading comprehension subtest refers to the "passage," students must know what a *passage* is. Make a list of these terms and share them among teachers.

Using Bubble-In Sheets for Daily Work

Make occasional use of an answer sheet for classroom tests. Create it so that bubbling is necessary. Include multiple columns so that students will gain practice in keeping their place.

The Issue of Last-Second Bubble-Ins

Because there is no penalty for guessing on group achievement tests, students should be counseled never to leave a test item blank. Some educators argue that this policy inflates scores. Remember, however, that the creators of achievement tests do not base scores on mastery of objectives, but on comparisons with the norming group. Were students in the national sample likely to have left items blank? This is the real issue, and whatever policy you adopt is ultimately your call.

Special Suggestions for Reading Comprehension Tests

We encourage literacy coaches to share the following dos and don'ts with their teachers. They pertain specifically to reading comprehension subtests based on passages and questions.

"Don't Read the Questions First!"

Do not encourage students to read the questions first. They tend to make little sense without the context of the passage.

Stressing Inferential Questions

Make sure students understand that many answers cannot be located in the passages. Inferential questions are the dominant type used in standardized assessments, so getting this point across is critical. The passage will always contain the basis of an answer, even if the answer itself is not explicitly stated.

What to Do about Hard Words

When reading a passage on a comprehension subtest, students must avoid becoming bogged down on individual words. This is especially true of proper names. Tell them to keep reading and to try to get the gist of a sentence. Laboring over one or two unfamiliar words can not only cause frustration, but may well prevent a student from correctly answering those test items that do not concern these words.

Going Back and Forth

When answering questions about a reading passage, students should go back to the passage actively. Make them realize that the idea is not to test their memories. It's "fair" to go back and ferret out answers.

Modeling the Process

Try modeling this process by making a transparency of a passage and one or more multiple-choice questions. Use a marker to indicate portions of the passage that pertain to each question.

Steps for Making Sure Students Give Their Best Effort

Discussing How the Results May Be Used

Test results are generally a factor in instructional placements, especially as students get older. A literacy coach might discuss the implications of doing one's best in terms of these prospects. Students who do their best will be rewarded by placements that are appropriate for them.

Counseling Individual Students

Identify students who scored extremely poorly last year, but whose ability as indicated by other data is clearly higher. Counsel these students prior to the next standardized test administration. Test them in small groups with direct supervision. For example, one of our second-grade teachers had two such children in her class. She seated them at the same table, in a corner (though it could have been in a conference room with a paraprofessional or volunteer sitting next to them). On the subtest of reading comprehension, the teacher watched to be sure they'd read the first passage *before* she handed them their pencils.

Providing Snacks

Provide juice or milk before testing and during breaks. It can be dispensed at a table in the hall. If possible, provide breakfast, but without syrup, doughnuts, or other sugary foods. Try getting one of your school's business partners to contribute the goodies.

Encouraging Students to Review Answers

Teachers should tell students that if they finish before time is called, *they are not through!* They should spend the remaining time reviewing their answers. Everyone should be working from start to finish.

Sending a Parent Letter

Make sure a letter goes home to parents prior to testing. It should stress making sure that children get plenty of sleep, having them eat a good breakfast, and avoiding family quarrels. A version you might use as a model appears in Figure 4.6. Keep the letter short; the longer it is, the less likely parents are to read it. Use a large type size and paper of an unusual color to attract attention. Sign the letters individually. Add handwritten notes where appropriate. Such a letter should also include the days of testing and the subjects to be tested.

Sending a Practice "Test" for Parents

Try sending home the practice "test" for parents that appears in Figure 4.7. It's fun and might make them think!

Special Steps Coaches and Administrators Can Take

Producing a Testing Policy

Establish a clear testing policy that embodies as many of the preceding suggestions as you feel are warranted in your school. This policy must not be a document that is shelved and forgotten, however. It must be composed with input from teachers and discussed with them in detail, so that all faculty members understand what is expected.

Individualized Testing for Some

Check the state, district, and test guidelines governing when individual administration is permitted. If the guidelines permit individual assessment of children you suspect of merely marking their answer sheets at random, or who are likely to be disruptive, then by all means arrange for these children to be tested individually. Students on 504 plans can be tested individually, but the plan must have been established in advance; there should be no flood of last-minute classifications!

Motivational Focus Sessions

Prior to the testing week, conduct small-group focus sessions with less able students. These students need to be encouraged to try their best and not give up in the midst of a subtest. For many, testing is a frustrating experience; these students (and others) may lack the motivation to do well. Confronting such attitudes proactively can help, especially when the focus groups are led by an experienced counselor or by a role model.

Dear Parent,

Next week we will begin our yearly testing. It is important for all children to do their best. You can help make this happen! Here's how:

- Make sure your child gets to bed early. A good night's sleep is important.
- Every child should eat a good breakfast. It takes energy to perform well!
- Have a talk with your child the night before the test. Stress the importance of trying hard.

Sincerely,

Your friendly literacy coach

FIGURE 4.6. Sample parent letter, asking for assistance for an upcoming test.

PRACTICE TEST FOR PARENTS

Instructions: Circle T (True) or F (False) for each statement.

T   F   1. Tell your child the tests are going to be so hard he or she couldn't possibly pass them.

T   F   2. Have a big fight in your family the night before the test. It won't make any difference the next day when your child takes the test.

T   F   3. Go to visit friends the night before the test and get home late. It won't make any difference the next day when your child takes the test.

T   F   4. Make sure your child goes to bed early and gets plenty of rest on the nights before testing.

T   F   5. Tell your child about how much you hated taking tests when you were in school.

T   F   6. Make sure your child's clothes and shoes are set aside on the evening before a testing day.

T   F   7. Tell your child he or she had better do well on the tests—or else.

T   F   8. Think of something nice you can do for your child after the testing is over.

T   F   9. Make sure that when you're talking about testing with your child, the conversation is positive.

T   F   10. Assure your child that the most important thing is to try hard and do his or her best.

Answers: Let's hope that the answers to these questions are obvious. But just in case, here they are!

    1. F   2. F   3. F   4. T   5. F   6. T   7. F   8. T   9. T   10. T

FIGURE 4.7. Practice "test" to be sent home to parents.

Posttesting Meeting

Once testing is concluded, the natural tendency is to put it out of one's mind and to get back to the business of teaching. But while memories are still fresh, it is a good practice to meet in grade groups or subject-matter teams in order to compare notes about what occurred. Teachers can reflect on item formats, offer observations about test content, and share experiences concerning the administration of the test. In the process, they can also provide support to one another and shore up sagging morale.

The MBWA Approach

Tom Peters and Robert Waterman, in their 1982 bestseller *In Search of Excellence,* coined the acronym "MBWA" to describe the administrative style of effective middle managers. MBWA—"management by walking around"—reflects an especially salient finding: Good managers are seldom at their desks, but are moving around making sure that the right things are happening. The lesson for building-level administrators and literacy coaches is clear. They must be frequent visitors in classrooms during assessments, checking to be sure that teachers and students are in fact doing what they are supposed to be doing and providing support when they are not.

A FINAL WORD

There is an old saying that you cannot fatten a cow by weighing it. Ironically, America's preoccupation with testing may actually threaten achievement by causing us to devote too much time to test preparation and too much worrisome attention to the scales we use to "weigh" our students. It is for this reason that we offer some of the preceding suggestions about standardized testing half-heartedly. It is, of course, only natural to look for Band-Aid approaches to such testing—approaches that appear to hold the promise of improved results at little or no cost. And it does make sense for a literacy coach to lead the effort to revisit the school's policies concerning how this type of testing is conducted. However, screening, diagnostic, and progress-monitoring assessments should not be viewed in that way; they must become essential to everyone in the school community to understand the needs of students and address them in instruction. Bear in mind that there is only one satisfactory remedy for low achievement scores in literacy: increasing literacy achievement. Teachers who are focused on this goal, and who employ instructional strategies known to be effective in attaining it, can be confident that test scores will take care of themselves. It is up to the literacy coach to help maintain this focus.

CHAPTER 5

Instructional Schedules

In this chapter, we will present some sample schedules that educators at real schools have constructed to facilitate teaching and learning. Schedules are constrained by building-level realities, such as the number of classroom teachers, the number of intervention teachers, and the number of teachers for "specials" (e.g., physical education, art, and music). It is unlikely that any one school's schedule can be transported directly into another setting. However, it is possible that elements of these schedules might be useful in crafting a schedule that improves opportunities for teachers and children.

Several issues must be considered prior to designing a schedule. None of these can be decided through examination of research; they are all potentially good decisions if they are right for the setting. One is the total length of the literacy block. We have worked with schools reserving anywhere from 2 to 3 hours for literacy instruction. Another is the flexible grouping strategy that will be used to differentiate instruction to address children's needs. As we have mentioned in Chapter 2, we have worked with schools grouping within the classroom, within each grade level, or across the grade levels. All of these grouping plans can work; all have an effect on the master schedule. Another decision to make up front is what time will be used for intervention—the type of intervention that actually provides additional instruction in literacy for students with serious literacy deficits. Some schools choose to provide intervention during regular school hours, and they interrupt instruction in other content areas; other schools choose to extend time, either by creating after-school programs or by adding days to the school year. Finally, a decision has to be made about the ideal time and place for professional development and collaboration. Again, some schools choose to do these things during the regular school day, and others choose after-school hours. We frame our presentations of model schedules around the answers to these questions.

PORTER HIGHLAND SCHOOL

Our first school schedule was designed by a team working at Porter Highland School (all school schedules are real, but the names are pseudonyms) to reform the curriculum of a fairly small school with very generous resources. This school had four classrooms at each grade level, kindergarten through third grade. Together, the team members made decisions that supported literacy teaching and learning by drastically changing their master instructional schedule. The first decision they made was that they would allocate 90 minutes each day for whole-group and needs-based instruction for all children, and then 30 additional minutes each day for students whose instructional level was below grade level.

The team members realized that 90 minutes was not a lot of time, and this consideration influenced their decisions about grouping. In the kindergarten and first-grade classrooms, teachers had paraprofessionals who received professional development alongside them and who worked as instructional partners. Because each teacher and paraprofessional could work with two groups at once, the team members decided that within-class grouping was preferable at these grade levels.

In the second and third grades, paraprofessional partners were not available. Because of the short time allotted for literacy instruction, the team members chose a within-grade-level regrouping plan for these grades. Each teacher would spend 1 hour with a group comprising children with similar literacy profiles, from any of the homeroom classes. Three Title I reading specialists would join each grade-level team, taking the three lowest-performing instructional groups in the grade level. After that hour, the children would have 30 minutes of fluency practice in their heterogeneous homeroom classes, and also a whole-class read-aloud to develop comprehension strategies later in the school day.

The school assessment profile showed that large numbers of children required intervention: Their initial literacy achievement was below grade level, so they were unlikely to achieve literacy acceleration without drastic measures. The team decided that kindergarten and first-grade children should have daily small-group intervention time, and that this should come during science and social studies time, protecting math instruction for all. For the second and third grades, the team decided that intervention should come during the school day for those with the largest deficits; again, it would come from science and social studies time, when the curriculum materials were too difficult to serve these children's needs well. They would not sacrifice all of their science and social studies content, though. The team members decided that intervention could only come three times each week, and that they would use content-area trade books matched to the state standards for science and social studies in their read-alouds. In addition, they decided to provide intervention opportunities for those children who were only slightly below grade level. They organized a late bus schedule for two after-school sessions each week to serve these children.

The team members were committed to learning together during the school day through team planning and with their literacy coach. They decided that they wanted to spend some of their professional development time in grade-level teams and some of their time as a whole faculty. Grade-level meetings were scheduled during the day, with each grade level meeting weekly at a different time while children were in specials. The team members modified their weekly work schedule so that they could leave earlier several days each week, in order to make up for an hour of planning time devoted to professional development. They alternated this planning time with two sessions each month to work with the literacy coach and two to work on curriculum mapping with a gifted education specialist. Through grant funds, the school was able to set aside money to pay the teachers and paraprofessionals to stay for an additional hour three times each month; this time was reserved for whole-school professional development led by the literacy coach.

Figure 5.1 presents the master schedule for Porter Highland School. One thing to notice is that the lunch schedule at this school was the same for all, because there was no cafeteria. All students ate in their rooms. Because of the decisions described above, creating the schedule was like solving a logic puzzle. The team members started by considering the weekly professional development time. In order for that to work, each grade level had to have an hour of specials at the same time 1 day each week, and of course these times could not overlap because of the personnel. The specials began in third grade, first thing in the morning, and then moved down through the grades. Second graders went next, first graders were third, and kindergartners had their specials at the end of the day.

Once the specials were planned, the focus was on creating the literacy block time. To allow the intervention team (three teachers in all) to work effectively as part of team reading instruction, this block had to allow for different instructional times in second and third grades. To trace the work of a single intervention teacher, then, the schedule enabled her to teach one needs-based group at second grade for an hour, and then to teach another needs-based group at third grade for an hour. During the reading practice times, all children were back in their homerooms, which were heterogeneous in terms of achievement.

Finally, the team planned the intervention time. Since the intervention providers were already teaching needs-based groups from 9:00 to 11:00, interventions could not begin until after that time. The three teachers assumed different responsibilities. One spent her afternoon with consecutive groups of kindergartners. Another spent her time with first graders. The third spent her time with struggling second and third graders, and also managed the after-school program for those two grade levels.

This schedule was a huge departure from "business as usual" at this school. In fact, in order to use time and personnel in more carefully planned and coordinated ways, all teachers gave up autonomy about when they taught what. The sacrifice

Time	K	1	2	3
9:00–10:00	Reading block (teacher and assistant)	Reading block (teacher and assistant)	Team reading instruction	Specials
10:00–10:30	Reading block	Reading block	Reading practice	Team reading instruction
10:30–11:00	Recess	Recess	Specials	Read-aloud and writing
11:00–12:00	Math	Math	Read-aloud and writing	Reading practice
12:00–12:30	Lunch	Lunch	Lunch	Lunch
12:30–1:00	Intervention, science, or social studies	Specials	Intervention, science, or social studies (3/week)	Math
1:00–1:30	Intervention, science, or social studies	Writing	Intervention, science, or social studies (3/week)	Math
1:30–2:00	Specials	Intervention, science, or social studies	Math	Intervention, science, or social studies (3/week)
2:00–2:30	Centers	Intervention, science, or social studies	Math	Intervention, science, or social studies (3/week)
2:30–3:00	Intervention or centers	Intervention, science, or social studies	Writing	Writing
3:00–4:15	Writing	Writing	After-school session (2/week)	After-school session (2/week)

FIGURE 5.1. Schedule for Porter Highland School.

of this freedom was worthwhile. The adults in the school learned to build a program by putting the needs of children first.

McMILLAN ACADEMY

McMillan Academy, also a small school (12 classrooms, three each in kindergarten through fifth grade) made different decisions, and these decisions drove the creation of a different master schedule. First, the team members decided to devote 3 hours each day to reading and writing. They made arrangements for after-school professional development (again by paying teachers overtime). Since their literacy block was long, they chose a within-classroom grouping strategy, with 30 minutes of teacher instruction for each group while the other group worked at literacy centers. Finally, they decided to use extended time options (intersessions in their modified calendar, as well as summer school) to provide intervention, rather than building it into the school day. The schedule they devised is presented in Figure 5.2.

BRADENTON ELEMENTARY

The team at Bradenton Elementary, a much larger school with seven sections at each grade level (kindergarten through fifth grade), made different basic decisions and created a different master schedule; this is presented in Figure 5.3. At Bradenton, time for literacy instruction included 90 minutes of needs-based time

Time	K	1	2	3	4	5
8:15–9:15	Whole-group literacy	Whole-group literacy	Whole-group literacy	Whole-group literacy	Specials	Specials
9:15–10:15	Needs-based literacy	Needs-based literacy	Needs-based literacy	Needs-based literacy	Whole-group literacy	Whole-group literacy
10:15–11:15	Math	Math	Specials	Math	Science/ social studies	Science/ social studies
11:15–12:15	Specials	Lunch Writing	Writing Lunch	Specials	Math	Math
12:15–1:15	Lunch Writing	Specials	Math	Science/ social studies Lunch	Lunch Science/ social studies	Science/ social studies Lunch
1:15–2:00	Needs-based literacy	Needs-based literacy	Needs-based literacy	Needs-based literacy	Needs-based literacy	Needs-based literacy
2:00–2:30	Science/ social studies	Science/ social studies	Science/ social studies	Writing	Writing	Writing

FIGURE 5.2. Schedule for McMillan Academy.

Time	K	1	2	3	4	5
8:00–8:30	Opening	Opening	Opening	Opening	Opening	Opening
8:30–9:00	Literacy block	Within-grade-level regrouping	Cross-grade-level regrouping	Cross-grade-level regrouping	Cross-grade-level regrouping	Cross-grade-level regrouping
9:00–9:30						
9:30–10:00						
10:00–10:30	Specials	Grade-level literacy instruction	Grade-level literacy instruction	Grade-level literacy instruction	Grade-level literacy instruction	Science/ social studies
10:30–11:00	Lunch					Specials
11:00–11:30	Thematic curriculum	Lunch			Specials	Grade-level literacy instruction
11:30–12:00		Math	Lunch	Specials	Lunch	
12:00–12:30			Math	Lunch	Math	
12:30–1:00				Math		Lunch
1:00–1:30		Science/ social studies	Specials		Science/ social studies	Math
1:30–2:00		Specials	Science/ social studies	Science/ social studies		
2:00–2:30	Read-aloud	Read-aloud	Read-aloud	Read-aloud	Read-aloud	Read-aloud

FIGURE 5.3. Schedule for Bradenton Elementary.

and 90 minutes of grade-level time. As a result, there was little time for other work—60 minutes for math, 30 minutes for science or social studies, and 30 minutes for a content-area read-aloud.

Like the team at Porter Highland, the Bradenton team members chose different grouping strategies for different grade levels. They chose within-class strategies for the kindergartners and the first graders. For the older children, though, they chose cross-grade regrouping. They did this because they had such large groups of children functioning 2 or more years below grade level, and they had to serve them all with extended time and limited personnel. Taken together, the weakest-performing fourth and fifth graders had skills similar to those of an existing group of third graders. All of these children could be served in the same group, and then regrouped and moved as their skills improved. At the same time, these struggling older children needed to learn grade-level vocabulary and comprehension strategies; they did this during grade-level literacy instruction.

This huge commitment to literacy instruction made further intervention time during the school day impossible; extending the school year for struggling children was a more viable option. For teachers, scheduling professional development time during the day was impossible. Instead, the principal contracted with a group of seven substitutes to spend time learning a set of curriculum practices at each grade level, and to come to substitute on the same day every week. They spent the first 3 hours of that day at one grade level, while those teachers collaborated and had time for staff development with their literacy coach; in the afternoon, the substitutes moved to another grade level. In this way, each grade-level team had a 3-hour block of professional development time every 3 weeks. The fact that the substitutes were there every week integrated them into the school team and cut down on wasted time and on behavior problems. It also provided a loyal and experienced cadre of substitutes to address the need for substitutes on other days.

WHITE OAK SCHOOL

The principal and literacy coach at White Oak School had a big-school problem in a small-school setting: Their instructional day was so fragmented that teaching and learning were compromised. In this kindergarten-through-fourth-grade school, intervention providers (including Title I teachers, special educators, physical therapists, psychologists, and counselors) traveled between two schools, each with an independent schedule. This created a scheduling nightmare for the front office and a sense of helplessness for teachers trying to set up literacy instruction schedules. The principal made a bold decision. He decided that all literacy instruction would happen at the same time—8:20–11:20—and that no interruptions would be permitted. He scheduled both the instruction and the intervention during those 3 hours, and asked all other intervention providers to use their morning hours at the other school. Although this plan was controversial at first, it was better for both sites in the end.

Another significant change came in the physical education schedule. The school had no resources for art or music; physical education was the only special. Each classroom was traditionally scheduled for 30 minutes in the gym twice each week. With no interruptions before 11:20, this would not be possible. Also, the tenured gym teacher would have nothing to do in the mornings. The gym teacher took matters into his own hands. He enrolled in a reading endorsement program through a local university and joined the intervention team in the morning literacy block. Then he doubled up in his own schedule, meeting two classes at a time instead of one, so that the children still had physical education twice each week. Because he was an excellent manager, the principal told us that the gym program ran just as before, and the children who worked in reading interventions with the gym-teacher-turned-interventionist were highly motivated.

TIME FOR TEACHING

The work that these (and many other) schools did at the school level made a difference to instruction at the classroom level. Here is a snapshot. The schedules that follow (Figures 5.4–5.7) are displayed outside the doors of classrooms at Christiansberg Elementary School. Here there is a direct connection between the literacy coach and principal's efforts to focus attention on using time wisely and the teachers' instructional schedules. School-level efforts make it easier for teachers to attend to scientifically based reading research (SBRR). In Chapter 6, we will describe instructional procedures that teachers at these grade levels would use in these precious minutes.

Kindergarten

The instructional team in kindergarten includes a teacher and a paraprofessional partner. The two work together to divide the class into two instructional groups as often as possible (for writing, for phonemic awareness, for reading decodable text, and during the literacy rotation). The schedule, reproduced in Figure 5.4, allows the children to move both physically and mentally from whole-group activities to small-group activities. In the afternoon literacy rotation, the groups are even smaller. The intervention teacher comes into the classroom for an hour to work with children who are struggling, and therefore three adults meet with groups at the same time.

First Grade

The first-grade teachers have the support of paraprofessionals through 10:40, so that is when they do the bulk of their literacy work (see Figure 5.5). Compared with the kindergarten team, the first-grade team devotes more time to writing. As with the kindergartners, the school schedule allows an intervention teacher to come into the classroom for 1 hour—the hour used for fluency groups. During that hour, the weakest-performing children work together with the intervention provider, and the rest of the class rotates among the teacher, the paraprofessional, and a literacy center.

Second Grade

In order to accommodate the rest of the school's needs, the second-grade teachers begin the day with math instruction. The schedule is presented in Figure 5.6. The second two blocks, phonics instruction/reading practice and a writer's workshop, are run by the teachers working alone. The fluency groups, which start next, are linked to the intervention time; again, an intervention provider comes into the

7:45–8:00	Announcements, pledge, calendar
8:00–8:30	Read-aloud (whole group) Writing in response to reading (small groups)
8:30–9:05	Phonemic awareness activities (whole group) Phonemic awareness activities (small groups)
9:05–9:30	Shared reading (whole group)
9:30–10:00	Recess
10:00–10:45	Math
10:45–11:15	Lunch
11:20–11:50	Science/social studies
11:50–12:30	Phonics (whole group) Reading decodable texts (small groups)
12:30–1:30	Literacy rotation and intervention (small groups)
1:30–2:10	Activity period
2:15	Dismissal

FIGURE 5.4. Kindergarten daily schedule: Christiansberg Elementary.

7:45–8:00	Partner reading (take-home books)
8:00–8:30	Phonics and reading decodable books (whole group, small groups)
8:30–9:00	Shared reading (whole group)
9:00–9:40	Writer's workshop (whole-group mini-lesson, individual writing)
9:40–10:40	Fluency groups and intervention (small groups)
10:45–11:15	Lunch
11:20–11:45	Science/social studies
11:45–12:45	Math
12:45–1:25	Activity period
1:25–1:45	Recess
1:50–2:10	Read-aloud
2:15	Dismissal

FIGURE 5.5. First-grade daily schedule: Christiansberg Elementary.

room and spends that entire time working with the weakest-performing children. The teacher rotates the rest of the children through work with her and work at literacy centers. Afternoon literacy time in second grade is whole-group, and the focus is on comprehension instruction, both in narrative texts and in information texts that comprise the focus on content-area reading strategies.

Third Grade

The third-grade team has the support of an intervention provider first thing in the morning, so that is the time for fluency groups (see Figure 5.7). As in second grade, the weakest-performing children spend the whole block with the intervention teacher, while the rest of the children rotate between literacy centers and the teacher. There is still time for shared reading, when all children are working with the teacher from the third-grade basal anthology. Since many children have decoding needs, decoding and spelling are built into the daily plan. Science and social studies time may include text, either with leveled sets of texts on the same topic or with read-alouds from appropriate information text.

A WORD TO THE WISE

Scheduling is important to teaching and learning. Seeing beyond the current schedule into all of the possible schedules is not easy. Visiting other schools, especially schools where decisions that affect the schedule (the length of the literacy block, the grouping strategies, the times for intervention and for professional develop-

7:45–8:00	Partner reading
8:00–9:00	Math
9:00–9:30	Phonics and reading practice
9:30–10:15	Writer's workshop
10:15–11:15	Fluency groups and intervention
11:15–11:45	Lunch
12:00–12:40	Activity period
12:45–1:15	Shared reading/read-aloud
1:15–1:45	Content-area reading
1:50–2:10	Recess
2:15	Dismissal

FIGURE 5.6. Second-grade daily schedule: Christiansberg Elementary.

7:45–8:00	Partner reading
8:00–9:00	Fluency groups and intervention
9:00–9:30	Shared reading
9:30–10:00	Phonics and spelling
10:05–10:45	Activity period
10:45–11:45	Math
11:45–12:15	Luntch
12:20–1:10	Writer's workshop
1:10–1:30	Recess
1:30–2:10	Social studies/science
2:15	Dismissal

FIGURE 5.7. Third-grade daily schedule: Christiansberg Elementary.

ment) have been different, can open up possibilities. In the end, though, the realities of time, space, and personnel and curriculum in a particular building are what set the scheduling parameters. Investigating scheduling options is a fall task; making a new schedule is a spring task; implementing a new schedule is once again a fall task.

In Figure 5.8, we restate the important questions that might guide your work. Answers to each question are important. If you have a very long literacy block, then a within-class regrouping scheme is easier to accomplish; there is ample time for both needs-based instruction for each group and grade-level instruction for all. If you have a shorter literacy block, consider the potential benefits of within-grade or across-grade regrouping. That way, you can provide needs-based instruction for all groups at the same time. If you will have intervention teachers moving into classrooms during the literacy block, consider stacking the blocks so that these teachers can work efficiently. If you want to provide intervention and professional development and collaboration during the day, then either stack your enrichment or specials so that teachers have planning at the same time at least once each week, or arrange for substitutes to be trained and working in classrooms on a regular schedule. Take the time to think the schedule through.

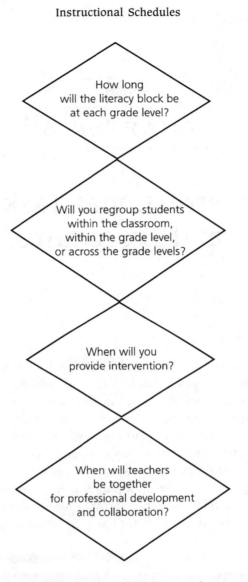

FIGURE 5.8. Scheduling guide.

CHAPTER 6

Instructional Tasks
and Procedures

In this chapter, we take some of the research that has been presented in Chapter 3 and use it to provide some grade-level-specific snapshots. Many literacy coaches have been excellent classroom teachers, but few have experience at all of the elementary grade levels; we paint the K–3 years here in broad strokes. We also briefly review stage theories in learning to read and spell. We do this here, before we discuss the selection of commercial materials in the next chapter. One of the difficulties literacy coaches tend to face at the start of their work is the large numbers of very low-performing readers in the upper grades. Stage theories are important because the only way to accelerate literacy growth for children who are behind is to acknowledge their needs—needs that are likely to be quite inconsistent with their grade-level curriculum.

We take the position here that literacy coaches should support teachers in providing some grade-level instruction to the whole group and some needs-based instruction to groups formed and reformed by achievement levels. Although it may seem counterintuitive to say so, many teachers are uncomfortable providing direct instruction to small groups of children. Part of the reason for this may be that core program materials typically address whole-group instruction only, with very little attention to grouping or needs-based-group instruction. In fact, in a review of seven basal series, researchers found fewer than 200 directions to teachers for leading small groups themselves and over 1,000 each for employing student-led groups or paired formats (Moody, Schumm, Fischer, & Jean-Francois, 1999). Another reason may be their lack of experience with managing groups efficiently. A vision of what should happen in whole-group settings and in needs-based settings is essential to the literacy coach.

STAGE THEORIES IN READING AND SPELLING

What are *stages*? What does it mean to be in one stage or another? There are actually some specific conditions that must be met in order for any developmental trajectory to be characterized by stages. We must be able to identify a specific set of indicators that are found in all individuals in that stage; there must be a watershed break that separates one stage from another; and the differences between stages must be qualitative—individuals in a higher stage have to do something different, rather than just do something better or faster (Bjorklund, 1995). This is not to suggest that stages are so sharply delineated that a child may be in one stage on Tuesday and the next on Wednesday. Nevertheless, the distinctions are real, and a literacy coach's ability to anticipate and recognize progress from one stage to the next is crucial. Understanding the indicators is central to actually developing a program that both serves children's current needs and accelerates growth for those who are struggling.

Connie Juel (1991) has reviewed stage theories in beginning reading. They have evolved differently, and there are some minor differences in the stage descriptions, but there is remarkable consistency across the theories. The general progression is this: Children move from attending to some aspect of the physical shape of words, to processing some of the letters, to processing all of the letters, to recognizing most words automatically. At first, when children begin to read words, they focus their attention on only one salient aspect of the word (e.g., the picture or font as in reading environmental print, or some part of the shape of the word). They leave this stage when they have enough phonemic awareness and enough alphabet knowledge to focus on partial alphabet cues—typically, initial and final consonants. They leave this stage when they know and are able to use letter sounds, including the vowels in the middle, to decode words. Finally, they recognize familiar words automatically, with no need for decoding.

These stages are much easier to see in children's spelling. Bear and Templeton (1998) have identified four stages in beginning spelling. In the *prephonemic* stage, children engage in pretend writing, theorizing that writing represents meaning directly with no reference to sound. With rudimentary phonemic awareness and some alphabet knowledge, they are in the *semiphonemic* stage—theorizing that writing does represent sound, but lacking the skills to fully analyze words. At this stage, they might spell *monster* "M" or "MR." With additional development, they move into the *letter name* stage. At this stage, they use what they know about letter names (rather than sounds) to spell. They spell *wet* "YAT," confusing the letter name Y with the letter sound /w/, the letter name A with the letter sound /e/, and correctly representing the letter sound T, since its name contains its sound. By the fourth stage, within-word pattern, they spell single-syllable, short vowel words conventionally.

Understanding these basic stage theories is essential to crafting a building-level program. We have focused our attention on developing knowledge of spelling

Spelling stages
1) prephonemic
2) semiphonemic
3) letter name
4) within word

stages as the foundation of our work with literacy coaches, because spelling stages are easy to see in children's work. We did this through a study group with the book *Words Their Way: Word Study for Phonics, Vocabulary, and Spelling* (Bear, Invernizzi, Templeton, & Johnston, 2004). Literacy coaches then introduced stage theories to their teachers by asking them to give and score a developmental spelling assessment (Ganske, 2000). The power of this type of data collection in exposing teachers to the very real instructional needs of their children should not be underestimated. Unfortunately, though, neither should teachers' panic. In the sections that follow, we offer examples of particular instructional methods appropriate for readers at different ages and stages. As you read, consider the grade-level organization as the goal, but the developmental level as the potential reality. For example, when we describe instructional procedures appropriate for developing decoding in first grade, those same procedures are also appropriate for third graders whose decoding development is at the first-grade level—those children in your intervention programs. In Chapter 8, we address the need for intensive literacy acceleration for these children whose developmental level is below grade level.

INSTRUCTIONAL EMPHASES

Before we describe particular instructional procedures we see as essential to literacy development at various ages and stages of reading development, we need to contextualize them within the broader structure of the reading program. First, various components of literacy instruction are nested within grouping configurations. Figure 6.1 provides some guidance. The realities of classrooms and schools (as well as what we know about development of vocabulary and comprehension) demand that we situate some aspects of instruction in undifferentiated, whole-group settings. The realities of children's literacy needs demand that we situate other aspects of instruction in differentiated, needs-based settings.

Reading programs also involve days and minutes devoted to specific activities. Time matters. Before we address specific instructional procedures, we want to provide an overview of how they might work together to provide a healthy diet of literacy instruction for children at different ages and stages. Unlike the old U.S. Department of Agriculture food pyramid, which has been criticized of late, instructional diets are still quite sound. We are influenced by the work of researchers who got their start at the McGuffey Reading Center at the University of Virginia (e.g., Mary Abouzied, Donald Bear, Janet Bloodgood, Kathy Ganske, Marcia Invernizzi, Darryl Morris, and Shane Templeton), who have consistently recommended that reading instruction be based on choices that together constitute a healthy diet for children. The components of this diet should shift as children's literacy skills increase.

	Phonemic awareness	Decoding	Fluency	Vocabulary	Comprehension strategies
K	Needs-based group	Whole group and needs-based group	Whole group and needs-based group	Whole group	Whole group
1	Needs-based group	Whole group and needs-based group	Whole group and needs-based group	Whole group	Whole group
2	Intervention only	Needs-based group	Whole group and needs-based group	Whole group	Whole group and needs-based group
3		Intervention only	Whole group and needs-based group	Whole group and needs-based group	Whole group and needs-based group

FIGURE 6.1. A model for grouping by grade level and component.

Figure 6.2 provides our own "instructional diet," a concept that must be interpreted by grade level for normally achieving students or by skills level for struggling students. Because literacy coaches need to address literacy development, we include both reading and writing in our model for how to use time. There follow some instructional procedures that literacy coaches can nest within grouping configurations and within the allowable time for instruction as they design their reading program. Thoughtful decision making (rather than direct reference to scientifically based reading research [SBRR]) is necessary here. In actuality, the ideal combination of instructional procedures, times, groups, and ages is a question both central to the work of a literacy coach and also impossible to answer through research. We believe that a general overview of instructional practices aligned with SBRR and with high utility in classrooms is important before selection of specific

	Phonemic awareness	Decoding	Fluency	Vocabulary	Comprehension strategies	Writing
K	20%	10%	20%	30%	10%	10%
1	10%	20%	20%	20%	10%	20%
2		10%	30%	10%	30%	20%
3			20%	20%	30%	30%

FIGURE 6.2. A model for instructional time by grade level.

instructional materials—a topic we take up in the next chapter. As you read this chapter, then, keep in mind that we are identifying typical research-based practices to help you look across the elementary school years.

INSTRUCTION FOR KINDERGARTEN READERS AND WRITERS

Whole Class Activities

Kindergartners surely spend some of their instructional day in whole-class activities. Ideally, those activities are *active*—allowing kindergarten readers and writers both the space and the opportunity to respond physically, to respond orally, and to read and write together.

Decoding

In order for kindergartners to learn to decode, they must develop alphabet knowledge. Typically, whole-group time in kindergarten includes time for learning and reviewing letter names, letter sounds, and letter formation. Kindergartners should learn quickly to sing the full alphabet, to track it while singing, to say the alphabet, and to track it while saying it. They also need to learn to recognize and produce the sound for any letter in isolation. This proficiency is not developed quickly. The traditional "letter-a-week" approach is insufficient. Alternative approaches include emphases on comparing and contrasting letters in predetermined small sets (selected for their specific visual and phonemic contrasts rather than their place in the alphabet, such as a focus on *b, m, r,* and *s*), and also built-in reinforcement and review of sets of letters previously introduced.

Kindergartners can and should read while they are developing their letter knowledge. Two kinds of reading are important: reading to learn to track print, and reading to apply letter–sound knowledge in text that allows it. For kindergarten readers, learning to track print is essential to later success in decoding (Morris, 1981). Kindergartners learn to track print by reading text that they have already memorized. For example, they may learn to sing a simple song, then learn to touch the words as they sing it. They can also learn to track print in specially designed texts with repeated sentences or phrases and/or with extremely supportive pictures. This type of reading of predictable text is easy to accomplish in whole-group settings by using big books or chart paper poems and stories.

Fluency

Typically, in this text, we have defined *fluency* as the application of automatic word recognition in text so that it can be read with appropriate rhetorical phrasing and rhythms (prosody). In kindergarten, fluency with lower-level processes (i.e., below the level of text) is a necessary precursor to text-based fluency. Kindergarten readers and writers need to develop automatic, effortless access to the recognition of both letters and the sounds they commonly represent. In whole-group settings, this access can be developed through daily playful review, through songs, and through the use of letter manipulatives (plastic letters, games, puzzles, and flashcards).

Vocabulary

Vocabulary development is absolutely essential in the kindergarten classroom. Vocabulary development in kindergarten must not be confused with development of word recognition: Kindergarten children might learn to read the word *run*, but they might also learn the meanings of *prance, wobble*, and *tiptoe*—words that they cannot yet read. The best source of words to teach children is the literature that they hear read aloud. Beck, McKeown, and Kucan (2002) present an instructional framework for such vocabulary development:

1. Tell a word in its context from a story.
2. Ask children to repeat the word, so that they represent its sound.
3. Explain the meaning of the word.
4. Provide another context, outside of the story.
5. Support children as they generate their own context.
6. Ask children to say the word again.

This simple procedure embeds what we know about vocabulary learning, reviewed in Chapter 3, within an essential component of the kindergarten day—the read-aloud.

Comprehension

As with vocabulary learning, kindergarten children must develop their comprehension skills and strategies far ahead of their decoding strategies. Again, the read-aloud is the perfect context. One strategy particularly appropriate for the whole-group read-aloud in kindergarten is *retelling*.

Retellings in kindergarten allow young children to develop their oral language skills, as well as the rudimentary knowledge of story structure that is so important to comprehension. Retellings are personal oral representations of text that has been read (and perhaps reread) aloud. For kindergartners, they must be scaffolded by the teacher (Morrow, 1984). Temporal prompts (such as beginning, middle, and end) or narrative prompts (such as who, when, and where) help children to formulate retellings that develop their comprehension skills.

Writing

Kindergarten children usually come to school without the alphabet knowledge necessary for writing, but they develop that knowledge over the course of the year. This does not mean that they should wait to write. At the beginning of the year, shared writing experiences (where teachers transcribe children's oral language, transforming talk into text) help children to learn the conventions of writing and to become engaged in the process. These shared writing experiences are also opportunities to develop phonemic awareness and alphabet knowledge, as teachers model the isolation of speech sounds and their matches to letters.

Kindergarten children can also do their own writing by drawing and labeling. This is particularly appropriate in whole-class settings, because it allows each child to work at the edge of his or her competence. For example, a child with high levels of phonemic awareness and alphabet knowledge may represent many sounds correctly, while a child with less competence in these basic skills may engage in pretend writing or scribbling. A continuum of more difficult tasks across the year—moving from simple labeling, to use of frame sentences, to writing of sentences and stories—ensures that children use what they are learning about the alphabetic principle to write.

Needs-Based Group Activities

Phonemic Awareness

Kindergarten children benefit from direct instruction aimed at developing phonemic awareness, and this instruction is best provided in small groups. *Picture sorts,* where children physically manipulate small sets of pictures to compare and contrast sounds, both engage and challenge kindergartners. Bear et al. (2004) suggest many variations of picture sorts—sorting pictures by initial-consonant sound, final-consonant sound, or short-vowel word family. An *oddity task* is a targeted variation of a picture sort: Children presented with three pictures decide which one is not like the others.

Decoding

Kindergartners who can track print confidently, who are developing phonemic awareness, and who know many of their letter sounds should also read books that allow them to stretch their decoding "muscles" in decodable text. For decodable text to be appropriate, its demands must be coordinated with the phonics knowledge that is being developed in the curriculum. Specially designed little books are available for this work. For kindergarten children to get maximum benefit from this work, they must all be reading at the same time, but not chorally. In essence, then, this is individual work that the teacher can support better in a small-group setting.

Fluency

The key to developing fluency for kindergartners is simply practice. Kindergartners need practice with phonemic awareness tasks (e.g., segmenting and blending), with decoding tasks (at both the word and text levels), with writing and spelling, and with oral language tasks (e.g., retelling). Some time in small groups, facilitated by a teacher, should be spent with practice of particular components introduced to the whole class.

INSTRUCTION FOR FIRST-GRADE READERS AND WRITERS

The first-grade year is the watershed opportunity for development of the essential foundational skills that underlie future literacy success. In order for the curriculum to ensure maximum success, every moment counts. Planned use of time and groupings is essential.

Whole-Class Activities

Progress in reading in first grade can range from steady, incremental increases to huge stalls and leaps. Whole-class activities in first grade lay the foundation for many children's successful move to conventional reading and writing.

Decoding

First graders must develop the knowledge and skills to understand and use the alphabetic principle to read and spell. Their decoding instruction, then, must be targeted to developing this knowledge and to using it to read and spell words. The scope and sequence of instruction are both important; instruction must be clear, direct, and progressive. Unfortunately, research does not tell us exactly what the ideal sequence should be. Rather, it tells us that it must be explicit and systematic. Some characteristics of the ideal scope and sequence can be inferred from developmental research. It must include review of letter sounds from the kindergarten curriculum, a focus on reading and spelling short-vowel sounds correctly, mastery of *r*-controlled vowels, and early work with long-vowel patterns. At the same time, first graders must learn to recognize and spell many high-frequency words with uncommon spelling patterns (e.g., *love*). The focus of the decoding curriculum must be (1) on using letter–sound and spelling pattern knowledge to recognize unknown words, and (2) on building an essential sight word vocabulary.

The decoding curriculum must include attention to the strategies that good readers use. The tricky issue is the role of context. The fact is that struggling readers do use context to guess what words might be; often they are correct when they guess. They use context to compensate for their lack of proficiency in decoding. As they become more skillful, context will be used chiefly to infer the intended meanings of multiple-meaning words. As proficient adult readers, we use context for this purpose alone, and not to guess the identity of a word without decoding it. Therefore, *teaching* children to guess is not an appropriate focus for the first-grade decoding curriculum. The primary focus of the decoding curriculum is on developing knowledge of letter sounds and patterns and strategies for using them to read words.

Fluency

First graders need to move from sound-by-sound decoding strategies to automatic word recognition. The only way for them to do this is to engage in extended reading practice. First graders must read and reread. They must read words in isolation, and they must read words in text. In whole-class settings, teachers provide both support and opportunity for this rereading. They use different reading formats (such as choral reading, echo reading, and paired reading) to facilitate reading practice.

First graders can also develop fluency by reading and rereading books that are carefully selected for them. Any book that has been previously read in an instructional setting, or any book that contains phonics elements previously taught, is a book eligible for fluency work. Another way to build fluency for these beginning readers is to build in time for practice reading. In first grade, this practice reading is anything but silent; for all children, reading aloud to themselves to build fluency is noisy business.

Vocabulary and Comprehension Strategies

For first graders, we combine vocabulary and comprehension strategies, because both can be developed effectively during the classroom read-aloud—if it is viewed as an active instructional context. Again, as with kindergartners, vocabulary and comprehension instruction for first graders is best situated within the read-aloud, because they can develop these skills and strategies far outside of their competence for reading text. In essence, we ask teachers to keep in mind that children learn to understand words and text structures orally so that they can read them later.

Children do learn new words from listening (Elley, 1989). They can also learn much more about text and how it works from read-alouds, but only if these are interactive. Smolkin and Donovan (2001) have described the interactive read-aloud as a context for comprehension acquisition in first grade, particularly when information texts are read aloud. Children who ask and answer questions, who listen to their teacher modeling thinking skills, and who make connections to other texts and to past experiences during read-alouds in which they are expected to learn new concepts are participating in a mediated instructional setting.

We have worked with teachers to use cognitive language during these read-aloud sessions. We borrow from the work of Gerald Duffy and colleagues (Duffy et al., 1986, 1987) in direct explanation, described in Chapter 3, when we encourage teachers to use strategy procedures (telling what strategies are, and how, when, and why readers use them) and strategy names. Figure 6.3 provides information about an acronym, "PICTURE," which we have devised with teachers for use in teaching multiple comprehension strategies. Each of these strategies comes from the research literature on comprehension; naming these strategies, and pro-

PICTURE a Good Reader:
First-Grade Performance Benchmarks

Predict: What do I think will happen next?
- Students predict from title and pictures before read-alouds.
- Students evaluate and change predictions during read-alouds.
- Students predict from title and pictures before they read.
- Students evaluate and change predictions during their reading.

Imagine: Can I imagine what is happening?
- Students visualize story events during read-alouds.
- Students visualize story events during their reading.

Clarify: Does this make sense?
- Students ask questions during read-alouds when something does not make sense.
- Students ask questions during their own reading when something does not make sense.

Try: Can I ask myself "how" and "why" questions?
- Students answer inferential questions during read-alouds.
- Students answer inferential questions during their own reading.

Use: What do I know already?
- Students use prior knowledge to help them understand texts read aloud.
- Students use prior knowledge to help them understand texts that they are reading.

Review: Can I summarize?
- Students retell a story after a read-aloud—including beginning, middle, and end, and characters, setting, problem, and solution.

Evaluate: Would I recommend this book to someone else?
- Students discuss and write in response to fiction.
- Students discuss and write in response to nonfiction.

FIGURE 6.3. Comprehension strategy language and benchmarks, first grade.

viding children extended exposure to modeling and guided practice with them within and across the elementary school years, are essential to developing strategy knowledge. For first graders, the read-aloud is the best context for this.

Writing

First graders write in school for many reasons. They write to learn to form letters easily. They write to practice segmenting oral language and representing letter sounds with letters. They write to practice spelling high-frequency words and spelling patterns. They write to document their experience. They write to demonstrate comprehension. They write to learn to write, and they write to learn to read. We are particularly interested in writing as a whole-class activity, because it is essentially a teacher-directed, individual activity.

Shared writing, described above in the section on kindergarten, is also part of first-grade literacy instruction. We encourage teachers to extend the writing curriculum in first grade. First graders who copy writing from the board are practicing letter formation and also learning how to copy. They are not learning how to read or spell. For that, teachers can include dictation. Dictated sentences allow teachers to see how their beginning readers and writers are integrating their learning of high-frequency words (such as *the*) and phonetically regular words (such as *cat*). Writing instruction that includes a daily dictated sentence (e.g., "The cat is sad.") helps first graders to use what they are learning in reading and spelling to write.

Dictation is surely not composition. First graders should generate texts to express themselves. They need support to do this. First graders can learn to compose their own texts in direct connection with their learning to understand the texts composed by others. During read-alouds, they can learn that stories have beginnings, middles, and ends. They can then use that same structure to begin to write their own stories with beginnings, middles, and ends. Writer's workshop, where children compose and share their own texts, should have its rudimentary beginnings in first grade.

Needs-Based Group Activities

Phonemic Awareness

First graders who have not developed phonemic awareness by the end of kindergarten need more phonemic awareness instruction. One task that is particularly effective for developing phonemic awareness is the use of manipulatives and Elkonin boxes (rows of two, three, or four consecutive boxes, each representing one sound) to "push and say it" (Blackman, Ball, Black, & Tangel, 1994). This procedure is found in many programs for developing phonemic awareness. Children repeat target words, then segment them, moving a token into a square to represent each speech sound. Then they blend the speech sounds again. This procedure has very high utility. It can be adapted to children's developmental knowledge by asking them first to push and say only the initial phoneme, then the onset and rime, and finally the initial, medial, and final phoneme. It also allows every student to respond to every item, making good use of precious time in needs-based groups. It can also be adapted to include letters rather than tokens, connecting phonemic awareness activities directly to decoding and spelling activities.

Decoding

Needs-based decoding groups in first grade must build upon phonemic awareness activities and link them directly to letter–sound activities. We favor phonemic awareness instruction and phonics instruction that are carefully coordinated. For decoding instruction to be effective for needs-based groups, it has to be more than just systematic and explicit (the requirements for the whole-group instruction). It also has to be diagnostic. That is, the instruction must be linked directly to the children's understanding.

There are two ways to organize diagnostic work in decoding. First, the whole-class decoding curriculum can be reviewed. In essence, based on evidence of the children's understanding of the elements previously taught, teachers can go back into the curriculum to reteach. An alternative is to provide an additional curriculum, linked in philosophy and sequence to the whole-class guide, but providing additional targeted work in both phonemic awareness and decoding. Either way, needs-based decoding instruction must include work with words in isolation, carefully selected for their phonic elements, and carefully sequenced to provide children with mastery of the alphabetic principle.

Fluency

Needs-based fluency work in first grade is the mainstay of the successful curriculum. The ideal fluency work builds directly upon work in phonemic awareness and decoding. In fact, the ideal needs-based curriculum in first grade combines all three elements. Here is a framework for that time:

- Children orally segment and blend target sounds and patterns.
- Children read and spell words in isolation with those same target sounds and patterns.
- Teachers preview a text that contains many words with those same sounds and patterns, briefly preteaching any words that are irregular or that contain phonics elements not previously taught.
- Children read and reread the target text orally, moving from decoding to fluency.

In our experience, successful needs-based fluency work in first grade is organized so that children are reading and writing for 75% of the instructional time; unfortunately, typical work is organized so that teachers are talking for 75% of the instructional time.

INSTRUCTION FOR SECOND-GRADE
READERS AND WRITERS

Whole-Class Activities

The second-grade curriculum is a bridge between fluency and comprehension. Children reading second-grade material are able to decode most common spelling patterns, although they cannot yet spell them all correctly. They have large sight word vocabularies, and they use them in texts of increasing complexity.

Fluency

Fluency, in second grade as in all grades, demands practice reading and rereading. The trick is designing reading practice so that it is both engaged and efficient. There are many ways to do that. A procedure called *readers' theater* provides that practice and also focuses on oral reading performance in a way that is engaging to children. Readers' Theater uses scripts, with parts for individual readers. Children split into theater troupes and practice the parts of the scripts, switching parts at each rereading over several days, and then perform their play (without fanfare or costumes) for the rest of the class. This procedure has been used in many classrooms; Martinez, Roser, and Strecker (1999) have used it successfully to build fluency in second grade.

Vocabulary

The texts that second graders read are different from the texts that first graders read, in that they contain new words—words that children may be able to decode, but for which they do not actually know the meanings. Vocabulary instruction has the aim of developing fully accessible, decontextualized knowledge of word meanings. In fact, knowledge of individual word meanings grows incrementally—from no knowledge, to some knowledge, to knowledge in context, to decontextualized knowledge. Vocabulary instruction, then, is key to developing both children's vocabulary and their successful comprehension. For that instruction to be effective and efficient, it must include clear definition and context, chances for children to use the words, and discussion (Stahl, 1999). Before reading, then, a few words should be taught well.

Second graders also continue to learn concepts in science and social studies that are outside their decoding competence. These concepts are perfect targets for rich vocabulary instruction. Semantic maps, semantic feature analyses, and concept-of-definition maps all use graphic displays to indicate how concepts are related to other concepts and to prior knowledge (Stahl, 1999). Meaningful, planned, coordinated knowledge building is essential to reading success as children get older.

Comprehension Strategies

Figure 6.4 illustrates the shift from read-alouds in first grade to reading in second grade for real comprehension work. Texts that second graders can read are richer contexts for comprehension than those they read in first grade; settings, plots, and

PICTURE a Good Reader:
Second-Grade Performance Benchmarks

Predict: What do I think will happen next?
- Students predict and justify predictions before they read and during reading.
- Students evaluate and change predictions during and after their reading.

Imagine: Can I imagine what is happening?
- Students create mental pictures during reading in direct relationship to text ideas.
- Students can describe their own mental pictures.
- Students can identify specific sources in the text that they are using to create mental pictures.

Clarify: Does this make sense?
- Students can identify specific parts in a text that are disrupting their comprehension during reading.

Try: Can I ask myself "how" and "why" questions?
- Students ask "how" and "why" questions during guided reading.

Use: What do I know already?
- Students use prior knowledge from personal experience, previously read text, and instruction to help them understand texts that they are reading.

Review: Can I summarize?
- Students retell a story read independently, including characters, setting, problem, events, and solution.

Evaluate: Would I recommend this book to someone else?
- Students write evaluations of story themes after reading fiction.
- Students write evaluations of text content after reading nonfiction.

FIGURE 6.4. Comprehension strategy language and benchmarks, second grade.

characters are more fully developed, and there are more twists and surprises. One instructional procedure that we have found particularly useful to whole-group instruction in second grade is *question–answer relationships* (QARs; Raphael, 1986). In QARs, teachers teach children to answer questions, and then to determine how they did it. They determine that some answers are explicit; they are "right there in the text." Other answers demand inferences within the text; these are "think-and-search" questions. Still other answers demand inferences between text information and the reader's knowledge; they are "author and you." And finally some questions spring from text, but they are really about personal knowledge and experience; they are "on your own." Like the PICTURE acronym, QARs provide consistent strategy talk and procedures that can be used across text; this is the type of comprehension work that second-grade readers need.

Writing

Second graders can learn strategies in writing that actually develop their reading comprehension as well, and that link the curriculum in meaningful (and efficient) ways. Teaching story elements (e.g., setting, characters, events, problem, solution) directly improves reading comprehension. Clearly, story elements can be taught (and used) in both reading and writing. Therefore, writing instruction in which children are taught to use story maps to understand and plan to write stories develops comprehension skills that transfer to narrative texts written by others.

Needs-Based Group Activities

Decoding

Beginning in second grade, understanding of reading stages is essential to addressing individual needs in decoding. In a typical heterogeneous second-grade classroom, especially prior to the institution of a research-based curriculum in kindergarten and first grade, decoding needs are likely to represent all reading and spelling stages. Second graders who are struggling require the needs-based instruction described in the sections for kindergarten and first grade. The need for assessment data for diagnosis, described in Chapter 4, will be evident here. We refer below to the needs of typical second graders who are developing their decoding skills.

Proficient first graders are comfortable with applying basic patterns in single-syllable words. Lower-frequency patterns (e.g., *-ight, au, aw*) are appropriate for second graders, and they should be taught for both reading and spelling words. A clear focus on decoding longer words is also appropriate for second graders. Explicit instruction in identification of common prefixes and suffixes as a strategy for reading longer words is appropriate.

Fluency

Samuels (1979) developed the method of *repeated readings* for fluency building. Second graders need extensive reading practice in order to move from decoding to automaticity; they are also able to work effectively in pairs with minimal supervision. Repeated readings use short passages that pairs of children can read, albeit slowly at first. During each session, one child in each pair reads and the other tracks time, and sometimes errors. That same child rereads twice, with the other tracking the decreased time and the decreased errors. Then the partners switch roles. Daily progress across the three readings is documented on a chart. In a daily repeated-reading session, the teacher could pair with a different child each day, collecting assessment data. There are other models of repeated readings, but repetition is the active ingredient in all of them. For example, a stronger- and a weaker-performing reader might be paired. The stronger-performing reader reads a paragraph while the other listens. Then the struggling reader reads the same paragraph, decoding having been supported in advance by the abler reader.

Comprehension Strategies

For first grade, we have provided a "package" of activities to consider during needs-based fluency time. Here we provide a "package" for comprehension instruction. Second-grade readers need to work on integrating reading and thinking. They will do this best when they read new text that is challenging for them in a setting with support from a teacher and interaction with peers (Dowhower, 1999; Pressley et al., 1992). This needs-based instruction can target the strategies presented in Figure 6.4 and follows a general lesson structure:

- Direct instruction in the meaning and/or pronunciation of new words essential to text understanding.
- Direct instruction in a comprehension strategy that will be useful in understanding of the day's text or text segment.
- Alternation of reading of specific text segments with discussions and/or writing to facilitate text comprehension.
- Silent reading of specific text segments by all children, plus oral reading for individual children to allow the teacher to evaluate oral reading accuracy and to promote decoding strategies. This can be accomplished without round-robin reading if the teacher moves to listen to individuals reading orally while the rest of the group reads silently.

- Rereading of longer text segments to promote fluency and comprehension.
- Discussion of the overall text content, focusing on comprehension.

INSTRUCTION FOR THIRD-GRADE READERS AND WRITERS

Whole-Class Activities

Third graders are capitalizing on the growth in their decoding skills and their fluency to devote almost all of their cognitive attention to comprehension. At the same time, they are meeting increasingly challenging texts and tasks. Whole-class strategies for them reinforce their learning and stretch it.

Fluency

Rereading is still important for third graders. Since they are able to read more text in one instructional sitting, a planned cycle of rereading it before the next day's lesson will build both fluency and comprehension. To promote this growth, teachers may ask third graders to reread in pairs; each pair begins with one partner reading orally and the other silently, and the roles are then reversed.

Repeated readings, described above for needs-based instruction in second grade, are also appropriate for the whole group in third grade. General gains in independence make facilitation of the repeated-readings procedure possible with the larger group. Third graders enjoy timing one another and tracking growth.

Vocabulary

Third graders see many new words in text, and they must learn to learn new words during reading. Understanding word roots and discovering how to use them to learn new words (morphemic analysis) are important for third-grade readers. Vocabulary instruction for third graders, then, in addition to the important prereading instruction that second graders need, should include instruction in sets of words related by meaning. For example, third graders might learn the similar derivations of the words *unison, unicycle,* and *uniform,* and might begin to ask themselves about other such possible relationships when they encounter new words.

Comprehension Strategies

Figure 6.5 takes the PICTURE acronym and moves it forward into third grade. The comprehension demands on third graders are great; the need for explanation and modeling of the thinking that happens during reading is even greater. *Ques-*

PICTURE a Good Reader:
Third-Grade Performance Benchmarks

Predict: What do I think will happen next?
- Students predict and justify predictions before they read and during reading.
- Students evaluate and change predictions during and after their reading.

Imagine: Can I imagine what is happening?
- Students create mental pictures during reading in direct relationship to text ideas.
- Students can describe their own mental pictures.
- Students can identify specific sources in the text that they are using to create mental pictures.

Clarify: Does this make sense?
- Students can describe strategies that good readers use to construct meaning.

Try: Can I ask myself "how" and "why" questions?
- Students ask and answer "how" and "why" questions during guided reading.

Use: What do I know already?
- Students use prior knowledge from personal experience, previously read text, and instruction to help them understand texts that they are reading.

Review: Can I summarize?
- Students write summaries of stories read independently, including characters, setting, problem, events, and solution, with the support of a graphic organizer.

Evaluate: Would I recommend this book to someone else?
- Students write paragraphs to compare or contrast two texts based on their story elements or their information, with the support of a graphic organizer.

FIGURE 6.5. Comprehension strategy language and benchmarks, third grade.

tioning the author (Beck, McKeown, Hamilton, & Kucan, 1997) is one procedure that directs attention to this during-reading thinking. Teachers ask children generic, inference-building questions during reading that direct them to make connections—both inside the text and between the text and their prior knowledge. Examples of these during-reading queries include the following:

- "What is the author trying to say here?"
- "Did the author explain this clearly?"
- "Does this make sense with what the author told us before?"
- "Why do you think the author tells us this?"

For third grade, comprehension instruction must include an emphasis on the cognitive work that readers do during reading.

Writing

Teaching children to write information texts, using the common text structures that they will find when they read these texts, serves to develop strategies for both reading and writing. Third graders can write texts to compare and contrast, to persuade, to show a sequence or chronology, or to show a problem and its resolution. If these text structures are taught with graphic organizers, these can be used both to understand text that is read and to plan text that is written.

Needs-Based Group Activities

Fluency

Children who can decode words in isolation, but struggle to read with adequate rate and prosody, need more reading practice. By the third grade, a needs-based fluency group may need more teacher support during this practice. In addition to the routine for building fluency described for second graders, struggling third graders may need a modeling layer. That is, teachers may need to read the text to them so that they can hear what adequate speed and phrasing sound like. This support can also be accomplished through the use of audiotapes or computer-based readings of the text. The task for each student, then, is to reread until he or she can replicate the fluency of the teacher model.

Vocabulary and Comprehension Strategies

Third graders may be able to decode, and to do so with fluency, and still be unable to really understand. One possibility is that they have inadequate knowledge of the meanings of the words in the text. Preteaching words most central to text meaning—using Stahl's (1999) frame of definition and context, children's use of the words, and discussion—is essential. This should happen before reading.

Teaching summarization is a high-utility focus for third graders who decode but don't necessarily understand. It has the bonus element of including both reading and writing, and it can be used with many different texts. The important characteristic of needs-based work for third-grade readers is that it includes instruction in how to summarize, rather than just a steady diet of summarization tasks. There are steps to summarization that can be taught. For example, Brown and Day (1983) suggest the following:

- Delete redundant information.
- Delete unimportant information.
- Replace lists with more general terms.
- Identify a topic sentence.
- Invent a topic sentence if none is provided.

A technique commonly taught for summarizing narratives is called *who-wants-but-so*. A child begins with the main character (*who*), states his or her goal (*wants*), identifies the problem that prevents immediately reaching that goal (*but*), and then tells how the character attempts to solve the problem (*so*). A simple summary of just a sentence or two can be produced this way for many stories.

Instruction and practice in summarization force deep processing of the text and the use of many comprehension strategies. They also result in student products that can be used to document the students' comprehension growth.

BUILDING A PROGRAM

Before we turn our attention in the next chapter to analyzing and selecting instructional materials, we want to stress that a knowledge of the instructional implications of SBRR (which we have reviewed in Chapter 3) and an understanding of the ways that they can play out across the elementary grades (which we have described here) are essential to the role of the literacy coach. Literacy coaches must be informed consumers themselves, and they must be creative and responsive leaders through the very difficult tasks of addressing student and teacher needs by selecting materials likely to support both. As we focus on that task in the next chapter, we caution literacy coaches to bring information from their reading so far and from their experience with children and teachers into the task ahead.

CHAPTER 7

Selecting Materials and Programs

If you attended elementary school in the United States, the odds are greater than 9 to 1 that you were taught to read with a basal reading series. A *basal series*, now often called a *core program*, has long been the mainstay of American reading instruction. Basal adoption is a strange game, but it is one that a literacy coach must understand and lead. In this chapter, we review some of the history and controversy over adoption procedures; we then provide you with tools that we have developed to guide your own selection process, as well as other resources to support you.

Rosa Martinez learned about basal adoption firsthand as an elementary school administrator in 1999–2000. She had just finished an advanced degree in reading, with a focus on beginning reading, and she was anxious to use what she had learned to help her teachers. During that year, she was working with her staff to choose new materials for first grade. She first called publishers to get examination materials. The response was astounding. Every day for almost a month, the small office of the school was filled to the ceiling with boxes. Excitement about the potential for new materials was quickly replaced with dismay; it was literally impossible to unpack and organize these materials at school because of their physical size and contents (e.g., puppets, CD-ROMs, classroom libraries, manipulatives). This problem was solved by establishing a protocol to find only the teacher's editions for each series and to store the rest of the boxes on the school stage. Dismay turned to disbelief as Rosa and her principal acknowledged the sheer physical size of the materials to be examined and estimated the time that would be required to conduct a thorough, school-level evaluation. They decided that they themselves would narrow the field to two and then engage the staff in a comparison.

For first grade, concerns about the type and quality of phonemic awareness and phonics instruction, and about opportunities to practice these concepts, were paramount. Rosa and her principal emerged from their examination with two programs that they considered to be superior in these areas to the one currently in use. They set these programs up in the library of the school for informal examination by the kindergarten and first-grade teachers. Next, they invited the publishers' representatives to make presentations. Then they conducted formal discussions of the merits of the two programs and elicited written feedback. Although the staff members were sophisticated in their knowledge of the development of beginning literacy, two issues surfaced that derailed the discussions: One publisher's representative was a more skillful presenter than the other, and one of the programs had a different number of books than the other. On the basis of those two issues, the decision was made. Neither issue was instructional in nature. Moreover, the core instructional issues of the type, quality, or amount of phonemic awareness instruction in the two programs—the concerns that Rosa and her principal had identified as essential—were not addressed.

This story is not an isolated one. In fact, the adoption process described above was rife with mistakes that others have identified as common. Traditionally, instructional materials are chosen via a combination of high-pressure sales presentations, use of poorly designed checklists, and a series of "flip tests" in which teachers flip quickly through the manuals and form opinions based on superficial characteristics of the materials. Teachers are not trained in advance to apply systematic standards to the programs they review. Insufficient time is allocated for real review, and it is done after school. The procedure is then usually finalized in a vote by all teachers, rather than the recommendation of a smaller committee with greater knowledge of the materials. These procedural mistakes can lead to selection of materials that are poorly matched to current research and poorly suited to the needs of children in the school (Stein, Stuen, Carnine, & Long, 2001).

The same problems occur in state-level adoptions, where a list of textbooks acceptable for the state is prepared by a central team. In surveys and interviews, members of state-level adoption teams reported that they relied on newspaper articles, personal contacts, television and radio, and popular-press magazines to keep abreast of current ideas about reading instruction—a strategy unlikely to engender deep knowledge of research and instruction. Not surprisingly, they also reported constraints (policy-oriented, political, and economic) that affected their work (Reutzel, Sudweeks, & Hollingsworth, 1994).

We will help you to avoid these common mistakes in this chapter. First, though, we present some history and some important descriptive terms. Then we turn to ways of actually sorting through and evaluating these materials.

A BRIEF HISTORY OF BASALS

What makes a basal a basal? The word *basal* denotes a sequence of activities that progresses from easy to difficult. The basic idea is that each child will be placed at the appropriate point on this spectrum and thereafter progress through the remainder of the sequence. For example, a new student will be preassessed using a placement test. He or she will then be placed in an appropriate reader and exposed to the corresponding instructional activities. The assumption behind a basal system is that once an appropriate placement is made, all easier objectives must have been accomplished and need not be repeated. In other words, a basal level has been established as a starting point for the new student.

This is the same rationale that is used in basal testing, such as intelligence measures and individually administered achievement tests. The examiner rarely starts with the easiest item, because doing so would take far too much time. This is also the idea behind a basal thermometer used to take a patient's temperature. Such a thermometer does not extend downward beyond a certain level, because it would be pointless to include temperatures below the range of living people. The manufacturer of such a thermometer simply assumes that a reasonable starting point can be set above a certain level.

The first multilevel series—clearly the forerunner of the modern basal reading series—was published by Noah Webster in 1783 and was eventually titled the *American Spelling Book* (Smith, 2002). It had three levels (beginning, intermediate, and advanced). It was used for teaching reading as well as spelling, for Webster saw spelling as a key to teaching children how to read. This series sold an amazing 24 million copies. Its moralistic tone is illustrated by the following excerpt:

> Be a good child; mind your book; love your school; strive to learn.
> Tell no tales; call no ill names; you must not lie, nor swear, nor cheat, nor steal.
> Play not with bad boys.
> Play no tricks on those that sit next to you; for if you do, good boys will shun you as they would a dog they knew would bite them.

Competing series such as the *Christmas School Primer* soon appeared, and all were similar to Webster's.

During the interval from 1840 to 1880, the first reading series that contained one book for each grade appeared. This was a natural development, given the adoption in the United States of the graded school system that began in Germany. The emphasis on patriotism diminished during these years, but the moralistic flavor remained. Illustrations were greatly improved because of advances in the technology of printing.

The famous McGuffey Readers appeared between 1836 and 1844 and dominated the latter half of the 19th century. The last editions appeared between 1896 and 1907. The McGuffey Readers were the first carefully defined and graded series. The religious tone persisted, but the literary quality of the selections was generally good. The orientation of the McGuffey Readers leaned heavily in the direction of systematic phonics instruction. However, this perspective was hotly contested even in that early era. Horace Mann, for example, opposed a decoding emphasis and once referred to letters as "skeleton-shaped, bloodless, ghostly apparitions" (cited in Adams, 1990, p. 22). During this time period, Josiah Bumstead developed a series of readers based on the whole-word, or "look–say," methodology advocated by Mann and others. Educators for the first time had choices of materials based on the pedagogy they preferred.

During the 1880s, the first supplementary materials appeared; by the turn of the 20th century, supplementary materials were becoming more prevalent as adjuncts to the individual student's reading book. Practice exercises to be done along with the reading of stories were notable in such programs as the Beacon Readers (1912–1922), produced by Ginn and Company. The 1920s brought the inclusion of specific, well-constructed teacher's manuals to accompany the children's reading books. There was also a change in the literature from predominantly fantasy-oriented fiction to nonfiction and realistic historical fiction. The expansion of supplemental materials continued during this period.

In the 1930s, a trend toward reducing the difficulty level of vocabulary and including more repetition of new words in introductory books began. In the 1940s, formal reading readiness programs became common components of reading series. More differentiation of the difficulty levels of the readers meant the inclusion of more books in a series. The artwork presented to children during this period was greatly improved and offered more varied and vivid color. The device of using story characters, like Dick and Jane, who recurred through the levels of the series was introduced during this period of time.

During the 1940s, the market-leading Scott, Foresman series (featuring Dick and Jane) emphasized a look–say (whole-word) approach. This perspective was evident in the limited phonics materials the series offered, and also in the repetition of high-frequency words. Here's a sample from the primer *Fun with Dick and Jane* (Gray, Artley, & Arbuthnot, 1951, pp. 6–7):

> Dick said, "Look, look.
> Look up.
> Look up, up, up."
> Jane said, "Run, run.
> Run, Dick, run.
> Run and see."

In this passage of only 20 words, *run* occurs 5 times, and *look* and *up* occur 4 times.

Phonics continued to be backburnered until Cold War fears led to a reexamination of the entire educational system. The *Reader's Digest* published critical articles with titles such as "Can Ivan Read Better Than Johnny?" Rudolph Flesch (1955), in his best-selling book *Why Johnny Can't Read,* placed the blame squarely on too little phonics instruction. In consequence, the 1960s saw a groundswell of phonics programs and a renewed emphasis on phonics within basal series. Some series, called *linguistic readers* (merely because their authors happened to be linguists), strictly controlled vocabulary, limiting the words a child saw to those that were regular and decodable. Irregular words (such as *of, have, come,* and *said*) had to be put off until the basics of phonics were mastered. This led to some cumbersome stories. Here's an example from a 1980 *Merrill Reader,* cited in Auckerman (1987):

> Nat is a cat.
> Is Nat a cat?
> Nat is a fat cat.

Despite evidence of the effectiveness of these materials, they tended to be boring and tedious. In addition, new theories of the reading process, introduced in the late 1960s by Kenneth Goodman and Frank Smith, challenged once again the importance of phonics. Basal publishers responded by removing vocabulary controls, so that far more difficult stories appeared in primary-level readers. Here's an excerpt from the 1981 Scott, Foresman primer (Jennings & Prince, 1981, pp. 8–9; published exactly 30 years after the excerpt from *Fun with Dick and Jane* quoted above):

> One time there was a mother bird.
> She had three little birds.
> She looked after her little ones.
> She found good things to eat.
> She found good things to drink.
> She would sing to her little birds.

Note that the vocabulary is more extensive. The repetition of words continues in this primer, but is subtler and aesthetically far more pleasing.

With the rise of the whole-language movement of the late 1980s and early 1990s, phonics was further minimized. Policy mandates in both California and Texas required adoption of reading materials consisting of unedited, authentic children's literature. Basal series were dominated by literature, and some were little more than anthologies. During the 1990s, however, it had become clear that basals and the methods they espoused were not successfully addressing the colossal reading problem faced by the United States as a nation. The basals of today employ far more decodable text, and they champion methods that have been empirically validated through scientific research. Their emphasis on phonics is strong, systematic, and sequential.

If you're interested in learning more about the history of reading materials, *American Reading Instruction*, by Nila Banton Smith (2002), provides a retrospective through the 1950s. James Hoffman (2002) tells the text story through the rest of the 20th century. The History of Literacy special-interest group of the International Reading Association maintains a Web site that may be of interest as well (http://www.historyliteracy.org).

TODAY'S BASAL BASICS

Before we offer a system for choosing materials, we want to help you sort through the components of a typical basal series, as well as some more recent choices and alternatives. Like the parts of an automobile, some of these components are standard equipment, while others are options that can be purchased at additional cost. And, as with an automobile purchase, wise selection and combination of these components require research.

Student Readers

Materials for students to read are organized into a sequence of progressively difficult readers. Each reader is an anthology of selections chosen to represent a variety of genres and to be of high interest to children at a given grade level. One of the issues confronting present-day basal publishers is how many readers to include in the series. Traditionally, the following organizational pattern has been used:

Grade 1:   Three preprimers, one primer, and a first reader
Grade 2:   A 2-1 reader and a 2-2 reader (for first and second semesters)
Grade 3:   A 3-1 reader and a 3-2 reader (for first and second semesters)
Grades 4–8: A single reader per year

Basal readers are rarely used beyond grade 5, despite their availability, because a literature anthology is offered in language arts materials.

Teacher's Editions

A teacher's edition accompanies each student reader in the series. It provides suggestions about ways to present a selection, possible questions to ask, and activities in which to engage the students. Some series are highly prescriptive, and the teacher's edition may provide detailed scripts of what the teacher is to say at all times. Scripting has become an issue of contention between those who argue that many teachers are ill prepared for the task of using basal materials and others who argue that scripting has the effect of deprofessionalizing ("deskilling") teachers. We will address this issue later.

Practice Materials

Every basal series offers student workbooks and reproducible masters that correspond to the reading selections. There is generally a wide variety of these materials, and the publisher's intent is not that all of them be used, but that they be viewed as a "smorgasbord" of possibilities.

Scope and Sequence

Each series is based on a system of educational objectives that are carefully sequenced from the most basic to the most sophisticated. The range of these objectives is referred to as the *scope,* while the order of the objectives is the *sequence.* Each commercial series offers a scope-and-sequence chart that spans the various grade levels and provides a master blueprint of the progress children should be making.

The scope and sequence of objectives are broken into several strands. These include a comprehension strand, a word recognition strand, a study skills strand, and possibly others. A teacher at a particular grade level may be largely unfamiliar with the portions of the scope and sequence associated with other grade levels. Of course, in addressing the needs of students who are above or below grade placement, a teacher may need to become familiar with the larger picture. An issue facing users of basal series concerns whether the objectives incorporated into the series are adequately aligned with the objectives that constitute the official curriculum of a state.

meet state standards?

Software

Every basal publisher now offers software closely aligned with the reading selections that children encounter. These programs provide a variety of experiences, often in game format, as a means of reinforcing the skills developed through the basal series. The software offered by the basal publishers began as little more than electronic workbooks in the mid-1980s, but its sophistication has increased considerably over the years. Purchasing options typically involve housing the software on a school's file server, so that teachers can use it as desired. Some systems offer record-keeping and assessment features as well.

Accessory Components

Every series offers optional components, such as wall charts, flashcards, letter cards, transparencies, big books, and other niceties that may make a teacher's life easier (if they are easy to organize and use) or harder (if they are cumbersome or superfluous to instructional goals). These components may be purchased or provided as part of the price of the student editions.

Little Books

Basals for kindergarten and first grade typically offer specially designed *little books* that are consistent with the decoding instruction in the program. These books are different from their trade book cousins, in that they are not meant to represent the full literary experience. They are constrained by the scope and sequence for word recognition of the curriculum. They are used for children to practice their decoding skills in a carefully designed context.

Trade Books

Many series now offer sets of trade books that teachers may wish to use in going beyond the anthologized selections. *Trade books* are simply full-text pieces of children's literature just as they are sold in a bookstore. They are typically offered as classroom libraries (for students to read on their own) or read-aloud libraries (for teachers to use to support themes in the series).

Leveled Books

Leveled books were inspired by the remedial program Reading Recovery, and they represent a sequence of progressively difficult trade books. Obviously, this is exactly what a basal series was originally designed to do. However, leveled books are distinct from student readers in two important respects. First, leveled books represent many more levels. They are chosen on the basis of the text demands (readability), the illustrations, and other subjective factors. Whereas the traditional basal series comprises 5 readers at grade 1, a sequence of leveled books may include as many as 10 levels. Second, leveled books are short paperbacks rather than hefty anthologies. Each lesson takes children from the beginning to the end of a single leveled book. They are easy to house in sets, and some schools have created a room for leveled books so that the teachers can share classroom sets.

Kits

Some publishers offer systems that are best described as kits. The Science Research Associates (SRA) Reading Laboratories, for instance, are boxes of cards with passages and activities arranged in order of progressive difficulty. Kits rarely claim to be everything a teacher needs, but are generally marketed as supplements to the core program. They often target specific portions of the reading diet and specific populations of struggling readers.

Integrated Learning Systems

The software that accompanies a basal series stops short of offering a comprehensive program, such as can be found in an *integrated learning system* (ILS). An ILS is a computerized system in which materials and assessments are built-in components, so that reading selections are prescribed based on student performance. Print materials in an ILS are generally unnecessary. Everything is digitized. It is little wonder that a basal publisher is not interested in producing a complete ILS, since doing so would mean that the student readers might not be needed!

Whole-School Reform Models

Whole-school reform models go beyond materials and more closely resemble the schoolwide program that we have described in Chapter 2. They often demand the services of an on-site literacy coach, or a facilitator who fills the role of the literacy coach as described in Chapter 1 by coordinating assessment, grouping, and program implementation specific to the reform model. Two current examples of whole-school reform models are Success for All (e.g., Slavin, Madden, Dolan, & Wasik, 1996) and Voyager Expanded Learning (http://www.iamvoyager.com). Although the instruction in a whole-school model is embedded within the larger system, a wise consumer will evaluate the content of the instructional program in the same way as a stand-alone basal program.

RESEARCHERS REACT

For the remainder of this chapter, we use the term *core program* to refer to the selection and combination of basal components with other supplementary programs defined above, or the whole-school reform model that is used during basic instruction in your reading program. Remember the lessons from Chapters 1 and 2: A literacy coach should be able to define a schoolwide reading program as much more than the materials that teachers use to teach or children use to learn to read.

Critics of core programs have argued that their use "deskills" teachers by taking control of their lesson selection and planning processes, and preventing them from making the decisions necessary for meeting the needs of students during instruction (Shannon, 1989, 1994; Goodman, Shannon, Freeman, & Murphy, 1988). This argument has been found wanting in both theoretical (Baumann, 1992) and empirical investigations. Baumann and Heubach (1996) surveyed 563 members of the International Reading Association, the vast majority of whom had advanced degrees in education and at least 10 years' teaching experience. They concluded that core programs supported teachers' instructional decision making in their classrooms, rather than controlling it.

Researchers have looked hard at core program materials for teaching beginning reading. From a conceptual standpoint, the exact balance of repetition, decodability, predictability, and accessibility has been debated (Hiebert, 1999). Adoption in the state of Texas has provided an important context in which to watch this debate play out. In Texas, the state board of education approves a list of commercial materials from which districts can choose. The board members "back-plan" that process by issuing a call to the publishers, with specific guidelines that will be used to review materials for inclusion on that list. In 1990, this call from the state included a specific focus on high-quality children's literature (Hoffman et al., 1994); in 1993, five publishers responded with new core programs approved for adoption in Texas.

Hoffman et al., (1994) examined these core programs in contrast to their 1986–1987 predecessors. They found marked differences: The 1993 imprints, overall, were more challenging to beginning readers. They contained fewer words (12,265 compared to 17,319), but more unique ones (1,680 compared to 962). On average, they scored higher on measures of readability (1.69 compared to 1.00), with more syllables per word (1.20 compared to 1.12) and more words per sentence (7.8 compared to 6.8). The new texts were also both more predictable and less decodable, especially early in the programs. Once these programs were actually implemented, researchers conducted case studies in 14 Texas classrooms and found that these new materials were used in classrooms in very different ways (Hoffman et al., 1998).

That was not the end of the story in Texas. In 1998, the state mandated that texts for beginning readers allow them to read words whose elements had been taught. In fact, 80% of the words had to be decodable by this definition. The 2000 texts, then, were more decodable again. Compared to the 1993 imprints, there were more unique words, more total words, and more controlled vocabulary and repetition. Words in the programs were more phonetically regular and also more directly connected to the instructional progression in phonics. Gone was the emphasis on predictability. Unfortunately, though, gone also was "engagingness": Texts with higher decodability were less engaging (Hoffman, Sailors, & Patterson, 2002).

Core programs have also been examined for support of specific areas of the literacy diet besides decoding. The results of these examinations have varied by area and by time. Smith et al. (2001) examined kindergarten programs published in 1991 and 1993 for their consistency with research on phonemic awareness instruction; they were found wanting. Schmitt and Hopkins (1993) searched for evidence that second-, fourth-, and sixth-grade programs published in 1989 contained comprehension skill and strategy instruction, and found evidence that they did. Jitendra, Chard, Hoppes, Renouf, and Gardill (2001) looked for evidence that programs published in 1995–1997 for second, fourth, and sixth grades taught comprehension of main ideas. They found evidence that the programs did teach this skill explicitly, but with very difficult passages and without the depth, repetition, or modeling indicated in the research literature. Franks, Mulhern, and Schillinger (1997) examined core programs for grades 1–8 as contexts for deductive reasoning. They found these programs to be rich contexts for children to make and observe these inferences, but no evidence that deductive reasoning was a skill explicitly taught or explained by teachers.

Where does this research lead us? Unfortunately, not to the place where literacy coaches need to go—to a blueprint for making a wise, research-based choice of a core program for a particular school. There are several reasons for this:

- Researchers are likely to look at only one aspect of a program; literacy coaches must examine the entire program.
- Core programs change over time, sometimes dramatically. Research on an older version of a program should not be applied to revisions of the program. (See Roser, Hoffman, & Carr, 2003.)
- Researchers are looking only at materials and manuals; they are not examining the match between program offerings and the local resources and needs.

The useful lesson in this research is this: In order to really know what a core program has to offer, a researcher (or a literacy coach) has to engage in a very carefully planned process, reading and evaluating the actual lessons with a clear and specific procedure.

THOUGHTFUL SYSTEMS FOR EVALUATING MATERIALS

One thing that we (and probably you) have learned the hard way is that thoughtful adoption of new materials takes time. One literacy coach with whom we work expressed frustration about this after working with us through the procedure that we introduce in this section. She reported, "Seriously, we seem to know what we need and are extremely excited about having money to do this. It's just about finding the time." In fact, thorough evaluation of materials takes an entire year. In Table 7.1, we have expanded upon the work of Stein et al. (2001) to help you to plan. Note that we see you working from the fall of year 1 to make a choice of a new core program to be implemented in the fall of year 2. We are trying to save you the frustration reported by one literacy coach: "Frustration has been a problem for many of my teachers. They feel like we should have had a planning year before implementing [the changes]."

Another missing link in materials selection is the training of the selection team. In the first quarter, your goal should be to develop the understanding needed to evaluate programs. We suggest that you first identify the members of

TABLE 7.1. Checklist for Materials Adoption

Time	Activities
First quarter	1. Select committee.
	2. Review federal, state, and local curriculum guidelines.
	3. Review assessments.
	4. Review relevant research.
	5. Specify financial constraints.
	6. Gather program materials for review.
	7. Gather input from all staff members.
Second quarter	1. Establish screening tool and procedure.
	2. Field-test screening tool and procedure.
	3. Edit screening tool and procedure.
Third quarter	1. Conduct initial screenings of all programs.
	2. Identify two to five finalists.
	3. Invite a publisher's representative for each finalist to make presentations to committee.
	4. Select core program.
	5. Secure district approval.
	6. Prepare grade-specific implementation guidelines.
Fourth quarter	1. Present plan to staff.
	2. Develop school purchase orders.
	3. Plan staff development.
Summer	1. Implement staff development.

your selection committee, and then either arrange release time or provide stipends so that they can do their job professionally. They will have to begin with the standards that apply to the particular adoption cycle—federal, state, and local guidelines that both support and constrain their work. For us, this also means a thorough understanding of the scientifically based reading research (SBRR) we have reviewed in Chapter 3, as well as the instructional implications of that research for readers in the elementary grade levels, which we have reviewed in Chapter 6. Finally, the identification and solicitation of materials to be reviewed should be completed early in the school year. In order to do that, you may have to screen programs to reduce a potentially very long list of choices to a manageable number.

The second quarter can then be devoted to developing, understanding, and pilot-testing a procedure for text evaluation. This work does not necessarily have to start from scratch; rather, it can be informed by existing procedures. In Figure 7.1 (pp. 133–153) we present a template for a procedure that we have developed and used. This procedure involves very careful examination of the materials. First, the team divides the tasks. Two team members take responsibility for reading and describing the scope and sequence of content and of instructional strategies presented in the program overview materials. In the same way, two team members take responsibility for describing the content at each grade level, choosing a specific week's instruction early in the program and another one later in the program. They look for evidence of specific content, and they describe the instructional context. When they are finished describing the materials, they summarize, focusing on program strengths and weaknesses within and between grade levels and on the evidence that the publishers provide of the materials' effectiveness. Finally, they apply what they know about the local context to make a decision about the program's match to local needs.

Other sources are available to you as well. In Table 7.2 (p. 154), we list additional sources with brief descriptions and information about how to find these documents. The main concern for your committee in the second quarter should be choosing a procedure, adapting it to include any special concerns in the locality, and trying it together in a pilot format. We recommend that you pilot-test your procedure on the materials that are currently in use. Those materials are likely to be more familiar to the committee members, so the procedure can be conducted more quickly. You will also be able to identify the weaknesses in your current program that must be remedied in the adoption process.

The third quarter of the year will be demanding. At this time, you will be applying the procedure that you have identified to all of the programs that you are considering. We recommend that you divide this task, with pairs of committee members responsible for individual programs. That way, you can devote the necessary time to actually reading the program materials. In our experience, a pair of trained evaluators need at least 4 hours to conduct a thorough evaluation of a comprehensive program, and a team needs at least 2 hours to share the results of evaluations across several programs.

After you have identified a short list of potential programs, you should invite representatives to make presentations. Since you will have reviewed the programs carefully, you can solicit specific types of presentations and present questions in advance to the representatives. That way, you can avoid the pressure of the high-powered sales talk, as well as the distraction of the prizes and incentives that are likely to be offered. Your final committee decision will be thoughtfully constructed to account for financial constraints; federal, state, and local guidelines; recent research; and grade-level instructional goals. With all of this up-front work, district approval should be easier to attain.

The third-quarter work is not yet finished. Staff members, some of whom have not served on the selection committee, will be implementing this program. In order for them to have a clear picture of what the program means for them and for their students, the committee will have to prepare grade-level-specific guidelines. We recommend that the committee spend time plotting out exactly how the new materials will fit into the structure of the school's reading program even before presenting its findings to teachers. For example, the committee can prepare grade-

[text resumes on p. 155]

DESCRIPTIVE TEMPLATE
FOR CORE READING PROGRAM MATERIALS

The purpose of the procedure outlined below is to provide specific descriptive information about commercial materials being considered for adoption. The procedure targets the domains of phonemic awareness, phonics, fluency, vocabulary development, and comprehension strategies at each grade level, K–3. This documentation will come from analysis of five specific lessons from early in the program and five from the end of the program for each of these grade levels, as well as an examination of the entire scope and sequence for each grade level. The quality of the information gathered in this process is directly proportional to the team's knowledge of reading development and commitment to be systematic. It is imperative that the description include only what the program explicitly directs the teacher to do, rather than what could be done. Done well, this procedure can be used by school districts to compare programs and select programs consistent with their local needs.

The full procedure is as follows:
- Read the descriptive template.
- Identify components of the program provided for examination.
- Read the program overview as a group.
- Identify all teacher's manuals for each grade level.
- Identify the program guide or overview that shows the scope and sequence or the entire grade level.
- Assign at least two team members to evaluate target lessons for each grade level.
  - Find the weekly planner pages that provide an overview for five lessons in a row.
  - Choose 1 week early in the program and 1 week later in the program for in-depth analysis.
  - Read each lesson from start to finish to get an overall picture.
  - Reread each lesson, documenting each instructional opportunity specifically included in the program.
- Assign at least two team members to evaluate the scope and sequence for the entire program.
  - Read the program's research base.
  - Find the program guide or overview that shows the scope and sequence for the entire grade level.

(continued)

FIGURE 7.1. Descriptive template for use in a materials selection procedure.

- Read descriptions of the program for each dimension, and then go to the teacher's manuals to see how the instruction is actually presented.
- Follow links to auxiliary materials if they are specified as part of the core program, but not if they are optional.
- Combine evidence collected by the two teams.
- Meet as a full team to discuss the strengths and weakness of the program.
- Finish the final pages of the descriptive template.

Describing Phonemic Awareness Content: Kindergarten and First Grade

Oral Language Play
How does the program encourage children to experiment with language?

Rhyming Activities
How does the program teach children to recognize and produce rhyming words?

Blending
How does the program teach children to blend sounds into words? Does it include the level of the sentence, syllable, onset and rime, and phoneme?

(continued)

Segmenting
How does the program teach children to segment words into sounds? Does the program teach segmenting at the level of the sentence, syllable, onset and rime, and phoneme?

Isolation
How does the program teach children to isolate sounds in words? Does it teach children to isolate initial sounds, final sounds, and medial sounds?

Describing Phonics/Decoding Content: Kindergarten and First Grade

Letter Names
How and in what order are letter names introduced and reviewed?

Letter Sounds
How and in what order are letter sounds introduced and reviewed?

Vowels
How, when, and in what order are vowels used for decoding and spelling?

(continued)

Consonant Digraphs

How, when, and in what order are consonant digraphs used for decoding and spelling?

Consonant Blends

How, when, and in what order are consonant blends used for decoding and spelling?

Word Families

How, when, and in what order are word families used for decoding and spelling?

Vowel-Consonant-Final E (VCE) Patterns

How, when, and in what order are VCE patterns used for decoding and spelling?

Vowel Digraphs

How, when, and in what are vowel digraphs used for decoding and spelling?

(continued)

R-Controlled Vowels
How, when, and in what order are *r*-controlled vowels used for decoding and spelling?

Irregular Words
How, when, and in what order are irregular words introduced and practiced for reading and spelling?

Decoding Strategies
How are synthetic decoding strategies used to decode or spell words?

How are analogy or rime-based strategies used to decode or spell words?

Automaticity
How is word recognition automaticity developed?

Describing Phonemic Awareness and Decoding Context: Kindergarten and First Grade

Describe the teacher preparation needed for full implementation. What does a teacher have to do or make before the lessons begin?

(continued)

Describe the materials provided in the program (e.g., songs, poems, objects, Elkonin boxes, markers, storybooks).

How long are the phonemic awareness lessons designed to last each day? Report or estimate in minutes per day.

How long are the phonics lessons designed to last each day? Report or estimate in minutes per day.

How explicit are the teacher directions? Give an example.

How are the phonemic awareness and phonics activities related? Give an example.

How, and how often, is progress in phonemic awareness monitored?

(continued)

How are teachers directed to group children for instruction?

How are teachers directed to differentiate instruction for students who are struggling?

Describe the texts provided for practicing phonics concepts.

How engaging are the materials and activities for children? Give an example.

Describing Vocabulary and Comprehension Content: Kindergarten and First Grade

Teaching New Words
How does the teacher provide definitions for new words?

How does the teacher provide context?

(continued)

How do children participate in learning new words?

Prediction
How are children taught to anticipate upcoming text events?

Visualization
How are children taught to make mental images?

Self-Monitoring
How are children taught to notice when comprehension is not certain?

Self-Questioning
How are children taught to ask themselves "how" and "why" questions?

Prior Knowledge
How are children taught to activate and use appropriate prior knowledge?

Summarization
How are children taught to retell and/or summarize during or after reading?

(continued)

Comprehension Skills
How are children taught other specific comprehension skills?

Describing Vocabulary and Comprehension Context: Kindergarten and First Grade

Where do the vocabulary items come from?

Describe the materials used for vocabulary development included in the program.

How explicit are the teacher directions for teaching vocabulary? Give an example.

How, and how often, is progress in vocabulary monitored?

How are new vocabulary items linked to one another and to the children's prior knowledge?

(continued)

Describe the materials used for developing comprehension.

Describe the texts used for developing comprehension.

How are the texts accessed by the children (e.g., independent reading, listening, shared reading)?

How closely does the comprehension instruction conform to a before–during–after reading structure? Give an example.

How closely does the comprehension instruction conform to a gradual-release model, with declarative, procedural, and condition strategy information? Give an example.

Describing Phonics Content: Second and Third Grades

Review
How are early phonics concepts reviewed and reinforced for decoding and spelling?

(continued)

VCE Patterns
How, when, and in what order are VCE patterns used for decoding
and spelling?

Vowel Digraphs
How, when, and in what order are vowel digraphs used for decoding
and spelling?

R-Controlled Vowels
How, when, and in what order are *r*-controlled vowels used for decoding and
spelling?

Consonant Blends
How are three-letter consonant blends used for decoding and spelling?

Other Long-Vowel Patterns
How are lower-frequency long-vowel patterns used for decoding and spelling?

Irregular Words
How are irregular words introduced for decoding and spelling?

(continued)

Root Words
How and when are root words identified for decoding and spelling?

Prefixes
How and when are prefixes used for decoding and spelling?

Suffixes
How and when are suffixes used for decoding and spelling?

Decoding Strategies
How and when are children taught to use synthetic decoding strategies for unknown words?

How and when are children taught to use spelling chunks or meaning chunks to decode unknown words?

Automaticity
How does the program develop automaticity in decoding words?

Self-Monitoring
How does the program teach children to use context to evaluate the accuracy of their decoding?

(continued)

Describing Phonics Context: Second and Third Grades

Describe the teacher preparation needed for full implementation. What does a teacher have to do or make before the lessons begin?

How long are the phonics lessons designed to last each day? Report or estimate in minutes per day.

How explicit are the teacher directions? Give an example.

How, and how often, is progress in phonics monitored?

What provisions are there to differentiate instruction for struggling readers?

What materials are provided for practicing phonics concepts?

How engaging are the materials and activities for children?

(continued)

Describing Fluency, Vocabulary, and Comprehension Content: Second and Third Grades

Fluency
What procedures are included to build fluency?

Wide Reading
What provisions are made to encourage wide reading in appropriate texts?

Teaching New Words
How does the teacher provide definitions for new words?

How does the teacher provide context?

How do children participate in learning new words?

How are graphic organizers used to build connections among word meanings?

(continued)

Vocabulary Learning Strategies
How are children taught to infer new word meanings from context?

How are they taught to analyze word parts to determine word meanings?

Setting a Purpose
How are children taught to set a specific purpose before reading?

Prediction
How are children taught to anticipate upcoming text events?

Visualization
How are children taught to make mental images?

Self-Monitoring
How are children taught to stop when comprehension is not certain?

Applying Fix-Up Strategies
How are children taught to take specific actions when comprehension breaks down?

(continued)

Self-Questioning
How are children taught to ask themselves "how" and "why" questions?

Prior Knowledge
How are children taught to activate and use appropriate prior knowledge?

Summarization
How are children taught to retell and/or summarize during or after reading?

Comprehension Skills
How are children taught other specific comprehension skills?

Describing Fluency, Vocabulary, and Comprehension Context: Second and Third Grade

Describe the materials for fluency building included in the program.

How explicit are teacher directions for building fluency?

How, and how often, is progress in fluency monitored?

(continued)

Where do the vocabulary items come from?

Describe the materials used for vocabulary development included in the program.

How explicit are the teacher directions for vocabulary instruction?

How, and how often, is progress in vocabulary monitored?

How are new vocabulary items linked to one another and to the children's prior knowledge?

Describe the materials used for developing comprehension.

Describe the texts used for developing comprehension.

(continued)

How closely does the comprehension instruction conform to a before–during–after reading structure? Give an example.

How closely does the instruction conform to a gradual-release model, with declarative, procedural, and condition strategy information? Give an example.

How often are children writing to demonstrate comprehension?

How often are children engaged in interactive discussions to demonstrate comprehension?

How, and how often, is progress in comprehension monitored?

How engaging are the materials and activities for children?

(continued)

Program Strengths: Looking across the Grade Levels

Phonemic Awareness			
Kindergarten	First grade		

Phonics and Decoding			
Kindergarten	First grade	Second grade	Third grade

Fluency			
		Second grade	Third grade

Vocabulary			
Kindergarten	First grade	Second grade	Third grade

Comprehension			
Kindergarten	First grade	Second grade	Third grade

(continued)

Program Weaknesses: Looking across the Grade Levels

Phonemic Awareness			
Kindergarten	First grade		

Phonics and Decoding			
Kindergarten	First grade	Second grade	Third grade

Fluency			
		Second grade	Third grade

Vocabulary			
Kindergarten	First grade	Second grade	Third grade

Comprehension			
Kindergarten	First grade	Second grade	Third grade

(continued)

Evidence of Effectiveness

What are the characteristics of the populations in which this program has been tested?

How was the effectiveness of the program measured?

Is there experimental or quasi-experimental evidence that the program is effective?

Is there case study evidence that the program is effective?

Local Implications for Adoption

What are the costs of full implementation of this program?

How well is this program matched to the needs of students in this school?

How well will this program meet the needs of at-risk children in the school?

What staff development would be needed for full implementation of this program?

TABLE 7.2. Other Sources to Guide Selection Committees

Source	Description
Simmons, D. C., and Kame'enui, E. J. (n.d). A consumer's guide to evaluating a core reading program grades K–3: A critical elements analysis. (Available at http://reading.uoregon.edu/appendices/consumer_guide_old.pdf)	This document identifies specific program characteristics for kindergarten (phonemic awareness, letter–sound association, decoding, irregular words, listening comprehension), first grade (phonemic awareness, decoding and word recognition, irregular words, passage reading, reading comprehension), second grade (decoding and word recognition, irregular words, vocabulary and concepts, passage reading, and reading comprehension), and third grade (decoding and word recognition, vocabulary and concepts, passage reading, and reading comprehension). Users apply a three-level rating system: "consistently meets/exceeds," "inconsistently meets/exceeds," and "does not satisfy." There is also attention to assessment, materials, and differentiation across the program.
Simmons, D. C., and Kame'enui, E. J. (2003, March).A consumer's guide to evaluating a core reading program grades K–3: A critical elements analysis [Update]. (Available at http://reading.uoregon.edu/appendices/con_guide_3.1.03.pdf)	This update of the document described above is a notable expansion. There are clear definitions for terms and citations to research. The authors provide guidance on how to use the system. Most notable is the direction to examine each item by looking within a sequence of 2–3 lessons, by analyzing the program's scope and sequence, or by completing a skills trace over 10 consecutive lessons.
Florida Center for Reading Research (FCRR) reports. (Available at http://www.fcrr.org/FCRRReports/reportslist.htm)	The FCRR has been analyzing reading curricula and materials available for use in Florida for their consistency with the Reading First legislation. Its Web site includes descriptive information on programs for initial instruction, for intervention, and for tutoring.
Reports of the What Works Clearinghouse (WWC), established by the U.S. Department of Education's Institute of Education Sciences to provide scientific information on educational programs. (Available at http://www.w-w-c.org)	The WWC is reviewing evidence on beginning reading interventions intended to increase phonemic awareness, phonics, reading fluency, vocabulary development, reading comprehension, or any combination of these reading skills. Reports on intervention programs for struggling readers are scheduled for release in 2004. Reports on intervention programs for general students will be released in spring 2004.

level-specific answer to the "hows," "whens," "whys," and "by whoms" of implementation.

The fourth quarter of the school year can be used to present and support the planned implementation. After the committee shares its findings with teachers in whole-staff and grade-level-specific presentations, purchase orders can be drafted so that materials are available well in advance of the new school year. Publishers will often include staff development support; this support should be provided during preplanning days, so that teachers are ready to start their year with their new materials in place.

THE PROBLEM OF LAYERING

The procedure described above can really help you to make reasoned choices about where to spend your materials money. But making such choices is not all you have to do to ensure that you are leading a schoolwide reading program. We have visited schools that look like museums of the history of educational materials. They have used their materials money wisely to purchase brand-new, research-based core programs. Teachers, though, mindful of the pendulum swings that they have experienced, cling to their old materials and create a hybrid program that combines elements of their old materials with elements of the new ones. We caution you to be proactive in preventing this practice, which is known as *layering*. Teachers need to know that the selection committee's members worked through a careful process, that they were mindful of the schoolwide context, and that they selected the core program for schoolwide use. New programs and materials should not simply be layered on top of old ones.

In fact, the Reading First legislation specifically forbids this layering process. Plans must be designed so that schools are doing the following things:

- Implementing instructional strategies based on SBRR.
- Selecting and implementing scientifically based comprehensive reading programs that provide instruction to all K–3 students.
- Using instructional strategies and programs that teach the five essential components of reading.
- Using instructional strategies and programs that will enable students to reach the level of reading proficiency.
- Implementing a clear and specific plan to use scientifically based instructional strategies to accelerate the performance and monitor the progress of students who are reading below grade level.
- Selecting and implementing scientifically based comprehensive reading programs, without layering selected programs on top of non-research-based programs already in use.

The same is true for technology-based programs and intervention programs. We urge you to take a schoolwide approach; to apply the descriptive rubric to all programs; to be careful to avoid layering; and to craft a reading program for your school that uses commercial materials in planned, thoughtful ways. In Figure 7.2 (pp. 157–159) we have provided a tool for you to use to evaluate computer-based programs. As with your core program evaluation, evaluation of a supplemental computer-based program should be conducted through a thoughtful examination of the actual lessons and a plan for how the computer-based program is an essential component of your schoolwide plan.

The use of leveled books in a reading program presents an additional challenge. We support the use of leveled books, but only if they are consistent with research on how children learn to read and with the basic scope and sequence of the core program. Leveled books are not useful unless the levels of the books match the reading levels of the children, *and* unless the skills and strategies needed to read these books are consistent with the skills and strategies taught in the core curriculum. To us, these are some broad concerns about leveled books:

- One leveling system (letters, numbers, colors) should be used throughout the school building—in classroom libraries, in the bookroom, in the library—to ensure that leveled books are used in a systematic way. The leveling system should be coordinated with the core program to avoid layering.
- Leveled books for emergent readers (ideally, children in the first part of kindergarten) must be predictable, to allow them to develop their ability to track print.
- Leveled books for beginning readers (ideally, children in the second part of kindergarten and the first part of first grade) must allow them to practice their decoding. That means that these books must be matched to the developmental level of the children and to the decoding curriculum in the core program.
- Leveled books for transitional and fluent readers (ideally, children from the middle of first grade through the first part of second grade) must allow them to gain fluency through access to a great number of high-frequency and decodable words.

The most widely used leveling system is derived from Reading Recovery. You can find book levels for many individual titles in *Guided Reading: Good First Teaching for All Children* (Fountas & Pinnell, 1996) or in *Matching Books to Readers: Using Leveled Books in Guided Reading, K–3* (Fountas, 1999). We find this system to be especially useful for organizing resources for emergent readers, transitional readers, and fluent readers. The problem comes in using this system for organizing and choosing books for beginning readers—readers who need to practice their decoding strategies in text. Books leveled in this system tend not to

A CONSUMER'S GUIDE TO EVALUATING READING SOFTWARE

This instrument is designed along the lines of "A Consumer's Guide to Evaluating a Core Reading Program Grades K–3" by Simmons and Kame'enui (see Table 7.2). This guide is intended to assist educators as they appraise software to determine how closely it is aligned with scientifically based reading research (SBRR). It is less concerned with the general design features typically appraised in all educational software. The rating symbols are similar to those adopted by Simmons and Kame'enui:

● Software consistently meets or exceeds the criterion.
◉ Software sometimes meets the criterion.
○ Software does not meet the criterion.
⊗ Software design is not relevant to this criterion.

The software is evaluated by first identifying the component(s) it addresses (phonemic awareness, phonics, etc.). The appropriate sections of this instrument are then used to appraise the software with respect to each criterion by circling or underlining the rating. Since the criteria are not necessarily of equal weight, and because some may in fact be irrelevant to a particular software design, there is no summative scoring. Rather, the ratings of all of the criteria judged must be weighed subjectively.

Phonemic Awareness

● ◉ ○ ⊗   Uses oral rather than written language.
● ◉ ○ ⊗   Progresses from awareness of larger phonological units (e.g., words, syllables, rhyme) to awareness of phonemes.
● ◉ ○ ⊗   Includes practice with blending.
● ◉ ○ ⊗   Includes practice with segmentation.
● ◉ ○ ⊗   Employs a format that minimizes the effects of guessing.
● ◉ ○ ⊗   Facilitates teacher monitoring of student performance.
● ◉ ○ ⊗   Prescribes activities on the basis of performance.
● ◉ ○ ⊗   Employs an engaging format.

(continued)

FIGURE 7.2. An instrument for use in evaluating computer-based programs.

Phonics

● ◉ ○ ⊗ Links phonics instruction to phonemic awareness.

● ◉ ○ ⊗ Includes practice with letter recognition if needed.

● ◉ ○ ⊗ Relies on direct approaches and minimizes the need to infer phonics content.

● ◉ ○ ⊗ Progresses from alphabetic (letter-by-letter) to orthographic (spelling-pattern) decoding.

● ◉ ○ ⊗ Emphasizes recognizing patterns, not learning rules.

● ◉ ○ ⊗ Stresses onset-and-rime decoding.

● ◉ ○ ⊗ Progresses from monosyllabic to polysyllabic words.

● ◉ ○ ⊗ Maximizes time actually spent learning and reinforcing skills.

● ◉ ○ ⊗ Teaches skills systematically and directly.

● ◉ ○ ⊗ Employs a format that minimizes the effects of guessing.

● ◉ ○ ⊗ Minimizes or eliminates jargon.

● ◉ ○ ⊗ Facilitates teacher monitoring of student performance.

● ◉ ○ ⊗ Prescribes activities on the basis of performance.

● ◉ ○ ⊗ Employs an engaging format.

Fluency

● ◉ ○ ⊗ Models appropriate phrasing and intonation (prosody).

● ◉ ○ ⊗ Stresses both speed and accuracy of decoding.

● ◉ ○ ⊗ Incorporates procedures for supporting reading, including repeated readings, choral reading, and echo reading.

● ◉ ○ ⊗ Facilitates teacher monitoring of student performance.

● ◉ ○ ⊗ Prescribes activities on the basis of performance.

● ◉ ○ ⊗ Employs an engaging format.

Vocabulary

● ◉ ○ ⊗ Teaches words in meaningful clusters.

● ◉ ○ ⊗ Employs graphic organizers to stress interrelationships.

● ◉ ○ ⊗ Selects vocabulary on the basis of utility and frequency.

● ◉ ○ ⊗ Provides for multiple exposures to words.

● ◉ ○ ⊗ Goes beyond simply learning definitions or synonyms.

● ◉ ○ ⊗ Incorporates validated instructional methods (including concept sorts, feature analysis, charting, webbing, possible sentences, list–group–label, etc.).

(continued)

● ◉ ○ ⊗   Stresses useful word elements (prefixes, suffixes, etc.).
● ◉ ○ ⊗   Combines definitions with contextual examples.
● ◉ ○ ⊗   Employs a format that minimizes the effects of guessing.
● ◉ ○ ⊗   Facilitates teacher monitoring of student performance.
● ◉ ○ ⊗   Prescribes activities on the basis of performance.
● ◉ ○ ⊗   Employs an engaging format.

Comprehension

● ◉ ○ ⊗   Provides interesting and engaging texts.
● ◉ ○ ⊗   Includes a variety of genres.
● ◉ ○ ⊗   Requires students to reach conclusions that draw on information in more than one sentence.
● ◉ ○ ⊗   Provides opportunities to transform the content of texts (e.g., into charts, summaries, graphic representations).
● ◉ ○ ⊗   Teaches effective strategies (e.g., activating prior knowledge, comprehension monitoring, predicting, generating questions, summarizing).
● ◉ ○ ⊗   Includes information about how, when, and why readers employ these strategies.
● ◉ ○ ⊗   Avoids a specific skill mastery approach (e.g., inferring a sequence of events, noting supporting details, etc.).
● ◉ ○ ⊗   Provides supported text to facilitate independent reading (e.g., online glossary, pronunciations, text simplifications, explanatory links, etc.).
● ◉ ○ ⊗   Includes only hidden media effects ("hot spots") that are germane to the story.
● ◉ ○ ⊗   Provides support before, during, and after reading.
● ◉ ○ ⊗   Provides a listening version of texts to support weak decoders.
● ◉ ○ ⊗   Recognizes prior knowledge limitations and attempts to accommodate them.
● ◉ ○ ⊗   Employs graphic and semantic organizers (e.g., timelines, story maps).
● ◉ ○ ⊗   Focuses on hypertext structures.
● ◉ ○ ⊗   Links comprehension to writing applications.
● ◉ ○ ⊗   Facilitates teacher monitoring of student performance.
● ◉ ○ ⊗   Prescribes activities on the basis of performance.

contain ample opportunities for beginning readers to strengthen their decoding strategies; they are more predictable than decodable in the levels targeted for first grade (C–I). Particular care must be taken to select and organize leveled books for beginning readers. In fact, to avoid layering, consider using little books published by or consistent with your core program's scope and sequence for phonics instruction (described above), rather than leveled books for beginning readers.

Organizing leveled books is a real challenge. Many literacy coaches have spent their first month on the job organizing materials full time. Although this may be tedious work, it is important work. In order for teachers to do their job well, they have to have easy access to their tools; we have visited many schools with new materials still in boxes in classrooms halfway through the school year. Literacy coaches must decide how to label and store materials so that the schoolwide program will truly be implemented schoolwide.

We have helped literacy coaches to establish shared-book rooms, so that teachers have access to more titles to use in their needs-based fluency instruction. This is a large undertaking. However, many literacy coaches have seen the shared-book room as their greatest accomplishment; because resources are pooled within the school, all teachers have more, and all children have the materials they need. In establishing a shared-book room, it is important to start with a plan. First, collect existing resources from classrooms and organize them, so that you can see what you already have. Next, compare these texts to the core program; you may find that the books that you have for kindergarten and first-grade children to use for practice are inconsistent with the instruction they are getting. It may be time to give those texts away. Finally, identify your needs and make a purchasing plan. Do you need more texts for children to practice phonics concepts? Do you need more leveled information texts? Do you need more easy chapter books for building fluency in second and third grades?

THE POLITICAL CONTEXT

Selection of core program materials remains a politically charged undertaking. We have worked with literacy coaches who have been hounded mercilessly by vendors trying to sell their wares without allowing a review process. We have worked with states threatened by vendors who regard the process of materials evaluation as a violation of their rights to sell their products (rather than a responsibility of informed consumers). We say to them that research-based reading programs need research-based instructional materials, and that the responsibility for materials selection lies at the local level. If we work together to become better consumers of instructional materials, the producers of instructional materials will respond quickly by increasing the quality of the products that they offer for sale.

The issue of defining *research-based* is particularly sticky when it comes to instructional materials. It is very, very difficult to locate SBRR on the effectiveness of specific materials. As we have noted in Chapter 3, the most convincing evidence would be experimental evidence. This would mean that programs were randomly assigned to schools, and then student achievement scores were combined for schools assigned to each program and then compared across programs. There are many reasons why this type of research evidence is not available. The most obvious one is that few school systems would allow their instructional materials to be assigned randomly.

The next level of evidence is the quasi-experiment. In a quasi-experiment, the materials are not assigned randomly. Instead, some settings agree to use one "treatment" and others agree to use another "treatment." Again, student achievement is compared across the treatments. Again, however, relatively little of this type of research is available. In addition to the difficulties involved in securing permission, as in experimental studies, even quasi-experiments comparing reading materials are extremely expensive and extremely difficult to conduct well.

The least "convincing" level of evidence is the case study, but this is the level most likely to be available. A wise consumer of case studies will ask these questions: Is growth the only measure (as in pre- and post-test designs)? How can we know whether the growth was enough? How can we know that the growth would not have occurred without the new materials? How closely matched are the characteristics of the site to our sites? Who conducted the research? Did that person or group have any personal or financial connection to any of the programs being evaluated?

Some literacy coaches and administrators will admonish the research community for not providing the evidence they need to make research-based decisions. We do not. We think that the role of the research community is to develop research-based principles (such as those we have summarized in Chapter 3). It is the role of local school district personnel to learn about those principles and to look for them in the materials they choose to buy for children in their care. There is no quick or easy road to materials selection.

CHAPTER 8

Intervention Programs

Even with systematic and explicit grade-level instruction and needs-based instruction as daily components in a schoolwide reading program, some children will need additional instruction. In this chapter, we review research on common contexts for intervention, and then provide guidance on evaluating their content. Our main goal is to guide literacy coaches to anticipate specific logjams in literacy growth at each grade level, and to coordinate personnel, materials, and schedules to address those logjams.

WHAT IS THE BEST INTERVENTION?

The best intervention is active, aggressive, and provided at the onset of a problem. It furnishes additional modeling, support, feedback, and practice in a particular domain. The best intervention is also intensive—usually daily, with no time wasted, provided individually or in very small groups. Moreover, the best intervention is specialized—provided by teachers with more and better training than typical classroom teachers. Finally, the best intervention is targeted—maximizing supported practice in a specific domain of need, rather than including all segments of the literacy diet.

Ann Duffy (2001) provided a definition of what she called *literacy acceleration* that we would like to co-opt for literacy coaches to characterize their interventions: "instruction that enables struggling readers to make rapid progress and read as well as or better than their peers not struggling in reading" (p. 70). Once Duffy personally conducted a summer intervention, she revisited that definition. She realized that she was able to do the difficult work of literacy acceleration because of her knowledge and her beliefs. As she was already an established university-based reading researcher, she had knowledge of best practices. This knowledge, though, was not what she reported as primary in her drive for literacy acceleration. Rather, it was her belief that success for children was her responsibility (not the responsibility of the students themselves or their families). She changed her own instruction to better meet the students' needs. She accepted what she called *instructional responsibility*. In a school-based program, the literacy coach must model, lead, and support a school-based notion of instructional responsibility.

WHY INTERVENE?

Robert Slavin and his colleagues (Slavin, Madden, Karweit, Dolan, & Wasik, 1991) tell a fictitious story that makes a striking point about the value of early intervention. Imagine a town in which 30% of the children became seriously ill from drinking contaminated water. Some of them died, while others were permanently disabled. Over the years, the town spent millions on medical care, but rejected an engineer's proposal to build a water treatment plant. The plant would be too expensive, the townspeople argued. And besides, 70% of the children never became ill at all. It may seem farfetched to compare reading intervention with a life-and-death scenario like this. After all, learning to read just isn't that important. Or is it?

Early literacy failure has long-term consequences. Marie Clay (1979), the New Zealand psychologist who developed the first-grade tutoring program Reading Recovery, has argued that the most efficient and effective time to prevent reading failure is right at the start of formal reading instruction, during first grade, when the achievement gap between normally developing and low-performing readers is smallest. She has reasoned that over time, the gap will widen, and the goal of the intervention will become more and more difficult to achieve.

Clay's charge to intervene early flies directly in the face of educational practices that are based on a developmental lag theory—the idea that children who are struggling with literacy at an early stage simply need more time to "catch up" with their peers. Children who are struggling with literacy are not simply developing more slowly; they are actually missing important knowledge and skills relative to their normally developing peers (Foorman, Francis, Shaywitz, Shaywitz, & Fletcher, 1997). Connie Juel (1988) reported that children who were struggling readers at the end of grade 1 had an 88% chance of struggling at the end of grade 4. The first years of school, then—kindergarten and first grade—are the prime time for intervention.

The *Matthew effect*, a term coined by Keith Stanovich (1986), captures the spiraling effects of reading failure. Children who struggle with reading avoid reading. This avoidance prevents development of fluency and vocabulary that come from wide reading. At the same time, children who read easily enjoy reading. They read more. Their fluency and vocabulary develop more and more quickly, and the difference between them and their struggling peers in reading knowledge, skills, and strategies becomes greater and greater each year. As a result, the gap between the best and worst readers widens each year until it is unbridgeable. In the early grades, however, when the gap is narrowest, appropriate intervention stands a chance of reaching struggling readers.

WHO NEEDS INTERVENTION?

In 1998, the National Research Council's report *Preventing Reading Difficulties in Young Children* (Snow, Burns, & Griffin, 1998) described factors predicting reading failure. First, it identified child-based factors (those that could be identified through individual assessment): severe cognitive deficiencies, severe hearing and language impairments, attention problems, depressed early language development, and depressed preschool literacy skills. Individual children exhibiting one or more of these factors are *potentially* at risk. Next, the report identified family-based factors (those that could be identified without any actual testing of a child): family history of reading problems, family environment with limited English-language proficiency, and low socioeconomic status (SES). Children living in environments with one or more of these factors are also *potentially* at risk. Finally, it identified community and school-based factors (those that could be identified without specific data on families): low SES at the neighborhood level, and placement in schools with a history of low achievement. Again, children living in such circumstances are *potentially* at risk.

Identification of individual-, family-, and community-based risk factors is actually an indictment of our schools' inabilities to adapt and respond to children's needs. At risk status does not *cause* reading failure. Individual children with disabled parents learn to read. Individual children with language impairments learn to read. Individual children with no English spoken at home learn to read. Individual children from very poor families, living in very poor neighborhoods, learn to read. In a schoolwide reading program, teachers must learn to provide especially expert instruction and to meet the needs of all children.

In fact, many children fail to learn to read because they receive poor instruction. This is one potential risk that can be removed. In a schoolwide reading program, no individual-, family-, or community-based risk excuses the school from responsibility for preventing reading failure and/or intervening as soon as the classroom curriculum fails to address the needs of individual children. Unfortunately, when schools fail to provide the necessary instruction and intervention, individuals point to risk factors outside the school to explain it. This leads to a damaging self-fulfilling prophecy, one that can become a series of mantras: "These children can't learn to read because they come to school at risk for failure," "The school is powerless in light of these outside circumstances," "The children failed to learn to read because they were initially at risk."

The total number of children who need intervention is a hotly contested issue, both within the literacy community and in the political arena. The broad message is a hopeful one: Many reading problems can be prevented altogether through consistent, research-based instruction in preschool and across the grade levels, and others can be remediated through specially targeted efforts. For a summary of this controversy, we describe the recent longitudinal work of Frank Vellutino and Donna Scanlon (e.g., Vellutino & Scanlon, 2001).

Vellutino and Scanlon's intervention studies were carefully designed. First, they tested over 1,000 kindergarten children with a variety of assessments (some of literacy achievement and others of cognitive skills) to investigate the potential underlying causes of reading problems. Next, they observed kindergarten instruction to describe this instruction, and later to investigate the potential relationship between the type and amount of instruction and achievement. Next they retested children in the middle of first grade to identify struggling readers and normally achieving readers. They provided tutoring to half of the struggling first graders. Finally, they retested children at the end of first grade, at the end of third grade, and at the end of fourth grade. This series of carefully integrated studies provides important insight into the potential effects of intervention. Here are some highlights of their findings:

- Literacy measures (letter identification and phoneme segmentation) in kindergarten were strong predictors of reading achievement at the end of first grade.
- Children who were initially rated as weak in letter identification in kindergarten were more likely to be rated as average or strong by their first-grade teachers if they came from kindergarten classrooms where more time was spent on phonemic awareness activities.
- Children who were initially rated as strong in letter identification in kindergarten were more likely to be rated as average or strong by their first-grade teachers if they came from kindergarten classrooms where more time was spent on shared reading activities.
- After only one semester of daily tutoring (rereading for fluency, reading new text, phonemic awareness, phonics, spelling for sounds), one-half of the tutored children scored in the average range on standardized measures of decoding and comprehension; this average range was maintained through fourth grade.

- Examining the progress of these children, the authors estimated that only 3% of children had reading impairments (standardized scores below the 30th percentile) and only 1.5% had severe impairments (standardized scores below the 15th percentile) after only one semester of tutoring.
- The ability to decode was not predictable from IQ scores. Children with both high and low IQ scores were normally achieving decoders; children with both high and low IQ scores were in the severely impaired groups.

Taken together, this longitudinal work is especially important for understanding the potential for intervention. First, instruction matters. In a heterogeneous kindergarten class, both code-based and meaning-based reading instruction are important, but to different groups of children. Intervention, if it is intensive, targeted, and provided early, can make meaningful differences in children's literacy performance in only one semester; given instruction and early intervention, very few children will fall into the category of severely impaired. We discuss the content of such interventions after we discuss issues of context.

CONTEXTS FOR INTERVENTION

We consider the contexts for intervention to include its places, times, and groupings, as well as the personnel who provide intervention as part of a schoolwide program. There is one broad theme that literacy coaches should recognize: Each of these intervention contexts has the potential to be an effective part of a schoolwide reading program, but each of these contexts is also a potentially ineffective one.

Classrooms

Although it is the major theme of this book, and surely the major role of a literacy coach in a schoolwide reading program, we will restate it here: The most important and effective part of an intervention program is increasing the amount and quality of classroom instruction, especially for struggling readers. No program of intervention, regardless of its quality, will be sufficient to counter the negative effects of poor classroom instruction.

Preschools

Provision of high-quality preschool experience is increasingly identified as an intervention strategy with the potential to produce an impressive yield in preventing reading failure. Unfortunately, though, not all preschool experiences are equal. Typically, poorly funded preschool programs designed to serve at-risk children, such as Head Start, are less effective than better-funded model programs (Barnett, 2001).

Preschools designed specifically to intervene provide children with extensive language and literacy experiences that are developmentally appropriate for them. Those preschools are busy, child-centered places. Literacy learning for very young children requires social interaction, joint participation, knowledge of and responsiveness to individual needs, opportunities for personal feedback, extended independent practice, easy access to materials, and attention to motivation (McGee & Richgels, 2003).

The physical environment in a high-quality preschool classroom allows for choice and exploration. Centers (e.g., library, post office, doctor's office, business office, and bank) allow children to engage in dramatic play, in settings that they may already know, including literacy materials. For example, a post office could contain writing utensils, envelopes, stickers, and postcards to facilitate children's experimentation with emergent writing and to motivate children to be interested in the alphabet.

High-quality preschools are filled with language. Teachers work with children in large groups, allowing them to interact and speak naturally, rather than teaching them the hand-raising conventions that will be useful later on. They work with children in small groups, modeling and expanding (rather than correcting) the language that the children use during dramatic play. They engage individual children in extended conversations about their own play and about their own lives.

High-quality preschools are filled with reading and writing. Like the rest of the staff in a schoolwide reading program, preschool teachers have high-quality classroom libraries and access to the school's library to select materials that are interesting to and appropriate for their students. Teachers read and reread books aloud, interactively. They engage children in shared and guided retellings, and help children to act out their favorite books. They allow children to handle books themselves, including chances for pretend readings of books previously read aloud. They model writing about what is read and about what is important to the life of the class.

These activities together (dramatic play, extended language interaction, and reading and writing) provide an authentic window into authentic introduction of letter names, letter sounds, and early phonemic awareness activities (e.g., rhyme, initial phoneme isolation) appropriate for very young children. A literacy-skills-only preschool (one that targets extensive drilling to mastery of early literacy skills) wastes the chance to intervene in language development in ways likely to produce lasting impact.

Family Literacy Models

Comprehensive school-based intervention may include family literacy programs. *Family literacy,* as defined by the federally funded programs in Even Start, has four components. The first, described above, is preschool. In a family literacy model, this preschool will also include high-quality, language-rich day care options for infants and toddlers. The second—adult education—typically involves programs to provide general equivalency diploma (GED) classes for parents who have not graduated from high school, training programs in basic computer- and/or job-related skills, and English-language courses for parents whose native language is not English. The third part of the Even Start model is parenting education—specific training for parents in supporting the physical and cognitive development of their children, beginning at birth. Finally, family literacy programs include programs to help parents support their children in school: specific programs about homework, about the importance of reading and writing, and about ways for parents to partner with their children's teachers. Reviews of comprehensive family literacy programs for their effects on adult and child outcomes have yielded promising early results (Wasik, Dobbins, & Herrmann, 2001).

One large-scale look at the effects of family literacy programs is available in the Chicago Longitudinal Study (Reynolds & Temple, 1998). The program provided support to over 500 low-income African American children and their families. Some children participated for 2 years (preschool and kindergarten), and others for up to 5 years. With long-term intervention, these potentially at-risk children were more successful in both math and reading at the third grade, and the advantage in reading was still significant in seventh grade. Children who participated in the long term were also less likely to be retained in a grade or placed in special education.

Family literacy programs are expensive. However, the separate components of family literacy are likely to be provided by various government agencies in the locality. One way a literacy coach can turn separate programs into a comprehensive intervention is to coordinate them for parents at an individual school and provide a parent education classroom at school. For example, parents of a school's preschoolers could be invited to a series of family literacy services provided at school: GED and parenting classes coordinated to be held at school while children are at day care and preschool, and a series of special parent and child classes to introduce those same parents to school life. The National Institute for Literacy (http://www.nifl.gov) and the Partnership for Reading (http://www.nifl.gov/nifl/pfr.html) provide information for schools on grants to support family literacy, as well as downloadable documents for parents about language and literacy development. The National Center for Family Literacy is a nonprofit organization supporting family literacy services that include training, programs, research, and advocacy. Its Web site (http://www.famlit.org) has excellent links.

Title I and Special Education

Title I and special education programs are traditional contexts for remediation; in a schoolwide program, they can become contexts for intervention. Both programs are federally funded, and both provide services to struggling readers. Title I, originally authorized by the Elementary and Secondary Education Act of 1965, was designed to provide additional support for poor children. Title I moneys are allocated based on the numbers of children qualifying for free or reduced-price lunches, and they are often used to hire reading teachers and paraprofessionals to work with struggling readers. Special education, funded beginning in 1975 through the Education for All Handicapped Children Act, targeted children struggling to learn because of cognitive and physical disabilities. These federal moneys for special education are used to fund extensive testing programs and to pay both school-based and itinerant teachers with special training in working with particular disabilities. Neither Title I nor special education funding has solved reading difficulties; both "programs" are fraught with problems (Klenk & Kibby, 2000; McGill-Franzen & Goatley, 2001).

Richard Allington and his colleagues have been sage but trenchant critics of Title I and special education as forming a "second system" of education that fragments children's learning opportunities and teachers' responsibility for that learning (e.g., Allington, 1994; Allington & McGill-Franzen, 1989; Walmsley & Allington, 1995; Johnston & Allington, 1991). The criticisms they have identified are central to the work of a literacy coach, who must ensure that these special programs are actually purposeful, integrated components of the schoolwide reading program. Here we take some of the criticisms and turn them into proactive statements for program planning:

- Special programs do not shift responsibility for educating struggling readers away from classroom teachers to specialists; special programs supplement and extend the already expert, targeted instruction provided by classroom teachers.
- Special programs need to be directly linked in philosophy and pacing to the school's core program.
- Special programs need the best available materials.
- Children in special programs cannot afford to lose any time in transitions; those programs should be incorporated into the classroom whenever possible.
- Children in special programs must actually read and write more during their time in these programs than their peers who are working with the classroom teacher.

Tutoring Models

One-to-one tutoring, especially for first graders, may be a part of an intervention effort. Tutoring programs can be effective, but not simply because they offer individualized instruction. Even tutoring programs with wide application and evidence of effectiveness do not work for every child, and some studies of tutoring efforts have failed to show any real gains (Shanahan, 1998). In considering tutoring programs, then, literacy coaches must be wise and informed consumers.

The most important variables to consider in implementing tutoring are the financial costs to the school's reading program in comparison to the benefits of effectively preventing reading failure for children. Wasik and Slavin (1993) reviewed 16 studies of five tutoring models and found evidence across models that tutored children made substantial progress. Particularly strong models used certified teachers. The largest-scale tutoring effort for beginning readers is Reading Recovery. A brief review of the research on this model highlights the complexities of developing and testing research-based intervention programs and of incorporating large-scale tutoring models into schoolwide programs.

Reading Recovery (Clay, 1993) is a one-to-one tutoring model for first graders. Hallmarks of the program include its use of a text gradient of natural-language texts, its emphasis on teaching beginning readers to use meaning-based self-monitoring and cross-checking strategies to recognize words, and its extensive supervised professional training. Reading Recovery teachers are trained weekly for an entire year while they begin tutoring children. After training, two teachers typically spend half of their time tutoring first graders and half of their time sharing responsibility for a classroom. Together, they are likely to serve 16 intervention students in a year, as well as to serve one classroom in regular instruction. Children's progress is evaluated daily through the collection of running records, and also frequently through the program's diagnostic measures. Successful children are discontinued from the program once they are reading on grade level, and new children are added. A smaller number of children are discontinued without success.

Research on Reading Recovery has been controversial. Reading Recovery has been evaluated in studies conducted by researchers who support it (e.g., Pinnell, 1989; Pinnell, Lyons, DeFord, Bryk, & Seltzer, 1994). Those studies have documented positive effects on the achievement of beginning readers. These results have been challenged, however: In a reanalysis of Reading Recovery data across sites, Hiebert (1994, 1996) found the program to be less effective than its advocates claimed.

Shanahan and Barr (1995) also conducted an independent evaluation of the effects of Reading Recovery. They concluded that Reading Recovery does work for many (but not all) students. They also concluded that Reading Recovery is expensive, potentially much more expensive than its developers have claimed. At its most generous (with 16 students served by one full-time teacher or two half-time teachers), they estimated the cost to be $2,890 per pupil. Applying a stricter criterion—one that computed the number of children who would effectively complete the program—they estimated Reading Recovery to cost $4,000 per pupil in 1994. That was 10 years ago as of this writing.

Iversen and Tunmer (1993) challenged Reading Recovery's top-down philosophy about word recognition. They added a phonological recoding portion to the lessons, explicitly teaching phonemic awareness and vowel phonograms. They compared their modified treatment to a traditional Reading Recovery treatment and to a small-group intervention. Both Reading Recovery treatments produced higher achievement than the small-group intervention. The main (and unexpected) difference in the study was in the number of lessons: The Reading Recovery treatment with the addition of the isolated phonemic awareness and phonics instruction was 37% more efficient. That is, students needed over one-third fewer lessons to reach the program's goals. Adding more of this type of instruction to the Reading Recovery model, then, is one way to reduce the expense. This is an important lesson about the characteristics of effective tutoring models.

Volunteer tutoring efforts have been developed to counter the high costs of tutoring models such as Reading Recovery. Wasik (1998) looked for evidence of the effectiveness of these programs in increasing reading achievement, but found relatively little. Although such programs attempt to document their effects, the difficulties in establishing control group comparisons (because of ethical concerns about denying treatment to struggling children) have prevented the gathering of experimental evidence. However, several important shared characteristics of volunteer tutoring efforts can inform the literacy coach:

1. Tutoring efforts must include assessments of children before, during, and after tutoring.
2. Tutors need the guidance of a reading specialist who creates lesson plans and evaluates student performance.
3. The need for training is inversely related to the explicitness of the lesson plans; tutoring programs with lesson plan frames that are individualized for each session need to plan for substantially more training than tutoring programs including a highly structured series of lessons.
4. Tutoring models for beginning readers must include rereading for fluency; work with letters, sounds, and words in isolation; text reading matched to children's growing expertise; and writing.
5. Each tutoring model's approach to instruction should be evaluated for its match to the school's classroom-based approach.

Since the analysis described above was conducted, one additional (and very different) tutoring model has been developed that may be of interest to the literacy coach. Start Making a Reader Today (SMART) is a tutoring model that serves many more children at a much lower cost than any of the other models we have reviewed (Baker, Gersten, & Keating, 2000). The lesson plan is greatly simplified, and much less training is provided to the tutors. Sessions are 30 minutes twice each week. There are four lesson strategies that the tutors may use: They read aloud to the children, they read chorally with the children, they read and then the children reread, and they ask the children questions during reading. Children receive two books each month to build a home library. Clearly, then, the SMART program is designed to build reading interest and motivation in the context of a one-on-one book-reading session; the program evaluation indicates that this approach also provides dividends in word recognition and fluency.

Small-Group Models

Extending group size from one-on-one tutoring to small groups is another way to address the need for intervention for a large number of children and to reduce the costs of providing such an intervention.

Hiebert, Colt, Catto, and Gury (1992) provided a small-group model when they restructured curriculum and instruction for first graders in an existing Chapter 1 project. Children were served in groups of six by a teacher and a paraprofessional for 30 minutes each day. First, the research team changed the responsibilities of the adults. Rather than have the teacher provide instruction and the paraprofessional assist children as needed, they divided the children into two groups, taught simultaneously. Midway through the intervention, the adults switched groups. Second, they changed the instructional diet to focus more attention on fluency and decoding. Children reread predictable texts for fluency, wrote lists of rhyming words and entries in their journals, and learned about word patterns.

Leslie and Allen (1999) also designed and evaluated a successful small-group model, The Literacy Project. Struggling readers in grades 1–4 were placed by reading level in groups of two to four and were taught by university students after school in 90-minute sessions for a total of 30 hours each semester. The intervention continued until children were reading on grade level or for as many as four semesters. Sessions included book sharing, with children retelling or responding to books read at home; shared or guided reading of literature; direct instruction in either word identification (using rimes to decode by analogy, and automatically recognizing high-frequency words) or comprehension strategies; and writing.

Several interesting aspects of research on The Literacy Project have implications for choosing small-group intervention models, especially because the researchers examined the contributions of particular components of the model. This intervention provided the greatest growth for children who began at mid- to late-first grade reading levels. The weakest-performing readers in this model were not as successful; the rime-based decoding instruction may have been insufficient for them. The total number of rimes taught for decoding was correlated with reading growth, but the number of high-frequency words was not. Perhaps teaching word recognition strategies is more powerful than teaching words. The amount of story structure instruction was significantly correlated with growth for children reading at second- and third-grade levels. This makes sense, given the ideas about reading development presented in Chapter 5. Recreational reading (total words read at home) predicted word-level and text-level outcome measures. This too makes sense, in light of research on the importance of fluency and motivation to reading achievement.

Technology-Based Models

Technology offers intervention possibilities with both promise and problems. Computer applications are hardly the panacea some once thought them to be, but they do possess the potential to supplement effective instruction. The question is how best to use computers.

Perhaps the most important lesson from research into classroom applications has been that immersing beginning readers into an integrated learning system (ILS; see Chapter 7) is no substitute for insightful teaching. Independent studies of two major ILSs raise doubts as to whether any ILS can deliver on the promise of higher comparative growth. IBM's Writing to Read, which linked reading and writing and also involved print activities, failed to produce comparative gains (Slavin, 1990). More recently, students using the Waterford Early Reading Program failed to outperform students receiving traditional instruction in K–1 classrooms (Patterson, Henry, O'Quin, Ceprano, & Blue, 2003). Given the high costs of such programs, we wonder whether there can be any rationale for purchasing them.

On the other hand, software that is more limited in scope can often fit seamlessly into classroom instruction and provide young children at risk with some of the extra help they need. Such uses can involve the sort of social interaction that is essential for early learning (Labbo & Ash, 1998) and yet too often lacking in an ILS setting (Patterson et al., 2003). The present state of best practice affords an important place for such applications (McKenna, Labbo, & Reinking, 2003). As early as kindergarten, children can use software to explore the alphabet and illustrate their stories. They can learn sight words and read stories at their listening levels through electronically supported text, which supplies pronunciations on a point-and-click basis. They can enhance their phonological awareness through programs like DaisyQuest, Earobics, and Lindamood Phoneme Sequencing. Well-designed decoding software, such as Simon Sounds It Out and Reading Mansion, can provide the additional reinforcement that some children require during this stage of their development (Fox & Mitchell, 2000; McKenna, 2002). Children who have difficulty attaining fluency can be helped by the speech recognition and recording capabilities of such programs as Reading Resource, by Soliloquy Learning.

Teachers can build applications like these into their daily planning without the curricular disconnections and lost time implicit in trips to the lab. A computer corner can afford one type of center and can also be used by children at other times during the day, according to their needs. The literacy coach is in the position to recommend purchases and monitor applications in classrooms. Remaining current is no easy matter, but most schools boast one or more "technophiles," who can be counted upon to keep up with developments. These individuals can become an important resource to the literacy coach.

After-School, Saturday School, and Summer School Programs

A comprehensive approach to intervention means a comprehensive approach to using all of the available time to extend opportunities for children who need them. The Beginning School Study (Alexander, Entwisle, & Olson, 2001) provides an intriguing data set and some common-sense policy implications. The study relied on a large sample of standardized test scores for each of 5 years. When these were looked at in traditional ways, as end-of-year scores, there were marked differences in achievement by SES: Children from poor families had lower achievement. When the scores were looked at in a different way, by analyzing individual growth during the year, the picture was different: There was little difference in the growth of academic skills during the year attributable to SES. The discrepancy came in the summer. Higher-SES children continued to develop their academic skills during those months (presumably because they had greater access to educational materials and experiences), while lower-SES children's development remained stagnant. A common-sense approach to this finding, then, would be to provide more school-based services during the summer to children from poor families; they would then be better able to maintain their academic growth, like their more advantaged peers.

Some schools combat the potential effects of the summer loss by changing their calendar (even with the same number of total school days). In a limited comparison of traditional-calendar schools (with an extended summer vacation) to alternative-calendar schools (with short breaks spaced throughout the school year and shortened summer vacation), children in the early primary grades fared better with the alternative calendar (Reese, Myers, Nofsinger, & Brown, 2000).

Other schools combat the effects of summer loss for all students through extended-year programs. Extending the year for 30 days (15 at the end of kindergarten and 15 at the beginning of first grade) was associated with greater achievement in both mathematics and reading at the beginning of first grade—a finding with significance for intervention design (Frazier & Morrison, 1998). Perhaps extending the year in this way for *struggling* students would be a way to reduce the achievement gap.

Another way that schools extend time for learning is through extended-day programs. Extended days have the potential to serve two purposes. First, they can provide a safe and supervised setting for children who would otherwise be home alone while their parents work. Second, they can provide additional instruction for children who need it, specifically targeting the achievement gap by providing more services. Neither purpose will be adequately served with an extended-day program, though, unless it is well run and well thought out. Schools may elect to run programs at the building level or the district level, or to outsource them to private companies. They can be funded either through the district budget, by charging parents directly, or through grant moneys. The federal government funds extended-day programs through the 21st Century Community Learning Grant (Joiner, 2000).

CONTENT OF INTERVENTION

We take an aggressive intervention approach here, anticipating the very specific struggles that readers may have at different ages and stages of development. We cannot automatically assume that children have had access to explicit, systematic, high-quality classroom instruction each year of their schooling. A literacy coach will quickly recognize the folly of that assumption. First, many struggling readers will transfer from one school to another. They are likely to have had curricular disruptions; they often come to their new school with academic "holes." Second, even the best-designed whole-school elementary reform effort takes 4 years to bear real fruit. In year 1, the kindergartners come to school and receive the instruction they deserve. A small number of them require intervention. Most of them move to grade 1 during year 2 with the skills and strategies they need to be successful. A smaller number of them require intervention. This cohort successfully moves to grade 2 during year 3; a few still require intervention. During year 4, this initial cohort is in third grade, having had 3 years of research-based reading instruction. By this time, the numbers who require intervention should be very few indeed. At the start of any schoolwide reform effort, then, the numbers of children who require intervention are unusually high. It is important to remember, though, that for many of those children, the intervention is necessary because of the ineffective classroom instruction that the children previously received in the building. Because of this, it may be necessary to provide "first-grade" interventions for second and third graders.

There are five instructional characteristics of interventions that can be applied to any intervention program (Coyne, Kame'enui, & Simmons, 2001):

1. *Conspicuous strategies.* Interventions teach and reinforce explicit, repetitive procedures that can be purposely followed to solve a problem or complete a task.

2. *Mediated scaffolding.* Interventions rely on a carefully coordinated set of materials and/or tasks progressing purposefully from easier to more complex, and from more to less teacher support, both within and across lessons.

3. *Strategic integration.* Interventions are designed to allow literacy progress in on   main to be integrated with and demonstrated in another domain.

4. *Primed background knowledge.* Interventions identify and remind children to use lower-level skills to achieve higher-level tasks.

5. *Judicious review.* Interventions include review that is targeted to both the needs of the learner and the demands of the task.

Below, we apply these characteristics to individual programs that have been developed and tested by researchers. These programs are identified as examples (rather than a recommended list) of potentially effective interventions.

As we read recent research on intervention efforts and reflected on the place of intervention in a schoolwide program, we found extensive support for Hiebert and Taylor's (2000) conclusion that the focus of the intervention changes in ways consistent with ages and stages of reading development. Many kindergarten interventions focus on basic skills underlying reading and writing, not on conventional reading and writing. Many first-grade interventions focus on developing knowledge of the alphabetic principle and application of the principle in reading appropriate text. Many second-grade interventions target fluency. And, finally, many third-grade interventions are more global, teaching children comprehension strategies to apply in increasingly complex text. Below we provide a description of one intervention of each type; these interventions are provided as samples of interventions that meet the criteria above (Coyne et al., 2001), rather than as recommendations. The job of the literacy coach will be to evaluate all possible interventions for their match to student needs in the building; for their potential to add value to the building's reading program; and for their systematic, explicit targeting.

Phonemic Awareness

Blackman, Ball, Black, and Tangel (1994, 2000) developed and tested a phonemic awareness intervention for kindergarten children. The 41-lesson intervention was conducted for 15–20 minutes each day for a small group of children during the second half of the kindergarten year. The lessons had three parts:

1. *Phoneme segmentation.* Teachers pronounced one-, two-, and three-phoneme words orally, and children segmented the sounds while moving disks to represent the sounds. This segment of the lesson progressed from easier to more difficult tasks (mediated scaffolding) and targeted one conspicuous strategy (using manipulatives to aid in phonemic segmentation). Gradually, as letter tiles were introduced for the target letters, the task included strategic integration. Letter sound knowledge, developed in isolation, was combined with segmentation strategies, developed without letters.

2. *Phoneme comparisons.* Using picture games and puppets, children analyzed words spoken orally by the teacher or presented in pictures (including segmenting and comparing their initial sounds). The target words in these tasks included

words in children's oral vocabularies (e.g., *ambulance, alligator*), which primed background knowledge of additional words sharing phonological characteristics of words targeted in phoneme segmentation tasks.

3. *Letter names and sounds. Children learned to recog*nize eight letters and to produce their individual letter sounds. Eventually, these letters and sounds were integrated into the phoneme segmentation part of the lessons. This segment of the lesson directed the teacher to use judicious review of these particular letters and sounds to build automaticity.

This intervention was refined over time, was used with both kindergarten and first-grade teachers, and was tested both for its effects on phonemic awareness for kindergartners and for its effects in combination with decoding instruction for first graders.

Language Development

Jordan, Snow, and Porche (2000) developed and tested Project EASE (Early Access to Success in Education) as a family literacy project for kindergarten children. The program targeted language development by teaching parents to engage in effective interactions with their children. Five units were prepared: vocabulary development, storybook reading, letters and sounds, narrative retelling, and nonfiction. The characteristics of intervention were apparent at two levels for this intervention; it was an intervention for parents so that they could provide an intervention for children. Each unit consisted of three parts:

1. *Parent education sessions.* These sessions were designed to teach parents specific concepts about literacy development for their children, as well as specific interactions that would facilitate this development. This part of the intervention was an example of conspicuous strategies and mediated scaffolding for the parents as both learners and teachers.

2. *At-school activities.* These sessions were designed to help parents to observe specific school-based literacy activities and then to engage in one-on-one interactions with their children at school. These interactions provided mediated scaffolding for both parents and children.

3. *At-home activities.* These activities included structure and support for engaging in language and literacy-rich activities at home. Specific books, and scripts for introducing and using them, provided all five aspects of intervention: conspicuous strategies, mediated scaffolding, strategic integration, primed background knowledge, and judicious review.

The Project EASE model was evaluated for its effects on children's language development.

Decoding

Vellutino and Scanlon (2002) developed and tested a tutoring model, Interactive Strategies, with struggling first graders. Their intervention was delivered by certified teachers with additional support and training. The domain of interest in the intervention was decoding. In order to support decoding, word knowledge and background knowledge of phonemic awareness were primed. Lessons included the following:

1. *Five minutes of rereading familiar texts.* The primary purpose of this section of the lesson was building automaticity in word recognition. The criterion of judicious review was met here; rereading allowed quick review of previous work in all areas of the lesson.

2. *Five minutes of phonological skills instruction.* This part of the lesson progressed through alphabet recognition, phonemic awareness, phonics, recognizing word families, and producing spelling patterns. The criterion of mediated scaffolding was met here, as the approach to developing phonological skills was progressive, and the lessons were tailored to the needs of the individual child. Once a child succeeded with alphabet recognition, this time was used for phonemic awareness; once a child was successful with phonemic awareness, this time was used for phonics instruction; and so forth. The criterion of conspicuous strategies was also met here, as this instruction included direct procedural information. For example, in developing phonemic awareness, the teacher first modeled saying the first sound in a target word and then directed the child to do so.

3. *Ten minutes of reading new text.* Children read new text each day, matched to their instructional level. Before reading, the teacher provided a short story introduction. During reading, the teacher intervened to prime background knowledge. For example, if a child was struggling to recognize a word with a previously studied phonogram, the teacher prompted, "Is there a word family you already know in that word?" The teacher also encouraged strategic integration during reading. For example, for a child working on basic phonics during the phonological skills instruction phase of the lesson, the teacher encouraged the child to make the sounds that he or she already knew and to think about words that would make sense, integrating synthetic decoding with comprehension-based monitoring. After reading, the teacher engaged the child in a very short response or evaluation of the story, to maintain his or her motivation to read.

4. *Five minutes of work with high-frequency words in isolation.* The teacher reviewed a corpus of words selected for their frequency in texts for beginning reading, many of which were phonetically irregular. This part of the lesson again provided mediated scaffolding (because the words were selected and ordered for their utility in reading) and also judicious review (because once individual words were recognized automatically, other words were added to the lesson).

5. *Five minutes of writing.* Again providing primed background knowledge

and strategic integration, the teacher engaged the child in some sort of writing task—either spelling a list of related words, dictating a story for the teacher to model writing and spelling, or eventually writing a sentence or simple story.

The Interactive Strategies intervention was evaluated for its effects on word reading, text reading, and spelling.

This tutoring model is very similar in content and focus to the tutoring models developed or tested by researchers trained at the McGuffey Reading Center at the University of Virginia: Book Buddies (Invernizzi, Rosemary, Juel, & Richards, 1997; Johnston, Invernizzi, & Juel, 1998), Howard Street (Morris, 1999; Morris, Shaw, & Perney, 1990), and Early Steps (Morris, Tyner, & Perney, 2000; Santa & Hoien, 1999). The main difference is in the personnel. Interactive Strategies tutoring was provided by certified teachers who were participating in an experiment. Book Buddies is an ongoing program provided by community volunteers and supervised by reading specialists, who write the lesson plans, train the tutors, and observe the lessons. Howard Street is an after-school program provided to second and third graders who are reading at the early-first-grade level. The program is located outside the school, staffed by volunteers, and supervised by reading specialists. Early Steps is provided by a school-based team: first-grade teachers, paraprofessionals, and reading teachers, supported by a trainer who conducts site visits to model lessons, observe, and provide help and feedback. We encourage literacy coaches to evaluate the needs of their site and the available personnel before choosing one any of these tutoring models.

All tutoring models for at-risk beginning readers owe a substantial debt to Reading Recovery (Clay, 1993). The main differences between the more recently developed models and Reading Recovery are the newer models' explicit and systematic attention to developing phonemic awareness and phonics knowledge, and their use of at least some phonetically regular (decodable) texts. Unlike Reading Recovery, each of the three first-grade tutoring models above (Interactive Strategies, Book Buddies, and Early Steps) includes decontextualized, explicit work with letters, sounds, phonograms, and words in isolation.

Word-Level Fluency

Retrieval Rate, Accuracy, and Vocabulary Elaboration (RAVE) is an intervention targeting fluency by developing word retrieval skills and broadening vocabulary knowledge for individual words in isolation (Wolf & Segal, 1999). The intervention was designed for small groups of children; it lasted 30 minutes, 4 days each week, for 8 weeks. The target population for this intervention consisted of children who had already learned basic phonics, including blending and segmenting, but were still struggling with fluency. Children in the experimental studies were in second and third grade.

RAVE lessons consisted of four parts:

1. *Direct instruction for target words, presented in a sequence for mediated scaffolding.* These words allowed teachers to use primed background knowledge as they drew attention to sources of prior knowledge of the words (either their sound, their spelling patterns, or their meaning).

2. *Word sleuth strategies.* Teachers taught children to use a series of strategies when they encountered unknown words (e.g., searching for clues, analyzing words into parts, and making a calculated guess) or when they had difficulty retrieving words (e.g., searching for clues, asking themselves what the word sounded like, asking themselves about the syllables, and saying a part of the word). These were examples of conspicuous strategies.

3. *Vocabulary development.* Teachers helped children define and categorize the week's words with many connections (semantic, syntactic, and phonological). They also taught strategies for learning and remembering new words (e.g., visualizing). The goal was to teach both the target words and generalizable vocabulary learning strategies. This part of the RAVE lesson allowed for both primed background knowledge and strategic integration.

4. *Retrieval games.* A series of games allowed children to practice retrieving words rapidly from memory. This series of activities was an example of mediated scaffolding and judicious review, as the activities were sequenced to allow children to review both the taught words and the taught strategies for learning and retrieving words.

RAVE was evaluated through measures of word retrieval, vocabulary knowledge, and naming speed.

Text-Level Fluency

QuickReads (Hiebert, 2003) is a repeated-reading program targeting the building of background knowledge and reading rate. The program begins at second grade and continues though third and fourth grades. Lessons are designed to last from 15 to 20 minutes. The materials consist of series of short passages constructed to combine high-frequency words and decodable words targeted to the grade level. They are arranged into thematically similar strands of five passages. This design is an example of mediated scaffolding and judicious review. There are four steps in the instructional plan.

1. The teacher introduces the passage and asks students to think about what they already know. Students then scan the passage for new words and underline them. Students read the passage silently, untimed. Students use a graphic organizer to help them remember the content of the passage. This part of the lesson provides primed background knowledge and strategic integration.

2. The teacher models fluent reading of the passage, with students following

along silently. There is a brief discussion of the passage meaning. Since this is a procedure used in every lesson, it emphasizes a conspicuous strategy for developing fluency through reading, listening, and rereading.

3. Students read the passage again, with a target of reading the entire passage in 1 minute. They mark and record their progress.

4. After every fifth lesson, students reread all of the passages related to that theme and complete a multiple-choice comprehension check. Again, this allows for judicious review.

QuickReads is a version of repeated readings (which we have discussed as a research-based part of classroom instruction). We categorize it as an intervention because of the careful attention to the word-level characteristics of the texts in the program. It has been evaluated (but only by its designer and publisher) on measures of reading rate, accuracy, and comprehension.

Comprehension Strategies

Palinscar and Brown (1984) developed and tested Reciprocal Teaching, a comprehension intervention designed to use a repetitive, strategy-based dialogue to support children's development of comprehension strategies. It is intended for small groups of children. Reciprocal Teaching was originally tested with older readers, but it has been used successfully with elementary-age children (e.g., Kelly, Moore, & Tuck, 1994; Hacker & Tenent, 2002). This approach takes text broken into segments (usually by the headings). Children read the text segment and then engage in the discussion. At first, the teacher leads the discussion. As children become familiar with the strategies, children take turns as leader, and the teacher scaffolds for them. This structure is itself a form of mediated scaffolding and allows for judicious review. Reciprocal Teaching relies on a structured discussion with four parts:

1. *Asking questions.* The teacher (or child leader) opens the discussion by asking questions related to the text content. If necessary, children reread to find answers; this provides another chance for teachers to engage children in judicious review.

2. *Summarizing.* The leader engages the group in a summary to bring closure to the questioning and to review the gist of the text. This is an example of a conspicuous strategy.

3. *Clarifying.* The leader engages in a discussion of what was difficult about understanding the text segment and how he or she solved the comprehension problem. This discussion allows both for primed background knowledge and for strategic integration.

4. *Predicting.* The leader ends the discussion segment by predicting the con-

tent of the next segment and explaining why and how he or she made that prediction, again using a conspicuous strategy.

Reciprocal Teaching has been evaluated both with measures of understanding of the texts used in the discussions and with standardized comprehension tests. Like repeated readings (mentioned above), Reciprocal Teaching could also be used as a classroom-based program. We characterize it as an intervention here because of its repetitive use of conspicuous strategies—a characteristic that literacy coaches will have to look for in any comprehension intervention.

CAVEAT

There are significant holes in the intervention literature as we see it informing the intervention segment of a schoolwide reading programs. First, there are few studies of interventions targeting English literacy achievement for young second-language learners, and certainly none that we can use as an intervention model. Although the National Research Council's *Preventing Reading Difficulties in Young Children* (Snow et al., 1998) finds flaws in the available research, it recommends initial literacy instruction in the native language, followed by literacy instruction in the second language once children have attained basic oral language.

The second hole is in vocabulary development studies. Vocabulary growth is key to literacy development; it is also quite difficult to change early growth trajectories (Hart & Risley, 1995). We know that literacy coaches are working with large numbers of children who have weak vocabularies, and that they are anxious to incorporate vocabulary interventions into their schoolwide programs. For both second-language learners and children with weak vocabularies, we recognize the need for intervention, but we cannot yet recommend intervention strategies or models from the research literature.

INTERVENTION PLANNING

There is more to intervention than meets the eye. Surely, all schools (even those not meeting the needs of their children) have intervention programs in place. For intervention, the trick is in the details. Many interventions simply do not work, especially when we define an intervention that *does* work in Ann Duffy's (2001) terms—as instruction that permits literacy acceleration. Interventions are ways in which we take instructional responsibility for every child. This is a very tall order.

When we think about the model interventions described above, though, they have some important things in common. First, they all use a very structured lesson plan that targets the literacy domain of interest directly. Second, they all have a specific notion of time—time during the lesson, and also days and weeks in the intervention. Third, they use specialized materials—materials that are designed to target the area of interest. Finally, interventions are interactive. During interventions, children read, write, talk about, and manipulate letters, words, and texts.

Figure 8.1 provides an intervention-planning matrix for the literacy coach. First, take stock of the current intervention programs. What are they? Who administers them at the district level? Engage those people in an honest discussion of the needs of students in your building and the focus of the curricular reforms. Ask them how their programs can help. This is likely to be a very difficult task; we will revisit it in Chapter 10, as we discuss leadership issues.

Next, move to your local personnel. Who are they? What specialized training do they have? Who do they typically serve, when, and why? How successful have they been in increasing student achievement? If your reading program's interventions are like many of the unsuccessful ones described in the research on intervention, it is likely that they will need an overhaul. As you work with the rest of your team to build your reading program, you may want to move your existing intervention personnel into classroom-based jobs (assessing children, teaching needs-based groups), using the materials that are the core of your program. In that way, your intervention team will come to understand the new program and to establish relationships with classroom teachers.

Once you have collected and summarized data on student achievement, work with grade-level teams to identify children for intervention and to describe their needs. Then locate materials that are matched directly to their needs, and set up a short-term intervention schedule. Work with the classroom teachers to be sure that the intervention schedule supplements (rather than supplants) their own instruction, in terms both of time and intensity.

At every marking period, when you have collected new data, evaluate the previous quarter's intervention decisions. Discontinue children who have made adequate progress with the combination of intervention and expert classroom instruction. Allow children who are now lagging behind to enter into interventions.

At the end of the school year, rethink your intervention plan. Consider all of the children who were not reading on grade level. Look for patterns in their performance, and go back to your grade-level teams to consider additional interventions. Intervention planning and evaluation are ongoing components of the job of a literacy coach. These components will be heavily influenced by state and local programs that provide funding to support additional services. For these components, understanding the context—local, state, and federal—is absolutely essential to success.

INTERVENTION-PLANNING GUIDE

	Time/place	Materials or curriculum	Personnel (district and local)	Number served	Evidence of effectiveness
Preschool					
Family literacy					
Title I					
Special education					
Kindergarten					
First grade					
Second grade					
Third grade					

FIGURE 8.1. Intervention-planning matrix for the literacy coach.

CHAPTER 9

Providing Professional Support

Designing and providing a professional support system for all adults who work with children in a school are key to pulling a schoolwide program together. We define *professional support* broadly to include all of the ways that literacy coaches assist teachers in understanding, implementing, and evaluating literacy development and the reading program. Literacy coaches must make professional support count for teachers in the building so that they can make instruction count for children in their building. In this chapter, we first review research about systems for professional support, and then suggest options for literacy coaches for specific decisions and activities that are pieces of the professional support puzzle.

RESEARCH ON PROFESSIONAL SUPPORT SYSTEMS

Educators you know may have a fairly skeptical view of professional support; they are probably thinking of the traditional, isolated, formal workshops that are collectively referred to as *professional development*. They are not wrong to be skeptical. There is virtually no evidence that such sessions effect any change at all.

The literature on professional development in general is not especially large or positive. In fact, Richardson's (1990) review traces some of the assumptions that underlie this literature—assumptions that are particularly important for literacy coaches to consider. First, research on "change" assumes that a target is identified, a process for meeting the target is implemented, and then teacher implementation of the target is measured. One problem with this approach is that it assumes that the change itself is necessarily good, and that teachers' inability to meet this target is evidence of resistance. This is certainly a harmful assumption, but it is inherent in most school-level reforms. A system in which a literacy coach "demands" that teachers change from "bad" practices to "good" practices is destined to fail. One possibility that Richardson suggests is to begin with a *situated goal*—a definition of a target practice that is located at the intersection of what the teachers bring in terms of practical knowledge and skills, and what research provides in terms of new theories, ideas, or methods. Involving the teachers and what they know is crucial to the development of a professional support system. A general belief that all teachers can learn and grow is also crucial, as is the assumption that many (but not all) of their current practices are likely to be effective.

The situation is far from hopeless. Evaluation of the largest-scale federally funded initiative—the Eisenhower Professional Development program—is consistent with the belief that teachers can learn and that building upon their existing good practices is effective. Eisenhower funding was provided for many programs, some of which teachers reported to be more effective than others. Effective Eisenhower initiatives were likely to be organized as reforms; to include extended time; to involve all teachers at a grade level or school; to focus on specific content; to provide for active learning by the teachers, including review of student work or feedback on actual teaching; and to be coherent with the curriculum and assessments at the building and the state levels (Birman, Desimone, Porter, & Garet, 2000; U.S. Department of Education, Office of the Under Secretary, 1999). Although Eisenhower funds are used for math and science initiatives, those characteristics of an effective program mesh directly with the initiation of a schoolwide reading program supported by a building-level system of professional support—the very thing we envision for the literacy coach.

Reading researchers have looked across studies for findings that might assist in planning effective inservice experiences in the area of literacy. Certain characteristics are present in many successful programs, and they are consistent with the findings in math and science. These efforts are both intensive and extensive. They include support at the implementation level, with planned systems for observing instruction and providing feedback. They are interactive; they engage teachers in reflection on their practices, including collaboration and discussion. They include elements of choice. They link teachers, administrators, and even researchers in efforts to solve building-level problems (Anders, Hoffman, & Duffy, 2000). How they actually do this is what literacy coaches probably want to know.

Seen in this way, professional support for teachers is a balancing act between the development of knowledge and the development of instructional skills, each addressed within a context of current knowledge and skills and within the learning environment of the school. Traditionally, professional development for inservice teachers has been targeted to address one or the other of those areas—either knowledge or skills. For example, a school or system may hire a researcher to come and give a lecture to develop knowledge in an area of concern. However, this researcher typically has no information or understanding of the curriculum or practices of the school or teachers in the audience. (We know this firsthand. We have provided such "fly-by" sessions.) The assumption behind these sessions is that knowledge building, without any reference to curriculum, will transfer to changed practice. At the other end of the spectrum, a school or system may hire a representative of a publisher or a master teacher to describe or even model the use of a particular set of commercial materials or a particular teaching technique. The assumption behind these sessions is that teachers will change their practice without building knowledge or understanding of literacy and its development in schools.

Many have challenged this either–or approach to professional development. Their general message is one embracing complexity and problem solving. Shulman (1998) has proposed the use of cases. Essentially, teachers start with samples of instruction embedded in the complex climate of the curriculum and the school, and then use them to examine and develop both knowledge and skills. Smylie (1996) has urged the building of professionalism in schools by focusing on long-term strategies that allow teachers to work together to engage in problem solving. These problems come from the daily work of the teachers and the students, and solving them builds both knowledge and skills. Both suggestions are examinations of practice deeply embedded within the complex context of real instruction. Literacy coaches are probably committed to this concept, but may need some nuts-and-bolts guidance about how to proceed.

Sparks and Loucks-Horsley (1990) have identified five existing how-to models. Figure 9.1 is a preview of these models. The *individually guided* model engages teachers in a process for designing and implementing a personal program. The model of *observation and feedback* provides teachers with data about their own practice, which they can use for improvement. The *curriculum development/improvement* model identifies a specific problem and then engages a group of teachers in addressing it through curriculum design and implementation. The *training* model identifies a target behavior or goal and then provides instruction and support to address the goal. Finally, the *inquiry* model involves teachers in the selection of an area of interest and the design of a system to investigate it.

Of these five models, only the training model has been investigated thoroughly enough to provide evidence that it is effective in changing teaching behaviors and student outcomes. However, in order to design a system of professional support for all of the adults involved in the reading program, a literacy coach is likely to have to create a hybrid model, drawing on elements of all five of these models. A comprehensive system will include mechanisms for individual support, informed by observation and feedback, all designed to develop curriculum and to train teachers to implement it, in a context of inquiry about the effects of the total program on teachers and children.

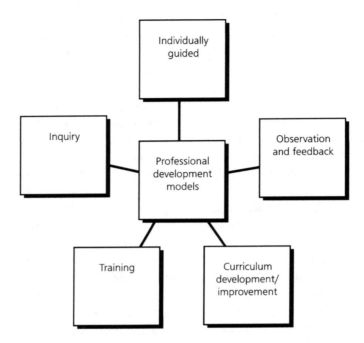

FIGURE 9.1. Models of professional development.

Creation of such a hybrid model is surely not an easy task. A literacy coach may find him- or herself in a 2- or 3-year reform in which a school building's staff must implement a totally new assessment system, a totally new schedule, and a totally new set of commercial materials. Typically, there is little time between the funding of the reform and the first day of school. In essence, some literacy coaches begin their professional support work in emergency mode—an ineffective mode for teaching and learning. Guskey (1986) has proposed a heuristic that is helpful even in the extremely difficult first months of such a reform. He has argued that staff development sessions be targeted directly to changing teacher practice, that data be collected to track the effects of that changed practice on student outcomes, and that these changes in student outcomes influence changes in teachers' beliefs and attitudes. This is a realistic model for literacy coaches at the start of their reform work. However, we agree with Hoffman and Pearson (2000) and with Little (1993) that training teachers to change their practice is only a first step. Literacy coaches can create real and sustainable learning communities—communities with the knowledge and skills to continue to develop and refine their practice.

Joyce and Showers (1988) have provided thorough analyses of the characteristics of professional development systems. What is especially striking about this work is its careful attention to context and to the development of the school as a learning community. Their analyses speak directly to the literacy coach:

- Professional development systems require new resource allocations; time, personnel, and budgetary decisions must be allocated to provide staff development within the school building and the school day.
- Professional development systems increase student learning.
- Virtually all teachers can learn within comprehensive systems for professional development.
- Professional development systems demand collaborative relationships between teachers and administrators.
- Professional development systems change the beliefs and practices of teachers.
- Professional development systems include cycles of theory, demonstration, practice, and feedback.

Designing and implementing comprehensive professional development systems have proven to be challenges for most of the literacy coaches we have worked with. We offer some guidelines here, but with this caveat: Professional support must actually be responsive to the needs of individuals in the building; it is impossible to plan it all in advance. Vacca (1989) proposed that staff development be planned and conducted at the building level, with clear and specific goals, in a collegial and collaborative environment, related directly to teachers' daily work, and respecting their time. We examine each of these principles in turn.

Literacy coaches must develop the knowledge and skills to provide professional development themselves in their own buildings. Many literacy coaches, themselves former excellent teachers, struggle with this responsibility because they are taking on a new role within an existing peer group. Literacy coaches can develop the knowledge and skills to engage adult learners.

The primary goal of a professional support system is increasing student achievement. Along the way, however, individual sessions may be aimed at other areas: increasing the self-esteem and efficacy of teachers, and promoting collegiality and trust within and across teams in the school. Achieving these goals is not as simple as it may sound, even if a literacy coach has taught or held another position within the same building. In fact, some literacy coaches have reported a frustration with familiarity:

"I would say [the biggest obstacle that I have had to overcome this year] probably is . . . the fact that they know me so well. And there are a few people here that I taught with for a long time."

As hard as it may be at first, literacy coaches need to assume new roles, sometimes in a context of old relationships.

Professional development must include collaboration. In a schoolwide program, collective responsibility for student achievement arises from collaborative work. Teachers respond to one another; they respect one another; together, they solve problems of implementation by sharing their own responses.

> "You know, if you walked in during lunch—if you walked into the work room—before we had professional development and we met on a regular basis, you might hear, 'Well, I can't believe so-and-so can't do that.' It was very negative. Lots of excuses were being made for why children couldn't do things. And now it's more about collegial collaboration. 'What are you doing? How are you doing that? Has it worked?' "

Professional development sessions must also be practical, in that teachers must expect to learn things that they can actually use with children. Although literacy coaches are charged with developing both knowledge and skills, knowledge-only professional development sessions are unlikely to be successful. Instead, constant attention to the question "What do I want teachers to *do* once they leave this session?" will help literacy coaches to embed the building of knowledge within the practical work of teaching children every day.

To create a truly comprehensive system of professional support, we urge literacy coaches to balance time providing support inside classrooms (through observations, feedback, and modeling) with time providing support outside the classroom (through knowledge-building sessions, data-based presentations, and book clubs). We urge literacy coaches to provide support both orally (through discussion) and in writing (through confidential, written feedback about teaching). We urge literacy coaches to provide support with curriculum materials (through assistance with understanding their organization and interpretation, and by locating new materials when they are needed for children). We deal first with sessions outside the classroom, and then move inside.

KNOWLEDGE-BUILDING SESSIONS

In order for a knowledge-building session to be productive, the literacy coach has to make decisions about what to teach and about how to teach it. In the beginning of the reform effort, literacy coaches must build knowledge of the nuts and bolts of the reading program: the schedule for instruction, the data collection schedule and tools, the commercial reading materials that will be used in the program, and the plans for differentiation and intervention. They must also address staff member's anxiety about the changes and build confidence. One literacy coach reported to us that her first concern in professional development was getting off to a good start. She asked herself this question before deciding on a focus for each session:

"[How] can we get [the change effort] going the fastest? How can we get it started at this point in a positive sort of way?"

Teachers have to situate themselves with their new children at the beginning of the year; they have to build community and establish classroom procedures. These are important things that will consume teachers' attention during the first weeks; time spent on anything else, however well designed, will be wasted. What happens during outside-the-classroom knowledge-building sessions must be connected directly to daily instruction. One literacy coach described this hectic time very well:

> "Well, this year has been the big rollout year. The first thing that we rolled out was [a new phonics program], and we spent all of our study groups and our meeting times on the phonics and the theory of it and then what we were going to use. And then we got down to the nitty-gritty part of it where we had a trainer that came in, and she trained [the teachers], and then we went out and we started it."

After attending to the basic schedule and procedures for instruction, literacy coaches can conduct knowledge-building sessions to target specific areas that teachers need to understand better. Some literacy coaches have knowledge of the school and its practices to guide them in this.

> "[In] this school, the emphasis on the past has been on phonics, so the teachers are kind of phonics-minded. So I wanted to get the other materials there first to start broadening their minds, thinking beyond phonics."

Other literacy coaches do not have this advance knowledge. Figure 9.2 (pp. 192–195) is a simple survey instrument that we have developed for reactions to an existing description of professional development opportunities (Learning First Alliance, 2000). We have used this survey with teachers and with literacy coaches. In both cases, we asked the participants to read the original piece (*Every Child Reading: A Professional Development Guide*; Learning First Alliance, 2000). Then they rated and commented on each potential professional development activity. Using such a survey, either before or during a reform effort, to target professional development builds a collegial spirit.

Once there is basic implementation of the reading program, and a basic understanding of the needs of individuals and of the school in general, the literacy coach can really tailor his or her knowledge-building sessions. For example, one literacy coach wanted to build knowledge of why and how teachers could develop knowledge of comprehension strategies during read-alouds. She started with the basics.

[text resumes on p. 196]

REACTION TO *EVERY CHILD READING: A PROFESSIONAL DEVELOPMENT GUIDE* (LEARNING FIRST ALLIANCE, 2000)

Please rate the following activities:

1 = Most beneficial to my professional growth

2 = Moderately beneficial to my professional growth

3 = Slightly beneficial to my professional growth

4 = Unnecessary for me

Phonemic Awareness, Letter Knowledge, and Concepts of Print		
Experience	Rating	Comment
Practice phoneme matching, identification, segmentation, blending, substitution and deletion.		
Order phonological awareness activities by difficulty level and developmental sequence.		
Practice and analyze letter–sound matching activities (identifying how letters and letter groups are used for representing speech sounds).		
Observe and critique live or videotaped student–teacher interactions during phonological awareness and alphabet instruction.		
Role-play the teaching of print concepts during interactive reading aloud.		
Discuss children's progress, using informal assessments, to obtain early help for those in need of it.		

(continued)

FIGURE 9.2. Professional development survey.

Phonics and Decoding

Experience	Rating	Comment
Practice various active techniques, including sound blending, structural word analysis, word building, and word sorting.		
Identify, on the basis of student reading and writing, the appropriate level at which to instruct.		
Observe, demonstrate, and practice error correction strategies.		
Search a text for examples of words that exemplify an orthographic concept; lead discussions about words.		
Review beginner texts to discuss their varying uses in reading instruction.		

Fluent, Automatic Reading of Text

Experience	Rating	Comment
Practice assessing and recording text-reading fluency of students in class.		
Organize classroom library and other support materials by topic and text difficulty; code for easy access by students, and track how much children are reading.		
Use informal assessment results to identify who needs to work on fluency.		
Devise a system for recording student progress toward reasonable goals.		
Conduct fluency-building activities with a mentor teacher.		

(continued)

Vocabulary		
Experience	Rating	Comment
Collaborate with team to select best read-aloud books, and share rationales.		
Select words from text for direct teaching, and give rationale for the choice.		
Devise exercises to involve students in constructive meaning of words, in understanding relationships among words, and in using and noticing uses of words beyond the classroom.		
Devise activities to help children understand the various ways that context can give clues to meaning, including the fact that often clues are very sparse and sometimes even misleading.		
Use a series of contexts to show how clues can accumulate.		

Text Comprehension		
Experience	Rating	Comment
Role-play and rehearse key research-supported strategies, such as questioning, summarizing, clarifying, and using graphic organizers.		
Discuss and plan to teach characteristics of both narrative and expository text.		
Consider student work and reading behavior (written responses, oral summaries, retellings, cloze tasks, recorded discussions) to determine where miscomprehension occurred and plan how to repair it.		

(continued)

Text Comprehension *(continued)*		
Experience	Rating	Comment
Interpret the effectiveness of instruction with video and examples of student work.		
Practice leading, scaffolding, and observing discussions in which students collaborate to form joint interpretations of text.		
Discuss and plan to teach ways of helping students call on or acquire relevant knowledge through defining concepts, presenting examples, and eliciting students' reactions to the concepts in ways that assess their understanding.		

> "First we had to make sure that [teachers] were doing read-alouds every day, and that it became a habit, and that it was a routine in their day. Everybody expected it, and there was nobody—nobody who didn't do one. And so we got the ritual and routine down of doing the read-alouds: when they were going to do them, how often, and how much time they were going to spend."

After that, she could really focus her knowledge-building sessions on strategies for making the read-alouds count as instruction. She conducted informal observations, once the read-alouds were part of the instructional routine, and then she made decisions about what to target during professional development time.

> "And then we had to see: What is the weakness there? Where do we need to go? Where are [the teachers] and where do we need to go with them?"

With routines came opportunities to build knowledge that could influence practice immediately.

DATA-BASED PRESENTATIONS

Presenting data as part of a professional support system is absolutely essential. Literacy coaches build knowledge when they assist teachers in understanding the data that have been collected in the building. In our experience, literacy coaches are expert in collecting data, and expert at interpreting data for an individual child, but reticent about looking for larger trends within or across grade levels. However, this type of knowledge-building session has been particularly powerful in the work of many literacy coaches.

> "I think what's happening is [that] teachers are seeing the scores and listening to the children read and seeing improvements that they're making. They're finally buying into it. I think you've got to tough it out at first. Let them see that it will happen. Then they believe, and they'll do it."

Time and time again, literacy coaches report that seeing improvements in student scores is powerful:

> "I believe the teachers are starting to express excitement about what they're seeing."

Over time, literacy coaches can direct knowledge-building sessions so that they address both what the teachers need and what the students need; it is at this intersection that professional support is likely to be most effective.

Knowledge-building sessions (whether they build knowledge of the reading program, of reading development, or of the building-level data) will never be quick fixes. In fact, for many literacy coaches, the second year of their work with a staff will involve revisiting ideas that were already covered. One literacy coach told us:

> "I'm looking forward to being able to go back and go over it all again, and for us to get deeper into it. You know we've skimmed the surface, and we've hit all the high points, but now I'm hoping that we can get deep, deep into it so that we're better and better and better."

Surely this type of repetition is evidence of a well-designed system rather than a failure of the first year's sessions. Another literacy coach described her first year's professional development efforts as "salesmanship." She was "selling" the new reading program to the teachers—describing its features in detail, and showing teachers how to use them. In the second year, she was able to shift her attention to "customer service"—tailoring her work more closely to the needs of individual teachers and children, and fine-tuning her support.

BOOK CLUBS AND STUDY GROUPS

Book clubs and study groups are other ways that literacy coaches provide professional support outside the classroom. We distinguish them from other types of knowledge-building sessions only because they involve work for teachers prior to each meeting. Book clubs and study groups are important because they establish a collegial climate for teaching and learning; all participants are reflecting together on ideas expressed in text, and all are making connections to their prior knowledge and experience and to the building's reading program. Practically speaking, the use of text for learning builds relationships and collegiality. A "research says" presentation conducted by a literacy coach establishes a power structure that is not conducive to building relationships. In fact, literacy coaches who "know it all" are unlikely to be effective in leading building-level change efforts (Vacca & Padak, 1990). A book club sends a different message: Literacy coaches and teachers are learners. They can work together to understand research and see how they can use it to inform their practice. Table 9.1 provides some practical tips for literacy coaches in planning and implementing book clubs.

Literacy coaches we have worked with use different strategies for identifying areas for study. At first blush, knowledge of the school and its history may provide guidance; a literacy coach may be in a position to know about specific domains in the reading program that have previously been ignored. For example, one school may really need to focus on developing knowledge and skills for supporting de-

TABLE 9.1. Practical Steps in Implementing Book Clubs

1. Identify specific areas for study.
2. Identify professional texts that address these areas and are consistent with research.
3. Purchase sets of these texts.
4. Facilitate whole-school, role-alike, or choice groups.
5. Establish a timeline for reading and a procedure for discussion.
6. Establish a procedure for sharing across groups.

coding or automatic word recognition. Another school may really need to focus on understanding of comprehension and its instruction. Still another strategy is to sort topics by grade level. For example, the kindergarten team may engage in a book club on developing phonemic awareness. First-grade teachers may work on decoding and spelling. Second-grade teachers may target fluency. Third-grade teachers may target comprehension strategy instruction. Some topics transcend a single grade level, of course, and may lend themselves to a combined study group. However, our experience is that a group works best when it is confined to a single grade level. The teachers already have a working relationship and tend to be more candid in their discussion. It is also easier for them to tailor their talk to concerns specific to their grade level.

As a school-level reading program evolves, a literacy coach makes much more targeted decisions, and relies on data to inform these decisions. Student achievement data, for example, may indicate that the youngest learners are proficient overall in phonemic awareness and decoding, but that their language development is limited. A book club on vocabulary development may be needed. Observational data constitute another potential source of ideas. As literacy coaches observe instruction, they will learn that teachers struggle with implementation in one or more areas of the program; book clubs can be planned to develop knowledge and expertise in those areas.

After a target area is identified, literacy coaches must locate resources. Since choice is important, it may be best to identify several different texts and then to allow teachers to choose the one they are most interested in reading. Text selection is crucial. Literacy coaches who do not monitor text selection for book clubs run the risk of engaging teachers in long-term work with ideas inconsistent with the principles of the building-level program. One literacy coach told us that she had trouble with teachers' not being able to see the inconsistencies between what they were reading and the goals of the schools' reading program:

> "They're so literal. They can't hear one person's spin on something and apply it to fit our model. They're not thinking about it. They just think, 'Okay. This is a clear step, so I'll just go do it.' "

That sort of inconsistency will derail the program right from the start. Table 9.2 (pp. 200–204) provides a list of texts that we have located and used in professional development, as well as suggested tasks and focus questions for study groups. This list is provided only as a start; researchers and teacher-educators are always writing new texts, and literacy coaches must develop the knowledge and skills for locating them and for evaluating their match to the school-level program. In addition, the mere fact that we have listed a particular title in Table 9.2 does not mean that it is fully consistent with the program you are attempting to implement. You must still read these books before recommending them to teachers for detailed study.

A professional organization such as a school should have a professional library. Literacy coaches should spend some of the building's resources in stocking this library. Book clubs are only successful if the members read the books; in a professional support system, these books must be provided. One way to build the library is to buy sets of texts (e.g., 10 copies) so that a small group can check them out for study and then return them for use by another group. In some cases, one text may be selected and copies purchased for the entire faculty. We have identified some potential texts for whole-school use. Such texts should offer a wide range of topics, each of which addresses the needs of a particular constituency within the program. In other cases, each grade-level team might read a different text.

Establishing a procedure for discussion up front is also important. One possibility is to move from a small-group format to a jigsaw format. We have learned that it is important to start with the text and then move to experience. For example, we have created discussion forms requiring that the book club members first summarize and write down important text ideas, then compare them with their experience, and finally formulate specific possibilities for applying the ideas in their own program and practice. If individual book clubs all engage in this procedure, the entire staff can then meet to hear about these discussions across clubs. In this sort of jigsaw discussion, small groups end their study of a particular text by preparing and presenting what they have learned to the larger group.

OBSERVATION AND FEEDBACK

Outside-the-classroom knowledge-building sessions and book clubs are not enough. Literacy coaches must move inside the classroom. One way that literacy coaches can focus their professional development efforts on the real daily work of teachers is to conduct formative observations. A formative observation is designed to guide an individual teacher to examine and improve his or her own practice. As a professional development tool, observation must be carefully defined and described to teachers. We have urged literacy coaches to establish a climate for observation by providing a direct explanation of the purpose of the observation and

[text resumes on p. 204]

TABLE 9.2. Texts and Tasks for Study Groups

Texts	Tasks
Schoolwide best practices	
Marzano, R. J. (2003). *What works in schools: Translating research into action.* Alexandria, VA: Association for Supervision and Curriculum Development. Grounded in scientifically based reading research (SBRR), this book addresses topics other than just reading. It provides an excellent (and very readable) synthesis of what SBRR tells us about such topics as parent involvement, effective instructional strategies, classroom management, curricular sequencing and pacing, overcoming a negative home environment, the problem of limited prior knowledge, and more.	This volume paints the big picture for teachers and literacy coaches alike. Consider using it with your leadership team to answer this question: What do we need to do across the school to maintain a climate that supports our goals for teaching and learning?
Barone, D. M., & Morrow, L. M. (Eds.). (2003). *Literacy and young children: Research-based practices.* New York: Guilford Press. This is a longer (318-page) edited book with 16 chapters contributed by individual authors. There is something for everyone here: preschool, kindergarten, phonics, fluency, comprehension.	This would be a good book to use in a true jigsaw format. Groups of teachers could select chapters to read based on their interests, and then report to the others in this format: The author's main argument here was: _____ He or she supported it by: _____ Here are some concrete things I learned that could inform teaching in this building:
Morrow, L. M., Gambrell, L. B., & Pressley, M. (Eds.). (2003). *Best practices in literacy instruction* (2nd ed.). New York: Guilford Press. This volume is a wide-ranging collection of 16 chapters, addressing such issues as balance, phonics, fluency, vocabulary, comprehension, technology use, and assessment.	Like those in the Barone and Morrow text, this book's chapters are suitable for jigsawing by teacher study groups. Consider the format provided above.
Morris, D., & Slavin, R. E. (2003). *Every child reading.* Boston: Allyn & Bacon. This is a text specifically aimed at your kindergarten and first-grade team. It has a chapter on kindergarten, a chapter on first grade, a chapter on intervention, and a chapter about a particular reading program (Success for All). It would be a good text to help a primary team work more collaboratively with intervention teachers.	This book lends itself to role-specific work. Everyone could read the introductory chapter and the final chapter, and then kindergarten, first-grade, and intervention teachers could each read the chapter that applies to them. What are the essentials for effective instruction for these readers? Where is our current practice strong? Why? Where do we need to revise our current practice? How can we do this together?

(continued)

TABLE 9.2. *(continued)*

Texts	Tasks

<u>Schoolwide best practices *(continued)*</u>

Spear-Swerling, L., and Sternberg, R. J. (1996). *Off track: When poor readers become "learning disabled."* Boulder, CO: Westview Press.

This seminal book challenges conventional ideas that 20% or more of U.S. children suffer from reading disabilities. The alternative described and documented here is that most struggling readers have simply failed to move successfully from one developmental stage to the next. Instead, they go "off track" at a certain point. Assessment should be geared toward identifying that stage for an individual child, and instruction should be aimed at bringing the child through that stage to the next.

This is a great title to use with your special education and intervention teachers. Consider inviting the directors of special education and Title I to read it with you in order to build collegiality and collective responsibility for crafting an intervention program.

McCormack, R. L., & Paratore, J. R. (Eds.). (2003). *After early intervention, then what?: Teaching struggling readers in grades 3 and beyond.* Newark, DE: International Reading Association.

This book contains 12 chapters designed to provide guidance to teachers in the upper grades, including middle school. Of particular concern are those children who continue to struggle.

Like other edited books, this one lends itself to a jigsaw format, with small groups of teachers choosing individual chapters to consider. This text might also be useful to initiate dialogue between early elementary teachers and upper elementary or middle school teachers.

<u>Phonemic awareness, decoding, and phonics</u>

Strickland, D. S. (1998). *Teaching phonics today: A primer for educators.* Newark, DE: International Reading Association.

This is a good book for the "phonics-phobe." It is easy to read and understand, uses classroom-based examples, and might help reluctant teachers to approach their own learning of phonics.

This would be a good book for a "KWL" strategy. As teachers reflect on the year's phonics instruction, have them ask themselves:

What do I know now about phonics?
What do I want to know?

After they read the text, have them ask themselves:

What did I learn?
What do I still need to learn?

Lyon, A., & Moore, P. (2003). *Sound systems: Explicit, systematic phonics in early literacy contexts.* Portland, ME: Stenhouse.

This is a step up from *Teaching Phonics Today* in terms of difficulty and coverage, but still a very accessible book (160 pages). The book has a great appendix of concepts to teach by grade level.

How consistent is our curriculum with the grade-level concepts in Appendix A?
What are the strengths of our current assessment system for beginning readers?
What would we like to improve?
How could we manage to collect and use data to inform our instruction?

(continued)

TABLE 9.2. *(continued)*

Texts	Tasks

Fluency

Rasinski, T. V., & Padak, N. D. (2001). *From phonics to fluency: Effective teaching of decoding and reading fluency in the elementary school.* New York: Longman.

This book is slightly longer than some of the others, but the chapters are quite short. It provides many, many engaging activities for developing phonemic awareness, phonics, spelling, and fluency. It would be a great book for helping teachers move away from a scripted, rules-based curriculum into more interactive activities.

This book would be good for a jigsaw format. The first three chapters could be read by all, and then the rest of the book could be divided up. Teachers could read a chapter, write a short description of that chapter, and then demonstrate one instructional strategy advocated there, telling why it is important to literacy development and how to prepare for it.

Opitz, M. F., & Rasinski, T. V. (1998). *Good-bye round robin: Twenty-five effective oral reading strategies.* Portsmouth, NH: Heinemann.

This is a great book to work specifically with teachers who continue to employ a round-robin format. They do that because they don't have any alternatives. This is also a good book to choose if your data indicate that children's decoding accuracy has reached acceptable levels, but their rate is still depressed.

Start with the last chapter in this book. It's about why we *shouldn't* engage in round-robin reading. Then go back through the chapters. Each teaching strategy includes recommended texts to use. Assign teachers to read the text, choose a strategy that would be helpful to their children, and model it to the others, using one of the recommended texts. Then they could provide their peers with a one-page summary of what the strategy is and how, when, and why it should be applied.

Vocabulary

Bishop, A., Yopp, R. H., & Yopp, H. K. (2000). *Ready for reading: A handbook for parents of preschoolers.* Boston: Allyn & Bacon.

This is a short book that would be good for teachers of preschool and/or paraprofessionals in the K–1 classroom. The book gives many examples of lessons with specific children's books, using a before–during–after reading format.

Teachers could do the following:

Find five books recommended in the text and role-play the activities.

Decide how to integrate these text-based activities into the current instructional schedule.

Gather materials and make "kits" for each book.

Heimlich, J. E., & Pittelman, S. D. (1986). *Semantic mapping: Classroom applications.* Newark, DE: International Reading Association.

This is a very short book (more like a pamphlet) about just one vocabulary strategy. Consider using this book and the two below with teachers of older children in a jigsaw format.

What is semantic mapping?
Why and how does it build vocabulary knowledge?
How can we use it during reading instruction?
How can we use it during writing instruction?
How can we use it in our content-area curriculum?

(continued)

TABLE 9.2. *(continued)*

Texts	Tasks

Vocabulary (continued)

Texts	Tasks
Pittelman, S. D., Heimlich, J. E., Berglund, R. L., & French, M. P. (1991). *Semantic feature analysis: Classroom applications.* Newark, DE: International Reading Association. Again, this is a very short book (more like a pamphlet) about just one vocabulary strategy.	What is semantic feature analysis? Why and how does it build vocabulary knowledge? How can we use it during reading instruction? How can we use it during writing instruction? How can we use it in our content-area curriculum?
Stahl, S. A., & Kapinus, B. (2001). *Word power: What every educator needs to know about teaching vocabulary.* Washington, DC: National Education Association. This is an overview of vocabulary research and strategies. It is very short, but quite easy to read and use.	What is the relationship between vocabulary development and reading comprehension? How do we learn words? What do we know about direct instruction in word meanings? How can we teach children to learn words on their own?

Comprehension

Texts	Tasks
Campbell, R. (2001). *Read-alouds with young children.* Newark, DE: International Reading Association. This is a short (100-page) and accessible book with chapters on interactive read-alouds, the importance of narratives and high-quality books, and classroom-based activities to use with read-alouds. No book list is provided, however.	How do read-alouds fit into our reading program? Describe the procedures currently used for selecting read-alouds. Describe the quality of the texts selected for read-alouds. Describe the procedures used to teach during read-alouds. How can we improve the quality of text selected for read-aloud time? How can we improve the teaching procedures used during read-alouds? Can we make a list of great books that children should hear read aloud at each grade level?
Duffy, G. G. (2003). *Explaining reading: A resource for teaching concepts, skills, and strategies.* New York: Guilford Press. This book is really teacher-friendly. It makes Duffy's research on how to explain comprehension processes by turning the basal "skills" into strategies accessible. It includes chapters on explaining vocabulary, separate chapters on explaining each of the comprehension strategies, and chapters on how to coach word recognition through explanation.	What is the instructional model that Duffy is advocating? Where does explanation currently occur in our reading program? How can we include more explanation in our read-alouds? How can we include more explanation in our reading instruction? How do we currently assist children with word recognition during reading? How can we include more explanation of decoding?

(continued)

TABLE 9.2. *(continued)*

Texts	Tasks
<div align="center">Comprehension *(continued)*</div>	
Readence, J. E., Moore, D. W., and Rickelman, R. J. (2000). *Prereading activities for content area reading and learning* (3rd ed.). Newark, DE: International Reading Association.	Consider using this book to address these questions:
This accessible paperback describes practical strategies for helping children comprehend nonfiction. It has been a leading International Reading Association title, and with good reason. Teachers in grades 2 and higher will profit from learning about the strategies presented.	What can we do during read-alouds to encourage real learning from text? What can we do during needs-based time to support children in understanding nonfiction?

of their role as observers. We call the literacy coach the "good cop." Unlike the "bad cop" partner (the principal), the literacy coach observes in order to learn how to help. There are several strategies you may find useful as a literacy coach in establishing a positive climate for observation:

- Never link professional development to evaluation.
- Never make documentation of observations public.
- Have a preobservation meeting in which you review your commitment to confidentiality and ask the teacher what he or she wants you to see.
- Tell the teacher exactly how the observation will be conducted and how and when he or she will receive feedback.

Although we stress that observation drives professional support, it also helps establish the building-level climate. Literacy coaches who do not observe find themselves making incorrect assumptions about instruction. Literacy coaches tell us that they spend too much time on outside-the-classroom activities, and then they realize that their professional development has gotten out of sync with teachers' practices:

> "I think the biggest obstacle that I've been facing is people telling me one thing that they're doing, and then they're not doing it when I go by."

Literacy coaches need to keep careful track of what teachers are actually able to take from professional development into their classrooms.

We have used two different strategies for observing. Both have been successful in providing real information about the needs of individual teachers and about trends in the reading program across teachers. One way to observe is to document the teacher's activity by time. In this system, a literacy coach may prepare a form with spaces at 5-minute intervals and simply document what is happening during that interval. Figure 9.3 is a sample form for observing instruction by time for 1 hour. A form like this can be printed, and a coach can bring it on a clipboard to the classroom; it can also be saved as a template on a laptop computer, and the coach can bring a laptop into the classroom.

Figure 9.4 (pp. 207–212) is a form for observation by domain. A form like this is useful once the reading program is well underway. In this system, a literacy coach first looks at the schedule for the reading program to see which part of the instructional diet is supposed to be addressed. This helps to target the observation from the start. When things are going well, the literacy coach will check both "Observed" and "Expected," meaning (for example), "From the schedule, I expected to see phonemic awareness and phonics instruction. When I began my observation, that is exactly what I saw." Once the observation is underway, the literacy coach is documenting what content is covered, what the teacher is doing, and what the students are doing. In some cases, multiple content areas will be covered in a single observation; in other cases, only one area may be covered. This type of observation system allows literacy coaches and teachers to see whether the specifics of a research-based instructional diet are actually evident during instruction.

Whether a literacy coach chooses to observe by domain or by time, the next step is for the coach to analyze and reflect. Two questions should be central to this thinking: "What have I learned about this teacher that I can use to make my professional support more effective?" and "What have I learned about our reading program that I can use to make my professional support more effective?" The answer to the first question is retrospective; it gives feedback to the literacy coach about the effectiveness of his or her professional development sessions to date. The answer to the second question is prospective; it gives direction to future professional development sessions. The answers to both questions allow literacy coaches actually to address the individual needs of their adult learners. One literacy coach shared this reflection with us:

> "To some people teaching is a job, and to others it is a profession. And I think that [in some cases there's a] lack of knowledge, because my teachers come from different colleges that have different philosophies, and I think that's part of it. They just don't have that knowledge, and they're not . . . either they're not self-motivated to find it, or they don't even know that they don't know. And I have to realize that they're just like kids, in that they're all in different places in their knowledge. We've made a lot of assumptions here about what kids know. We've assumed that they know things that they don't, and I . . . I have to get out of [making] that [assumption] with teachers. So it seems like I try to collect information and use that to drive the upcoming session."
>
> *[text resumes on p. 213]*

FORM FOR OBSERVING INSTRUCTION BY TIME FOR 60 MINUTES

Minutes	Teacher activity	Student activity	Comments and questions
0–5			
5–10			
10–15			
15–20			
20–25			
25–30			
30–35			
35–40			
40–45			
45–50			
50–55			
55–60			

FIGURE 9.3. Observation by time.

FORM FOR OBSERVING DIMENSIONS OF INSTRUCTION

Phonemic awareness: K–1	❑ Expected	❑ Observed
Content	Teacher role	Student response

❑ Oral language play
❑ Recognizing rhyme
❑ Producing rhyme
❑ Sentence blending
❑ Syllable blending
❑ Onset–rime blending
❑ Phoneme blending
❑ Sentence segmenting
❑ Syllable segmenting
❑ Onset–rime segmenting
❑ Phoneme segmenting
❑ Initial-sound isolation
❑ Final-sound isolation
❑ Medial-sound isolation
	❑ Giving directions
	❑ Telling
	   information
	❑ Questioning
	❑ Modeling
	❑ Assessing
		❑ Listening
		❑ Individual oral response
		❑ Every-pupil response, oral
		❑ Every-pupil response,
		   written
		❑ Using manipulatives

Phonics/decoding/fluency: K–1	❑ Expected	❑ Observed
Content	Teacher role	Student response

❑ Introducing letter names
❑ Reviewing letter names
❑ Introducing letter sounds
❑ Reviewing letter sounds
❑ Using consonant sounds
❑ Using vowel sounds
❑ Consonant digraphs
❑ Consonant blends
❑ Short-vowel word families
❑ Vowel–consonant–final e
❑ Long-vowel digraphs
❑ Irregular words
❑ Synthetic decoding strategies
❑ Analogy-based decoding
   strategies
❑ Rereading for fluency
	❑ Giving directions
	❑ Telling
	   information
	❑ Questioning
	❑ Modeling
	❑ Assessing
		❑ Listening
		❑ Reading orally
		❑ Individual oral response
		❑ Every-pupil response, oral
		❑ Individual written
		   response
		❑ Every-pupil response,
		   written
		❑ Using manipulatives

(continued)

FIGURE 9.4. Observation by dimension.

Vocabulary/comprehension: K–1	❏ Expected	❏ Observed
Content	Teacher role	Student response
❏ Developing oral language ❏ Learning new definitions ❏ Providing context for new words ❏ Using new words ❏ Prediction ❏ Visualization ❏ Self-monitoring ❏ Self-questioning ❏ Using prior knowledge ❏ Summarization ❏ Personal response ❏ Story elements ❏ Expository text structure	❏ Giving directions ❏ Telling information ❏ Questioning ❏ Modeling ❏ Assessing	❏ Listening ❏ Individual oral response ❏ Every-pupil response, oral ❏ Individual written response ❏ Every-pupil response, written ❏ Using manipulatives
Composition: K–1	❏ Expected	❏ Observed
Content	Teacher role	Student response
❏ Sentence structure ❏ Text structure	❏ Giving directions ❏ Telling information ❏ Providing feedback ❏ Questioning ❏ Modeling ❏ Assessing	❏ Listening ❏ Individual oral response ❏ Every-pupil response, oral ❏ Every-pupil response, written ❏ Using manipulatives ❏ Brainstorming ❏ Drafting ❏ Revising ❏ Editing ❏ Publishing

(continued)

	Text or curriculum materials	Grouping configuration	Engagement and pace
Phonemic awareness			
Phonics/decoding/ fluency			
Vocabulary/ comprehension			
Composition			

Comments:

Next steps:

(continued)

Phonics/decoding: 2–3	❏ Expected	❏ Observed
Content	Teacher role	Student response
❏ Vowel–consonant–Final *e* ❏ Long-vowel digraphs ❏ *R*-controlled vowels ❏ Complex consonant clusters ❏ Low-frequency vowel patterns ❏ Morphological analysis ❏ Prefixes ❏ Suffixes ❏ Irregular words ❏ Synthetic decoding strategies ❏ Analogy-based decoding strategies ❏ Self-monitoring strategies	❏ Giving directions ❏ Telling information ❏ Questioning ❏ Modeling ❏ Assessing	❏ Listening ❏ Reading silently ❏ Reading orally ❏ Individual oral response ❏ Every-pupil response, oral ❏ Individual written response ❏ Every-pupil response, written ❏ Using manipulatives
Fluency: 2–3	❏ Expected	❏ Observed
Content	Teacher role	Student response
❏ Guided oral reading ❏ Rereading for fluency	❏ Giving directions ❏ Telling information ❏ Questioning ❏ Modeling ❏ Assessing	❏ Listening ❏ Reading silently ❏ Reading orally ❏ Individual oral response ❏ Every-pupil response, oral ❏ Individual written response ❏ Every-pupil response, written ❏ Using manipulatives
Vocabulary/comprehension: 2–3	❏ Expected	❏ Observed
Content	Teacher role	Student response
❏ Learning new definitions ❏ Providing context for new words ❏ Using new words ❏ Setting a purpose ❏ Prediction ❏ Visualization	❏ Giving directions ❏ Telling information ❏ Questioning ❏ Modeling ❏ Assessing	❏ Listening ❏ Individual oral response ❏ Every-pupil response, oral ❏ Every-pupil response, written ❏ Using manipulatives

(continued)

❑ Self-monitoring ❑ Using fix-up strategies ❑ Self-questioning ❑ Using prior knowledge ❑ Summarization ❑ Personal response ❑ Story elements ❑ Expository text structure		
Composition: 2–3	❑ Expected	❑ Observed
Content	Teacher role	Student response
❑ Sentence structure ❑ Text structure	❑ Giving directions ❑ Telling information ❑ Providing feedback ❑ Questioning ❑ Modeling ❑ Assessing	❑ Listening ❑ Individual oral response ❑ Every-pupil response, oral ❑ Every-pupil response, written ❑ Using manipulatives ❑ Brainstorming ❑ Drafting ❑ Revising ❑ Editing ❑ Publishing

(continued)

	Text or curriculum materials	Grouping configuration	Engagement and pace
Phonics/decoding			
Fluency			
Vocabulary/ comprehension			
Composition			

Comments:

Next steps:

The best literacy coaches we know are able to make nonjudgmental use of the information that they get from observations:

> "Each teacher has a different weak . . . I shouldn't say weakness, but something that they need to work on. [The important things are] going in there and finding out what each teacher needs and being able to talk with them. And trying to develop a relationship with them so they won't think of me as the enemy."

The final, crucial step in the cycle of observation is sharing the information with the teacher. In our experience, teachers are very nervous about observations at first (mainly because their experience has consisted only of observations by an administrator for the purpose of evaluation). However, if feedback is quick and specific, they are very grateful. Feedback can be written or oral, but it should be provided quickly, before a teacher has forgotten his or her own goals and insights for the lesson. Feedback must include positive comments, but they have to be sincere ones. Feedback must center on application and implementation of ideas previously covered in professional development sessions. When literacy coaches are providing feedback, they should not "test" what they have not taught. Feedback should include suggestions for improving teaching and learning, but again these must be specific. Finally, feedback should include an offer from the literacy coach to the teacher. The session (or the written comments) should end with "How can I help you?" We have found Lyons and Pinnell's (2001) book *Systems for Change in Literacy Education* a useful source for coaches who are working to improve the talk that they use to provide feedback to teachers. That text provides many useful discussion starters to direct positive interactions between coaches and teachers.

Some literacy coaches establish individual protocols for conducting observations and providing feedback. One literacy coach shared her system for observation and feedback:

> "I took a laptop computer with me, and I have a little form that has three sections: a description of what I see, celebrations, and then considerations. I try to make the descriptions almost just like a script, as much as I can, as quickly as I can. The celebrations, that's pretty easy. I try to always make sure I give a little general one right from the onset. And then I try to get really specific things. And I don't think a day has passed yet that I've given the feedback that I haven't had a teacher approach me and say, 'I appreciate that.' If I don't write something that was a celebration, but I remembered to mention it to them later, then I think they really feel like 'She was watching when she was in there.' A lot of us have never been watched this way. You're the only one that's going to see [my observation]. That's the end of

it. What happens is [that] you read it and hopefully you benefit from it, and that's all. We'll carry on, and I'll give you another [observation] next time."

Self-Observation

Self-observation is another potentially powerful tool. Goldenberg and Gallimore (1991) used videotaped lessons during after-school professional development sessions. They reported that teachers were initially uncomfortable with the videotapes, opening feedback sessions with a host of disclaimers about why their lessons were failures. However, over time, the videos provided the vehicle for feedback from peers and powerful self-analysis that led to real changes in practice. We know literacy coaches who regularly videotape classroom instruction and use it during professional development sessions. The use of videotape—as a guide to either personal reflection, reflection with the support of the literacy coach, or group reflection during professional development—gives teachers real access to real teaching and learning, and supports the focus of discussion on the daily life of teachers and children.

Video also makes clear to teachers elements of their instruction that no amount of verbalizing can adequately describe. In one case, a third-grade teacher agreed to have herself videotaped. Her students were about evenly divided: boys and girls, blacks and whites. After the taping, we asked her why she had directed 90% of her questions to white girls. She looked at us with astonishment and flatly denied having done so. It was only after viewing the tape that she became convinced and was able to acknowledge and reflect productively upon her own practice. Finally, effective coaches may note that advances in technology are making video recorders smaller and less noticeable. Such developments now provide digital alternatives to tape that offer greater flexibility and convenience.

Peer Observation

Live peer observation is also powerful. Showers and Joyce (1996) have focused careful attention on the relationship between particular aspects of a staff development system and the likelihood of transfer to actual changes in teaching behaviors. These authors are working in schools without literacy coaches (a very important context to consider). In those settings, peer coaching has emerged as an especially important component. Showers and Joyce have defined *peer coaching* as establishment of a schoolwide system of collaboration where all teachers are organized into teams that plan together and into pairs where partners observe one another. During this observation, the definition of *coach* is counterintuitive. The *coach* is the one who is teaching; the *coached* is the one who is watching. Teachers support one another's growth in practice by demonstration rather than by giving any feedback.

There is no doubt that teachers can learn from watching one another. Dianne Sweeney (2003) has proposed a model for peer observation that she calls a *lab network*. This is a type of peer observation that involves identifying a small set of particularly effective teachers who also have the self-confidence to host visitors and to debrief them about their work after visits. As part of professional development, other teachers observe in these lab classrooms, sometimes across several days. They are directed to observe (without interacting with children and without interrupting instruction in any way), to take careful notes, and then to participate in planned debriefing sessions where the visitors can ask the lab teachers questions about their work.

Establishing a climate for observation and for collegial discussion of teaching and learning is one of the most powerful ways that a literacy coach can provide professional support. This type of climate can set a school community on the road to continual improvement—improvement that could (if necessary) continue even without the support of the literacy coach.

Four Sets of Eyes

We have discussed four possible observers, each with a unique agenda and perspective: the literacy coach, the principal, the peer, and the teacher. Each can make distinct contributions to the growth of a teacher. The literacy coach can gain a better idea of the potential of these observers by noting key similarities and differences among them. We have attempted to list these in Table 9.3. In designing the observation-and-feedback component of a professional support system, it is im-

TABLE 9.3. Four Possible Observers in the Classroom

	Literacy coach	Principal	Peer	Self
Metaphor	Good cop	Bad cop	Accomplice	Suspect
Expertise of the observer	High expertise relative to literacy	High general expertise	Expertise similar to the teacher's	Expertise identical to the teacher's
Primary purpose of the observer	To enhance effectiveness	To evaluate	To enhance effectiveness	To enhance effectiveness
Type of feedback	Formative	Both formative and summative	Formative	Formative
Status of the observer	Informal and unofficial	Formal and official	Informal and unofficial	Informal and unofficial

portant that teachers know the purposes of the observations, and especially the different purposes served by different sets of eyes.

MODELING

Literacy coaches often include modeling in their system for professional support. Typically, they model in two ways: First, they model instruction outside the classroom during small- and large-group sessions. This modeling is designed simply to introduce materials and techniques in the context of professional development. Since there are no students, this modeling is low-risk. However, since there are no students, this modeling is also insufficient for real understanding of the use of new materials or techniques. The second type of modeling that literacy coaches do is in the classroom; they teach children while individual teachers (or sometimes groups of teachers) watch them. Literacy coaches make very different choices about when and why they model in classrooms.

Some literacy coaches model so that they can really understand the commercial reading materials, especially if these are new; the understanding that they get this way is very powerful.

> "I started it myself. I went into a second-grade classroom. I stayed in there 2 weeks. I did the lessons. And then I had the other teachers come and watch me. And then I modeled for them, and then after that they went out, and I started observing them. That's how [I've started] every piece that we've brought in this year."

For literacy coaches who choose to work in this way, collegial relationships with teachers are established immediately. What better way is there to start out a system for observation and feedback than to have the leader be the first one observed?

Some literacy coaches model for all teachers. First, they target a part of the day or a part of the program and introduce it outside the classroom. Next, they set up a schedule to demonstrate it in every classroom. Then they observe the teachers as they implement it.

> "Usually the morning part of my day is spent coaching. So I'm observing, I'm modeling, I'm demonstrating lessons during those blocks of time. And whatever I'm teaching in staff development courses usually parallels what I'm modeling, demonstrating, or observing, so that it is a simultaneous kind of thing. I guess some transforming is the right word. But I try not to evaluate anything that I haven't already taught. And I don't want to observe and

I don't want to model anything that I haven't already taught before. I like it to be hand in hand."

Other literacy coaches model as needed. They initiate new goals and practices during outside-the-classroom professional development sessions, and then they observe teachers as they implement them. For teachers who are struggling, they model. At first, this may be uncomfortable; such teachers may feel singled out for poor practices. But later, it is likely that different teachers will need modeling for different aspects of the program.

> "I've had several teachers, interestingly enough, who have said, 'I would like for you to make recommendations. I want to try to implement them, and I want you to come back and see me again, and then I want you to model a lesson.' "

Over time, teachers appreciate such support and request modeling when they are struggling. At that point, literacy coaches can combine modeling, collaborating, and observing.

> "I had a teacher who was at the kindergarten level, and this was her first year. She really experienced some difficulty trying to manage her groups. So I went into her classroom and I administered a center, and as the children rotated, I sat in there for about 3 hours, and I helped her to develop some better ways of having her students transition and manage her classroom. And I actually took her to visit another school so that she could observe teachers teaching kindergarten, just to go to a different environment so that she wouldn't be intimidated. I went back into her class Monday just to ask her a question, and she had already started making changes in her class, and I thought that was wonderful. She was open-minded, and she was willing to accept change."

This type of support for adults in a school building is actually very much like the support that we are asking those adults to provide for children—whatever it takes.

Literacy coaches are likely to be juggling many responsibilities, so we urge them to make the best possible use of their modeling time. First, they should collect artifacts that can be shared in professional development sessions: videos, student work, preparation or lesson plans, reflections. A particularly powerful artifact would be an observation (conducted by the classroom teacher) using the format that the literacy coach will then use to observe others. Literacy coaches who allow themselves to be observed have the chance to establish a very positive support system. They can actually show teachers that they are human—they make mistakes, they learn as they go, they reflect on both successes and failures.

PROFESSIONAL RESOURCES

Literacy coaches themselves need access to professional resources. Ann Lieberman (1995) has proposed a cycle to reconceptualize professional learning in schools; we borrow her ideas and apply them directly to literacy coaches as learners. Lieberman has made the convincing argument that adults in schools are forced to learn about learning in ways that are inconsistent with what we know about learning. That is, whereas the goal of professional development is often to teach teachers to provide more active, self-directed contexts for students to learn, the format of the professional development sessions themselves (lectures from an outsider who knows nothing about the teachers or the students in the locality) is not actually consistent with such a context. Such presenters are often perceived as saying, "Do as I say, not as I do." An alternative would be to move away from the learning-from-outsiders approach to a learning-on-the-job approach augmented by the fostering of outside relationships. Figure 9.5 provides a conceptual model for this system.

Literacy coaches are likely to be required to move through the first two phases. For example, a literacy coach in a new initiative is likely to be involved in state- or federal-level technical assistance sessions, in which outsiders convey the "rules" of these large-scale reform efforts and summarize the research that must be addressed and included. Literacy coaches may also attend research conferences conducted essentially in the same way—with little or no interaction either between presenters and participants or among participants.

After this "outside" phase, the literacy coach is likely to engage in intensive on-the-job training, learning to do his or her job within his or her school. This learning is likely to be both invigorating and frustrating. Over time, it is likely to reveal areas in the literacy coach's own knowledge base that are weak. The literacy coaches we have worked with become uncomfortable when this happens, but we think it is a normal part of the reform process.

The final stage of learning in Lieberman's (1995) system—learning by connection to outside resources of the learner's own choice—is what we advocate here. One job of the literacy coach is to end the culture of isolation in schools by helping

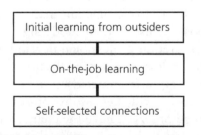

FIGURE 9.5. A model for literacy coaches' learning.

to create a collaborative learning community. However, the literacy coach him- or herself needs such a collaborative support system. Literacy coaches' connecting with one another to share ideas within and across school districts is a crucial step. As we work with literacy coaches, we see them establishing collegial support systems to share the wisdom of practice that each coach is gaining. This is essential to success in such a demanding job.

Literacy coaches also need to identify and connect with outside sources of professional development. Recently, we listened to literacy coaches sharing their experiences planning and conducting summer professional development institutes for teachers. The coaches identified outside consultants whose work was consistent with the needs of their teachers and their reading program. These experiences were empowering, both to the literacy coaches (who had created and shared professional networks) and to the teachers (whose professional training was geared directly to their needs by coaches who understood them).

University partnerships can be established. We urge literacy coaches to consider approaching university researchers (rather than waiting for the researchers to suggest projects). They can request a specific focus, a specific series of knowledge-building sessions, and specific follow-up visits for observation or modeling to inform teachers' application of knowledge in their practice. If a literacy coach is clear about the focus of the schoolwide reading program and about his or her (or the teachers') needs within that program, university partnerships can be one part of the professional support system. Researchers such as McCutchen and Berninger (1999) report that this type of partnership builds the relationships that are crucial to transforming university researchers from providers of workshops to real supporters of the work of teachers in schools.

Literacy coaches have to attend to their own learning, or they will not be able to attend to the learning of the adults in their building. Part of their own learning consists of getting organized, and this can be frustrating.

> "[The hardest thing about being a literacy coach is] being able to put your hand on the answers to the questions. There are a lot of questions coming from a lot of different directions. So I think a lot of that requires just getting organized, getting the tools organized. Tools like a workshop. You need your tools on a little peg so that you know where they are, and you need to be able to retrieve them quickly."

ESTABLISHING COHERENCE

No system of presentations, observations, coaching, modeling, or study groups will make a difference to teachers and children unless it directly and specifically supports a well-articulated, research-based, building-level program. We urge that literacy coaches constantly ask themselves to define the characteristics of their program and to compare these with research. We urge that they use a conceptual model (e.g., phonemic awareness, phonics, fluency, vocabulary, comprehension), surveys of teacher needs, observations of instruction, and analysis of student achievement data to determine foci for their professional development sessions. Finally, we urge that they consider three nested goals for professional development (Joyce & Showers, 1996): serving individual teachers within their school, serving the school community through study of the effects of the initiative on student achievement, and serving the district community by connecting and embedding all initiatives to serve students. A true system of professional support will provide powerful results.

> "[Teachers] are having a philosophy change. It's not a program. It's a way of believing that kids do have gaps. Even though [the teachers] knew that, they didn't address those facts. They're identifying the gaps. And now they know they've got to go back and paint in the holes. They're going to move forward with it. They just don't know how. They've always questioned why the kids stayed low. And now they're looking for ways to fix that."

CHAPTER 10

Leadership

We have begun this book with an overview of the many roles, some of them quite new, that literacy coaches are creating and assuming. Taken together, these new roles constitute a radically different definition of school-level curriculum leadership. Literacy coaches are in a unique position to direct and support changes at the level of the individual classroom, so that children's needs are served. These changes include an assessment system that informs instruction; a school-level and classroom-level instructional schedule that supports teaching and learning; a set of high-quality instructional materials; a well-integrated and flexible intervention plan; and a system of professional support that responds to the needs of all adults who work with children. To pull all of these changes off, literacy coaches must recognize and attend to their roles as leaders. In this chapter, we share what we have learned from literacy coaches and from the principals and district-level personnel who work with them.

CONCEPTUALIZING LEADERSHIP

Much has been said in the research literature about the role of the principal as instructional leader. Successful schools are in fact more likely to have principals with a deep knowledge of instruction and a commitment to time in the classrooms. Unsuccessful schools are more likely to have principals whose primary function is management of the building and personnel, and who take a bureaucratic stance toward teaching and learning. This state of affairs is no accident. During the 1970s and 1980s, research established a clear link between a principal's subject matter expertise and pupil achievement. In the famous "Federal Reserve Study," for example (Kean, Summers, Raivetz, & Farber, 1979), the reading achievement of a large number of Philadelphia fourth graders was examined for possible relationships with a host of factors. The principal's knowledge of reading instruction was among these significant factors: The more a principal knew about reading, the higher reading achievement tended to be, when other variables were controlled. Studies such as this led to calls for principals to lead the way for their teachers, with their personal expertise lighting the path ahead.

This notion of the principal's primary function has come to be called the *instructional leadership model*. Unfortunately, attempts to implement the model have proved somewhat disappointing. It has become clear that there is far more to raising achievement than enhancing the principal's expertise. Indeed, Hallinger, Bickman, and Davis (1996) concluded that there is no *direct* effect of a principal's expertise on reading. Rather, such expertise affects the decisions a principal makes.

An alternative is the *transformational model,* in which the principal facilitates a problem-solving approach. In this model, the principal acknowledges the expertise of teachers, particularly because of their proximity to and familiarity with the problems they face in their classrooms. The teachers no longer rely on the principal as the main repository of expertise. Instead, the principal draws upon and focuses the teachers' expertise in the process of addressing problems. This model may make it possible for principals to shift their focus from growth in teaching (driven by evaluative observations) to growth in learning (guided by team problem solving) (DuFour, 2002). However, many principals lack the interpersonal skills needed to make such a model work. In a study of 105 California superintendents, Davis (1997) found that more than 65% listed poor interpersonal skills as a reason principals failed. Of course, this does not negate the transformational model, but it does suggest that not everyone can implement it.

Which of these two models is better? This is certainly a Hobson's choice, in that both models have promising attributes. Indeed, a recent study by Marks and Printy (2003) led them to conclude that a hybrid model works best. The most effective principals know their subject *and* can facilitate the process of teacher growth.

Leadership in schools must be crafted at the building level, responding to the needs of adult and child learners in the school community. The Annenberg Institute for School Reform has been supporting the professional growth of instructional leaders and sharing information on the ways that these leaders are reconceptualizing their work. These "new" instructional leaders are "lead learners": They actually participate in professional development alongside teachers, and then provide follow-up sessions to direct the implementation and integration of new ideas in the building. They maintain the focus on collaborative time spent in teaching and learning (rather than on policies and procedures). They work to develop and distribute leadership responsibility within the whole school community. They create professional learning communities—where adults have regular time to meet and discuss teaching and learning, and where adults read to learn. They use data to inform their decisions, and they share that data with stakeholders both inside and outside the building. Finally, they use school-level resources (people, time, and money) creatively (King, 2002). The Annenberg leaders sound like literacy coaches. In fact, though, they are central office staff members, principals, and school-level professional development providers.

ISSUES OF AUTHORITY

Literacy coaches are unlikely to be successful if they do not attend to leadership issues at three levels: within the district, within the building-level administration, and within the faculty. Each of these three levels has its own set of leadership challenges; we fear that some literacy coaches will find their efforts thwarted because they do not take the time (or have the personal skills) to attend to leadership issues at one or more of these levels.

Leadership within the District

Literacy coaches must attend to their position in relation to central office staff members, particularly those who have previously had responsibility for some of the coaches' work. Many of the literacy coaches we have worked with have "special" positions in their schools; in the district, some schools have won federal grants to fund the work of literacy coaches and to pay for professional development and curriculum resources, while others have not. This situation is likely to breed resentment and mistrust. Literacy coaches must take steps to situate their work (and even the services they provide) at their schools as a part of the shared mission of the district to improve teaching and learning.

First, it is important to have regular contact with district-level personnel. Directors of Title I, directors of special education, assistant superintendents who coordinate instruction, and even superintendents must be included in building-level planning and informed about the status of the schoolwide program. Everything that is learned in the context of the change effort—how to collect and analyze data, how to evaluate and use new curriculum materials, how to schedule the school day and year, how to integrate and conduct professional development into the school community—should be shared with the central office staff.

Literacy coaches who can share this learning with humility are more likely to be successful at creating positive relationships within the district. We offer an important caveat, however. The politically astute literacy coach is ever aware of the line-and-staff organizational structure that defines supervisory relationships. Figure 10.1 illustrates the most typical structure. In this arrangement, the literacy coach reports to the building principal, who in turn reports to a central office offi-

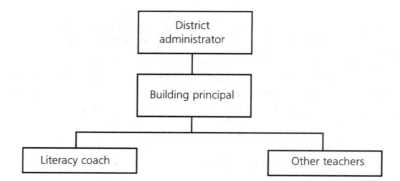

FIGURE 10.1. Typical line-and-staff organizational structure.

cial (often an assistant superintendent). The reason for keeping this "chain of command" in mind is that some principals may see direct contacts between the coach and the central office as jumping the chain and "going over the principal's head." The literacy coach must exercise tact by always clearing such contacts with the principal. The principal must never be caught unaware by a central office employee who has been dealing with the coach without the principal's knowledge.

Leadership within the Building-Level Administration

The ideal administrative team is collaborative. Although the principal and assistant principals in a large school building (we have worked in elementary schools with as many as 1,200 students) may by necessity have specialized roles, the "right hand" must know what the "left hand" is doing, and the focus on shared work to support teaching and learning must be maintained. One thing is certain: Literacy coaches can support change much more quickly and smoothly when they are part of an administrative team that makes decisions collaboratively and that provides collegial support.

Unfortunately, the reality of many schools precludes this ideal scenario. In some schools, principals are managers who leave literacy coaches to do the instructional work alone. In such a case, the literacy coach may be less effective, because the message to teachers is fragmented. The principal, who evaluates teachers' performance, does so with only incomplete knowledge of the goals of the schoolwide reading program.

What should a coach do in this situation? Even with the most reluctant principal, the literacy coach must relentlessly acknowledge that he or she works for the principal. A constant reminder of that relationship may help the principal to see his or her role as a partner over time. We have counseled many literacy coaches who struggle with this relationship to approach their principals frequently to ask two questions:

1. "How can I help you to do the work that you want to do in this building?"
2. "How will you help me to do that work more effectively?"

A principal may initially answer that the coach should know what he or she is supposed to be doing, and that it is not the principal's job to manage the coach. Over time, though, the principal may come to see that in supporting the coach, he or she is able to maintain "control" over the schoolwide program in new ways.

Leadership within the Staff

Negotiating leadership at the district level and within the administrative team is actually only a means to an end. This end is the real meat of the job—that is, leadership among teachers. There is a secret to developing a leadership position among teachers. It acknowledges and accommodates the many different personal styles and skills that literacy coaches bring to their work, and it allows them to have a common mission. The secret is not strength, wit, or knowledge of research. It is not administrative skill, research skill, teaching experience, or graduate training. The secret is service. Literacy coaches who see their mission as service to teachers, to make it easier for the teachers to provide service to children, are good leaders.

Visible, hands-on work on real issues of teaching and learning is key for literacy coaches who earn a leadership role on their staffs. They do it in many ways. In effect, they do whatever it takes: They unpack boxes, they copy, they make lesson plans, they make manipulatives, they assess children, they enter data, they bring snacks. They do these things without being asked and without much reward, especially at first. They make themselves useful to teachers, so that they can build the relationships that allow them to be real instructional leaders.

We have worked with literacy coaches who come from inside their schools, and who struggle with issues of leadership because the teachers are reluctant to acknowledge their new role. They may suffer from the "prophets in their own country" syndrome. We have also worked with literacy coaches who come from outside their schools, and who struggle with issues of leadership because the teachers are reluctant to trust them. Both sets of coaches become successful once the teachers really see them as providing a service—as responding to their individual and collective needs. And this level of "buy-in" gives the schoolwide program the momentum it needs.

SUPPORTING THE STRUGGLING TEACHER

The odds are high that a literacy coach will encounter some teachers whose skills are marginal. Citing both research and expert opinion, Tucker (2001) has stated bluntly that "5–15% of teachers in public classrooms perform at incompetent levels" (p. 52). Successful literacy coaches are willing to be supportive to all teachers and to differentiate this support for individual teachers the way that teachers differentiate support for individual children. The key to doing that is an absolute belief that teachers can learn, and that teachers who are struggling have the same rights as children who are struggling. They simply need more and sometimes different levels of support. Unfortunately, a struggling teacher often initially appears as a hostile teacher. To get through these dark days, a literacy coach has to look beyond the hostility and assume that the problem is simply that the teacher needs more help.

One literacy coach we know worked with a very difficult kindergarten teacher. The teacher was so resistant to the schoolwide effort that she actually turned her back during professional development sessions. She alienated the other members of her grade-level team to the point where she and they weren't speaking to each other; she thwarted the instruction and intervention schedule by having parents require that children take naps at the time designated for other things. She made every effort to insult the coach and to get other teachers to join in her rebellion.

The literacy coach was stymied, hurt, and angry. She tried to avoid this teacher, and she became physically flustered when this teacher approached her. At the January State of the School meeting, the literacy coach was sharing the grade-level assessment results. Individual teachers had copies of assessment results for their classes and were looking at the ways that their students compared with the results across classrooms. All but one of the children in need of intensive remediation came from one classroom—the difficult teacher's classroom, where children were sleeping while others received instruction and intervention. The literacy coach did not share this tidbit of information with the school, but since the reluctant teacher had her own data, she could see it for herself.

After the meeting, the teacher confronted the literacy coach. Initially, as always, she was angry and the coach was flustered. The coach steeled her resolve, though, and told the teacher that she really believed that it was not too late for the children—that they could work together immediately to rework the teacher's schedule and to change her focus. The teacher cried. The coach promised that she would teach for 1 week, to model. The coach also suggested that they meet that Friday to make a plan for that week. The teacher refused; she wanted to stay that evening and get on board the very next day.

What the coach learned was that the struggling teacher was hostile because she was afraid. This will usually be the case. When learners are afraid, they cannot learn. The literacy coach had not met the needs of this teacher, so she had become more and more afraid and hostile. This spiraling fear and hostility had caused the literacy coach herself to become afraid, so she became even less effective. We think that this is a common story. We urge literacy coaches to be effective leaders. To do so, they will have to step back from conflicts with teachers and ask themselves what they can do to support those teachers.

One thing to remember about working with teachers who are struggling is that the support for change must acknowledge and capitalize on what the teachers already know. Literacy coaches who start with teacher "deficits" rather than teacher "assets" are unlikely to be effective. This is an essential leadership quality; coaches must be able to see the strengths of their learners, and they must communicate those strengths to the learners in authentic and sincere ways.

WHAT ABOUT THE RESISTANT TEACHER?

There is a difference between "can't" and "won't." We have worked with coaches who focus almost all of their time and attention on particular teachers who simply will not participate in the schoolwide program. A few teachers will not collect data, will not participate in professional development sessions, will not open or use new materials, will not allow modeling, and will not accept observation and feedback. For many, as suggested above, this resistance will be the result of fear of change—fear that they will not be able to do what the coach is asking. Instead of admitting that fear (possibly even to themselves), these teachers may instead attempt to thwart the change by passively or actively resisting it. Given the relentless support that we are advocating, most teachers will gradually develop the confidence they need to become a part of the schoolwide effort. But not all will.

For a teacher with whom the literacy coach has exhausted all of his or her personal efforts at support to no effect, it is time to document these efforts and share them with the principal. Ultimately, it is the principal who makes administrative decisions about personnel, and who documents performance and evaluates the staff. A literacy coach cannot and should not take that evaluative work as part of his or her job; in Chapter 9 we have advocated that observation and feedback be given to teachers privately and in a nonthreatening way. Rarely, though, a literacy coach will have to admit that he or she has been unsuccessful with supporting a particular adult learner, and that it is time to ask for help from the principal.

We suggest that the literacy coach do this very formally, by writing a letter both to the teacher and to the principal that documents the general problem, the types (rather than specific details) of support the coach has provided, and the failure of that support. In this way, the literacy coach moves the locus of control into the front office; the teacher and principal will have to acknowledge that the literacy coach has failed with this teacher and decide what to do next. In some cases, the principal will be strong and supportive enough to counsel the teacher to transfer to a building where the requirements are more consistent with his or her beliefs and practices. In other cases, the literacy coach will simply have to acknowledge the failure with this particular teacher and try not to worry about it any more. This is easier said than done, but it is a reality of work in the complex environment of a school. Ultimately, it is a question of time. The coach must consider the time spent in futilely attempting to reach such a teacher, and realize that this time might be spent far more productively in working with other teachers.

MANY VOICES

Coaches Speak Out

Schoolwide change is difficult—very difficult. If you take on the role of literacy coach, you will have many difficult days. But you are likely to learn more about teaching and learning in this role then in any other you may have had. We know that this is where we have learned. Now listen to the voices of literacy coaches engaged in their first year's work. They work in many different settings: in large schools, small schools, urban schools, rural schools. Below, you will see the comments of different coaches, each answering the same two questions during different months in the same year:

1. "What is the biggest success you've had so far?"
2. "What has been the biggest obstacle for you?"

September

"The biggest success? It's really with the fluency. They taught the textbook. They put the lesson out every day. If the child wasn't learning, something's wrong with this kid, and we need to get him tested. Even just doing a little bit of fluency every day, the kids—the teachers start to see they're moving.

"The biggest obstacle? They won't come out in the open and be honest about the problems they're experiencing, and I know it's fear of change, but they try to undermine it in other ways."

"The biggest success? I think it was having our schedule organized for the beginning of the year. Our schedule is 60 minutes for whole-group phonics and read-aloud. Then we have another 60 minutes for small-group reading. Then we have another 60 minutes for writing.

"The biggest obstacle? To connect to them and make them want to change, without having to force them to change, which would make it more difficult, because when you make somebody do something, they're gonna resist and they're not gonna do as good a job as they would if they changed their mind."

October

"The biggest success? The positive enthusiasm among the teachers to want to learn. I think that's the biggest thing. And even the areas where I can see that—there are approximations at least.

"The biggest obstacle? It's a lot. It's a lot of teachers—31 teachers, total. Because of the responsibilities of ordering the classroom books and all of that, I mean, my name is called all the time. 'When are you gonna come to my room and do this?' And I want so bad to be everywhere, and that's the hardest part for me. And sometimes I drive myself crazy and work way too long and way too late and get way too tired."

"The biggest success? I think the dialogue is flowing more freely between the teachers and myself, and I feel like that's the door that I wanted to be sure was open, and that's open now.

"The biggest obstacle? There are a lot of questions coming from a lot of different directions. Different grade levels have a lot of different topics— a lot of different real, true concerns."

"The biggest success? I think I've earned some credibility with them. They see that I'm worked as hard as they are. I've done a lot of things for them.

"The biggest obstacle? The [district] policy-driven mindset that people have, whether it's really been forced upon them or whether they're creating it for themselves."

"The biggest success? I guess implementing a tutoring program [with] 144 kids, and [having] 113 tutors come in and visit those kids three times a week. I mean, that's a phenomenal thing in itself.

"The biggest obstacle? It's just an overwhelming task. It's just the sheer enormity of the school and the job."

November

"The biggest success? Really, it's the initiation of a lot of vocabulary things. I mean, I didn't think it would fly and I didn't think teachers would love it, but the kids love it and the teachers do too.

"The biggest obstacle? Coming from a middle school background, I did not understand [needs-based instruction]. And I'm not sure that I really understand it now, because I've only seen it done one way."

"The biggest success? A mother called me, and she was just really moved. You know, she said that her son was very unmotivated—that when he came home before he just hated to do his schoolwork, and he didn't want to come to school. And she said now he's excited about his schoolwork. He likes to read. She said when she walks in from work, he's already done his homework, and he's got his book in his hand waiting to read to her. She told me that we had changed her life.

"The biggest obstacle? Changing philosophies for some. People who have been in it for a long time. It's hard for me to go in and say, 'This is what you need to do,' when this person has taught for 25 years."

December

"The biggest success? The way our kindergarten got on board. They've already accomplished [with kids] now what they'd done at the end of the year last year.

"The biggest obstacle? Ugh. Time. Time is the worst thing. For me, for the teachers."

"The biggest success? My biggest success has been the reception that has been received from the teachers in administering [a developmental spelling test]. And getting that book room started and finished.

"The biggest obstacle? We need more books."

January

"The biggest success? Well, I think the shared-book room is a big success. And that the teachers have been accepting of trying to use it.

"The biggest obstacle? They're very friendly and open on one side, and then I think they go and close their door and do whatever they want to. And I cannot be in 12 rooms at any one time, so I'm going to have to do a lot more observations. I'm not spending enough time in the classrooms, and I'm not modeling enough."

"The biggest success? I've seen how difficult the change is, but . . . I believe the teachers are starting to express excitement about what they're seeing.

"The biggest obstacle? The biggest obstacle has been being the new kid on the block. Not being from here, not necessarily being included."

"The biggest success? Still being alive in January. No. I think really, everything's coming together. More teachers have bought into it and at least are making the effort. [It] may not be perfect, but [they're] at least making the effort.

"The biggest obstacle? It's just hard to get to 43 classrooms and take care of those teachers' needs."

"The biggest success? I think that my biggest success is just what I have learned. I just feel that I have learned so much since we began this process.

"The biggest obstacle? Time. Just not enough time to get everything done. And I think I have enough time. I just don't think that I use it wisely."

"The biggest success? Getting them to look at the assessment data, and getting them to use it and know what it means and be able to use that to guide their instruction. Because that's something that we've never really done.

"The biggest obstacle? The mindset of the teachers toward the students below grade level. Getting them to realize that you have two groups, [and that you must] now do two different lessons. If you're gonna do the same lesson, do it whole-group. Do different things in the small groups."

February

"The biggest success? The more we learn, the better we're able to understand where our weaknesses are as a school and as a system. We've found that when teachers look at their data and they see the growth in the children, that makes it all worthwhile.

"The biggest obstable? The job gets bigger every day. And having to prioritize what is the most important thing to do out of all the things that you have to do. I would say that's got to be the biggest thing."

"The biggest success? Winning over the teachers. I think that's the biggest success, because this is my first time doing something like this. I'm a different person because of this.

"The biggest obstacle? I think getting my data organized is an obstacle. I thought about that a lot. I wake up in the middle of the night thinking, 'What do I need to do to see this?' "

March

"The biggest success? Seeing the improvement. I love to see the growth.

"The biggest obstacle? Working with teachers who are less adaptive to change and are in denial, not wanting to step up to the plate."

"The biggest success? Working with the teachers.

"The biggest obstacle? Time. We have over 1,000 students, so sometimes I may have my day planned out, but something may come up."

"The biggest success? I guess it would be how well our kindergarten children are doing. Because those people gave me fits at first. The teachers were reluctant to step up the pace of instruction and to move to small-group instruction.

"The biggest obstacle? Setting up times for after-school study groups. We'll do that early on next year. You know, we're gonna have to protect those times."

May

"The biggest success? Actually seeing the teachers come on board has been wonderful.

"The biggest obstacle? [The] administration [is] not backing me, so [some] teachers [are] doing what they want to do. I was told to stop upsetting one teacher at one point."

"The biggest success? Our kids just seem to love to read.

"The biggest obstacle? Bringing all of the teachers over to one side. Convincing them that there is a different way, and it very well may be a better way than what they're used to doing."

"The biggest success? More people [teachers and paraprofessionals] working with children. There are two people working with children in the classroom. I think that the teachers can see where they were and the growth that their children are making.

"The biggest obstacle? Time. Meeting with them and getting them to where they need to be. I can't keep up."

Principals and Administrators Speak Out

Now listen to the voices of principals and district-level administrators. They are reflecting on the most important change that they've seen at each school after 1 year's schoolwide program and 1 year's collaboration with a literacy coach. They are responding in June, immediately following the year of change chronicled above. Remember that they are describing change, and assume that the opposite was true at the start of the reform effort.

"I think the most important change that I've seen is, I've focused on what the research tells us about literacy instruction."

"I think in the past we've done a lot of teaching because it was expected and somebody told us this was the nice thing to do. I think this year when they teach something, they know this is what they need to be teaching and this is how they need to be teaching it. We know why we're teaching what we're teaching."

"They were assigning tasks, and I think that's one of the most profound things that I've learned through the whole process is that they didn't teach—they assigned tasks."

"Over the course of the year, I think folks have become more and more re-laxed about expectations. They were real apprehensive about what kind of results they would get and were concerned that they may not have the re-sults that they expected."

"The most important change is a more consistent, concise focus on reading and the way that we have scheduled it into our day."

"The most important change is that the children have gained a love for read-ing. They really have."

"I guess the most dominant effect would be the attitudes of teachers and their joy and excitement teaching reading."

"I've seen a cohesiveness among the teachers. I've seen a lot of self-confi-dence among the teachers and more collaborative work going on, and I think that's as a result of all of the professional development."

"The most important change is professional development, which has caused change in the classroom."

"The most important change has been the climate—the climate in terms of accepting research."

"The most important change is that I see children reading."

This last change—"I see children reading"—is the bottom line for us.

References

Adams, M. J. (1990). *Beginning to read: Thinking and learning about print*. Cambridge, MA: MIT Press.

Alexander, K. L., Entwisle, D. R., & Olson, L. S. (2001). Schools, achievement, and inequality: A seasonal perspective. *Educational Evaluation and Policy Analysis, 23,* 171–191.

Allington, R. L. (1994). What's special about special programs for children who find learning to read difficult? *Journal of Reading Behavior, 26,* 1–21.

Allington, R. L., & Cunningham, P. M. (2002). *Schools that work: Where all children read and write*. Boston: Allyn & Bacon.

Allington, R. L., & McGill-Franzen, A. (1989). School response to reading failure: Chapter 1 and special education students in grades 2, 4, and 8. *Elementary School Journal, 89,* 529–542.

Allington, R. L., & McGill-Franzen, A. (1995). Flunking: Throwing good money after bad. In R. L. Allington & S. A. Walmsley (Eds.), *No quick fix: Rethinking literacy programs in America's elementary schools* (pp. 45–60). New York: Teachers College Press.

American Federation of Teachers. (1999). *Teaching reading is rocket science: What expert teachers of reading should know and be able to do*. Washington, DC: Author.

Anders, P. A., Hoffman, J. V., & Duffy, G. G. (2000). Teaching teachers to teach reading: Paradigm shifts, persistent problems, and challenges. In M. Kamil, P. Mosenthal, P. D. Pearson, & R. Barr (Eds.), *Handbook of reading research* (Vol. 3, pp. 721–744). Mahwah, NJ: Erlbaum.

Auckerman, R. (1987). *The basal reading approach to reading*. New York: Wiley.

Baker, L., Dreher, M. J., & Guthrie, J. T. (Eds.). (2000). *Engaging young readers: Promoting achievement and motivation*. New York: Guilford Press.

Baker, S., Gersten, R., & Keating, T. (2000). When less may be more: A 2-year longitudinal evaluation of a volunteer tutoring program requiring minimal training. *Reading Research Quarterly, 35,* 494–519.

Banks, J. A., & McGee Banks, C. A. (Eds.). (2002). *Handbook of research on multicultural education* (2nd ed.). San Francisco: Jossey-Bass.

Barnett, W. D. (2001). Preschool education for economically disadvantaged children: Effects on reading achievement and related outcomes. In S. B. Neuman & D. K. Dickinson (Eds.), *Handbook of early literacy research* (pp. 421–443). New York: Guilford Press.

Barone, D. M., & Morrow, L. M. (Eds.). (2003). *Literacy and young children: Research-based practices*. New York: Guilford Press.

Barr, R., Kamil, M. L., Mosenthal, P. B., & Pearson, P. D. (Eds.) (1991). *Handbook of reading research* (Vol. 2). White Plains, NY: Longman.

Baumann, J. F. (1992). Basal reading programs and the deskilling of teachers: A critical examination of the argument. *Reading Research Quarterly, 27,* 390–398.

Baumann, J. F., & Heubach, K. M. (1996). Do basal readers deskill teachers?: A national survey of educators' use and opinion of basals. *Elementary School Journal, 96,* 511–526.

Bear, D. R., Invernizzi, M. I., Templeton, S., & Johnston, F. (2004). *Words their way: Word study for phonics, vocabulary, and spelling instruction* (3rd ed.). Upper Saddle River, NJ: Merrill.

Bear, D. R., & Templeton, S. (1998). Explorations in developmental spelling: Foundations for learning and teaching phonics, spelling, and vocabulary. *The Reading Teacher, 52,* 222–242.

Beck, I. L., McKeown, M. G., Hamilton, R. L., & Kucan, L. (1997). *Questioning the author: An approach for enhancing student engagement with text.* Newark, DE: International Reading Association.

Beck, I. L., McKeown, M. G., & Kucan, L. (2002). *Bringing words to life: Robust vocabulary instruction.* New York: Guilford Press.

Birman, B. F., Desimone, L., Porter, A. C., & Garet, M. S. (2000, May). Designing professional development that works. *Educational Leadership,* pp. 28–33.

Bishop, A., Yopp, R. H., & Yopp, H. K. (2000). *Ready for reading: A handbook for parents of preschoolers.* Boston: Allyn & Bacon.

Bjorklund, D. (1995). *Children's thinking: Developmental function and individual difference* (2nd ed.). Pacific Grove, CA: Brooks/Cole.

Blackman, B. A., Ball, E., Black, R., & Tangel, D. (1994). Kindergarten teachers develop phonemic awareness in low-income, inner-city classrooms: Does it make a difference? *Reading and Writing: An Interdisciplinary Journal, 6,* 1–17.

Blackman, B. A., Ball, E., Black, R., & Tangel, D. (2000). *Road to the code: A phonological awareness program for young children.* Baltimore: Brookes.

Brown, A. L., & Day, J. D. (1983). Macrorules for summarizing texts: The development of expertise. *Journal of Verbal Learning and Verbal Behavior, 22,* 1–14.

Caldwell, J. S., & Ford, M. P. (2002). *Where have all the bluebirds gone?: How to soar with flexible grouping.* Portsmouth, NH: Heinemann.

Campbell, R. (2001). *Read-alouds with young children.* Newark, DE: International Reading Association.

Chall, J. S. (1967). *Learning to read: The great debate.* New York: McGraw-Hill.

Chall, J. S. (1996). *Learning to read: The great debate* (3rd ed.). Fort Worth, TX: Harcourt Brace College.

Clay, M. M. (1979). *The early detection of reading difficulties.* Auckland, New Zealand: Heinemann.

Clay, M. M. (1990). Research currents: What is and might be in evaluation. *Language Arts, 67,* 288–298.

Clay, M. M. (1993). *Reading Recovery: A guidebook for teachers in training.* Auckland, New Zealand: Heinemann.

Coyne, M. D., Kame'enui, E. J., & Simmons, D. C. (2001). Prevention and intervention in beginning reading: Two complex systems. *Learning Disabilities Research and Practice, 16,* 62–73.

Cunningham, P. A., Hall, D. P., & Sigmon, C. M. (1999). *The teacher's guide to the four blocks: A multimethod, multilevel framework for grades 1–3.* Greensboro, NC: Carson-Dellosa.

Cunningham, P. M., Hall, D. P., & Heggie, T. (1994). *Making words: Multilevel, hands-on developmentally appropriate spelling and phonics activities.* Torrance, CA: Apple.

Danielson, C. (2002). *Enhancing student achievement: A framework for school improvement.* Alexandra, VA: Association for Supervision and Curriculum Development.

Davis, S. H. (1997). The principal's paradox: Remaining secure in a precarious position. *National Association of Secondary School Principals Bulletin 81,* 592, 73–80.

Dowhower, S. L. (1999). Supporting a strategic stance in the classroom: A comprehension framework for helping teachers help students to be strategic. *The Reading Teacher, 52,* 672–683.

Duffy, A. M. (2001). Balance, literacy acceleration, and responsive teaching in a summer school literacy program for elementary struggling readers. *Reading Research and Instruction, 40,* 67–100.

Duffy, G. G. (2003). *Explaining reading: A resource for teaching concepts, skills, and strategies.* New York: Guilford Press.

Duffy, G. G., & Hoffman, J. V. (2002). Beating the odds in literacy education: Not the "betting on" but the "bettering of" schools and teachers? In B. M. Taylor & P. D. Pearson (Eds.), *Teaching reading: Effective schools, accomplished teachers* (pp. 375–388). Mahwah, NJ: Erlbaum.

Duffy G. G., Roehler, L. R., Meloth, M. S., Vavrus, L. G., Book, C., Putnam, J., & Wesselman, R. (1986). The relationship between explicit verbal explanations during reading skill instruction and student awareness and achievement: A study of reading teacher effects. *Reading Research Quarterly, 21,* 237–252.

Duffy, G. G., Roehler, L. R., Sivan, E., Rackliffe, G., Book, C., Meloth, M. S., Vavrus, L. G., Wesselman, R., Putnam, J., & Bassiri, D. (1987). Effects of explaining the reasoning associated with using reading strategies. *Reading Research Quarterly, 23,* 347–368.

DuFour, R. (2002). The learning-centered principal. *Educational Leadership, 59*(8), 12–15.

Ehri, L. C., Nunes, S., Stahl, S., & Willows, D. M. (2001). Systematic phonics instruction helps students learn to read: Evidence from the National Reading Panel's meta-analysis. *Review of Educational Research, 71,* 393–447.

Elley, W. B. (1989). Vocabulary acquisition from listening to stories. *Reading Research Quarterly, 24,* 174–187.

English, F. W. (1992). *Deciding what to teach and test: Developing, aligning, and auditing the curriculum.* Newbury Park, CA: Corwin Press.

Flesch, R. F. (1955). *Why Johnny can't read—and what you can do about it.* New York: Harper.

Flood, J., Lapp, D., Squire, J. R., & Jensen, J. (2003). *Handbook of research on teaching the English language arts* (2nd ed.). Mahwah, NJ: Erlbaum.

Foorman, B. R., Francis, D. J., Shaywitz, S. E., Shaywitz, B. A., & Fletcher, J. M. (1997). The case for early reading intervention. In B. Blachman (Ed.), *Foundations of reading acquisition and dyslexia: Implications for early intervention* (pp. 243–264). Mahwah, NJ: Erlbaum.

Fountas, I. C. (1999). *Matching books to readers: Using leveled books in guided reading, K–3.* Portsmouth, NH: Heinemann.

Fountas, I. C., & Pinnell, G. S. (1996). *Guided reading: Good first teaching for all children.* Portsmouth, NH: Heinemann.

Fox, B. J., & Mitchell, M. J. (2000). Using technology to support word recognition, spelling, and vocabulary acquisition. In S. B. Wepner, W. J. Valmont, & R. Thurlow (Eds.), *Linking literacy and technology: A guide for K–8 classrooms* (pp. 42–75). Newark, DE: International Reading Association.

Franks, B. A., Mulhern, S. L., & Schillinger, S. M. (1997). Reasoning in a reading context: Deductive inferences in basal reading series. *Reading and Writing: An Interdisciplinary Journal, 9,* 285–312.

Frazier, J. A., & Morrison, F. J. (1998). The influence of extended-year schooling on growth of achievement and perceived competence in early elementary schooling. *Child Development, 69,* 495–517.

Ganske, K. (2000). *Word journeys: Assessment-guided phonics, spelling, and vocabulary instruction.* New York: Guilford Press.

Gersten, R., Fuch, L. S., Williams, J. P., & Baker, S. (2001). Teaching reading comprehension strategies to students with learning disabilities: A review of research. *Review of Educational Research, 71,* 279–320.

Goldenburg, C., & Gallimore, R. (1991, November). Changing teaching takes more than a one-shot workshop. *Educational Leadership,* pp. 69–72.

Goodman, K. S., Shannon, P., Freeman, Y. S., & Murphy, S. (1988). *Report card on basal readers.* Katonah, NY: Owen.

Gray, W. S., Artley, A. S., & Arbuthnot, M. H. (1951). *The new fun with Dick and Jane.* Chicago: Scott, Foresman.

Guskey, T. R. (1986). Staff development and the process of teacher change. *Educational Researcher, 15*, 5–13.

Guzzetti, B. J. (Ed.). (2002). *Literacy in America: An encyclopedia of history, theory, and practice* (2 vols.). Santa Barbara, CA: ABC/CLIO.

Hacker, D. J., & Tenent, A. (2002). Implementing reciprocal teaching in the classroom: Overcoming obstacles and making modifications. *Journal of Educational Psychology, 94*, 699–718.

Hall, D. P., Cunningham, P. M., & McIntyre, C. (2002). *Month-by-month phonics for first grade: Sytematic, multilevel instruction.* Greensboro, NC: Carson-Dellosa.

Hall, N., Larson, J., & Marsh, J. (Eds.). (2003). *Handbook of early childhood literacy.* Thousand Oaks, CA: Sage.

Hallinger, P., Bickman, L., & Davis, K. (1996). School context, principal leadership, and student reading achievement. *Elementary School Journal, 96*, 527–549.

Hart, B., & Risley, T. R. (1995). *Meaningful differences in the everyday experience of young American children.* Baltimore: Brookes.

Heimlich, J. E., & Pittelman, S. D. (1986). *Semantic mapping: Classroom applications.* Newark, DE: International Reading Association.

Hiebert, E. H. (1994). Reading Recovery in the United States: What difference does it make to an age cohort? *Educational Researcher, 23*, 15–25.

Hiebert, E. H. (1996). Revisiting the question: What difference does Reading Recovery make to an age cohort? *Educational Research, 25*, 26–28.

Hiebert, E. H. (1999). Text matters in learning to read. *Reading Teacher, 52*, 552–556.

Hiebert, E. H. (2003). *QuickReads: A research-based fluency program.* Parsippany, NJ: Pearson Learning Group.

Hiebert, E. H., Colt, J., Catto, S., & Gury, E. (1992). Reading and writing of first grade students in a restructured Chapter 1 program. *American Educational Research Journal, 29*, 545–572.

Hiebert, E. H., & Taylor, B. M. (2000). Beginning reading instruction: Research on early interventions. In M. L. Kamil, P. B. Mosenthal, P. D. Pearson, & R. Barr (Eds.), *Handbook of reading research* (Vol. 3, pp. 455–482). Mahwah, NJ: Erlbaum.

Hoffman, J. V. (2002). WORDS (On words in leveled texts for beginning readers). In D. L. Shallert, C. M. Fairbanks, J. Worthy, B. Maloch, & J. V. Hoffman (Eds.), *51st yearbook of the National Reading Conference* (pp. 59–81). Oak Creek, WI: National Reading Conference.

Hoffman, J. V., McCarthey, S. J., Abbott, J., Christian, C., Corman, L., Curry, C., et al. (1998). So what's new in the new basals?: A focus on first grade. *Journal of Reading Behavior, 26*, 47–73.

Hoffman, J. V., McCarthey, S. J., Elliott, B., Bayles, D. L., Price, D. P., Ferree, A., et al. (1994). The literature-based basals in first-grade classrooms: Savior, Satan, or same-old, same-old? *Reading Research Quarterly, 33*, 168–197.

Hoffman, J. V., & Pearson, P. D. (2000). Reading teacher education in the next millennium: What your grandmother's teacher didn't know that your granddaughter's teacher should. *Reading Research Quarterly, 35*, 28–44.

Hoffman, J. V., Sailors, M., & Patterson, E. U. (2002). Decodable texts for beginning reading instruction: The year 2000 basals. *Journal of Literacy Research, 34*, 269–298.

International Reading Association & National Council of Teachers of English. (1996). *Standards for the English language arts.* Newark, DE: Authors.

International Reading Association, Professional Standards and Ethics Committee. (1998). *Standards for reading professionals* (rev. ed.). Newark, DE: Author.

International Reading Association, Professional Standards and Ethics Committee. (2000). *Teaching all children to read: The roles of the reading specialist. A position statement of the International Reading Association.* Newark, DE: Author.

International Reading Association, Professional Standards and Ethics Committee. (2004). *Standards for reading professionals—Revised 2003.* Newark, DE: Author.

Invernizzi, M., Rosemary, C., Juel, C., & Richards, H. C. (1997). At-risk readers and community volunteers: A 3-year perspective. *Scientific Studies of Reading, 1*, 277–300.

Iversen, S., & Tunmer, W. E. (1993). Phonological processing skills and the Reading Recovery program. *Journal of Educational Psychology, 85,* 112–126.

Jennings, R. E., & Prince, D. E. (Eds.). (1981). *Kick up your heels.* Chicago: Scott, Foresman.

Jitendra, A. K., Chard, D., Hoppes, M. K., Renouf, K., & Gardill, M. C. (2001). An evaluation of main idea strategy instruction in four commercial reading programs: Implications for students with learning problems. *Reading and Writing Quarterly, 17,* 53–73.

Johnson, J. F., Jr. (2002). High-performing, high-poverty, urban elementary schools. In B. M. Taylor & P. D. Pearson (Eds.), *Teaching reading: Effective schools, accomplished teachers* (pp. 89–114). Mahwah, NJ: Erlbaum.

Johnston, F. R., Invernizzi, M., & Juel, C. (1998). *Book Buddies: Guidelines for volunteer tutors of emergent and early readers.* New York: Guilford Press.

Johnston, P., & Allington, R. (1991). Remediation. In R. Barr, M. L. Kamil, P. Mosenthal, & P. D. Pearson (Eds.), *Handbook of reading research* (Vol. 2, pp. 984–1012). White Plains, NY: Longman.

Joiner, L. L. (2000, December). Dawn to dusk: School districts explore extended-day options. *American School Board Journal,* pp. 28–30.

Jordan, G. E., Snow, C. E., & Porche, M. V. (2000). Project EASE: The effect of a family literacy project on kindergarten students' early literacy skills. *Reading Research Quarterly, 35,* 524–546.

Joyce, B., & Showers, B. (1988). *Student achievement through staff development.* New York: Longman.

Joyce, B., & Showers, B. (1996). Staff development as a comprehensive service organization. *Journal of Staff Development, 17,* 2–6.

Juel, C. (1988). Learning to read and write: A longitudinal study of 54 children from first through fourth grades. *Journal of Educational Psychology, 80,* 437–447.

Juel, C. (1991). Beginning reading. In R. Barr, M. L. Kamil, P. B. Mosenthal, & P. D. Pearson (Eds.), *Handbook of reading research* (Vol. 2, pp. 759–788). White Plains, NY: Longman.

Kamil, M. L., Mosenthal, P. B., Pearson, P. D., & Barr, R. (Eds.). (2000). *Handbook of reading research* (Vol. 3). Mahwah, NJ: Erlbaum.

Kean, M., Summers, A., Raivetz, M., & Farber, I. (1979). *What works in reading?* Philadelphia: Office of Research and Evaluation and the U.S. Federal Reserve Bank.

Keene, E. O., & Zimmermann, S. (1997). *Mosaic of thought: Teaching comprehension in a reader's workshop.* Portsmouth, NH: Heinemann.

Kelly, M., Moore, D. W., & Tuck, B. F. (1994). Reciprocal teaching in a regular primary school classroom. *Journal of Educational Research, 88,* 53–61.

King, D. (2002). The changing shape of leadership. *Educational Leadership, 59,* 61–63.

Klenk, L., & Kibby, M. W. (2000). Re-mediating reading difficulties: Appraising the past, reconciling the present, constructing the future. In M. L. Kamil, P. B. Mosenthal, P. D. Pearson, & R. Barr (Eds.), *Handbook of reading research* (Vol. 3, pp. 667–690). Mahwah, NJ: Erlbaum.

Labbo, L. D., & Ash, G. E. (1998). Supporting young children's computer-related literacy development in classroom centers. In S. Neuman & K. Roskos (Eds.), *Children achieving: Instructional practices in early literacy* (pp. 180–197). Newark, DE: International Reading Association.

Learning First Alliance. (1998). *Every child reading: An action plan.* Washington, DC: Author.

Learning First Alliance. (2000). *Every child reading: A professional development guide.* Washington, DC: Author.

Leslie, L., & Allen, L. (1999). Factors that predict success in an early literacy intervention project. *Reading Research Quarterly, 34,* 404–424.

Lieberman, A. (1995). Practices that support teacher development. *Phi Delta Kappan, 76,* 591–604.

Little, J. W. (1993). Teachers' professional development in a climate of educational reform. *Educational Evaluation and Policy Analysis, 15,* 129–151.

Lou, Y., Abrami, P. C., Spence, J. C., Poulsen, C., Chambers, B., & d'Apollonia, S. (1996). Within-class grouping: A meta-analysis. *Review of Educational Research, 66,* 423–458.

Lyon, A., & Moore, P. (2003). *Sound systems: Explicit, systematic phonics in early literacy contexts.* Portland, ME: Stenhouse.

Lyons, C. A., & Pinnell, G. S. (2001). *Systems for change in literacy education: A guide to professional development*. Portsmouth, NH: Heinemann.

Marks, H. M., & Printy, S. M. (2003). Principal leadership and school performance: An integration of transformational and instructional leadership. *Educational Leadership Quarterly, 39*, 370–397.

Martinez, M. N., Roser, N. L., & Strecker, S. (1999). I never thought I could be a star: A reader's theater ticket to fluency. *The Reading Teacher, 52*, 326–334.

Marzano, R. J. (2003). *What works in schools: Translating research into action*. Alexandria, VA: Association for Supervision and Curriculum Development.

Marzano, R. J., Pickering, D. J., & Pollock, J. E. (2001). *Classroom instruction that works: Research-based strategies for increasing student achievement*. Alexandria, VA: Association for Supervision and Curriculum Development.

McCormack, R. L., & Paratore, J. R. (Eds.). (2003). *After early intervention, then what?: Teaching struggling readers in grades 3 and beyond*. Newark, DE: International Reading Association.

McCutchen, D., & Berninger, V. W. (1999). Those who know, teach well: Helping teachers master literacy-related subject-matter knowledge. *Learning Disabilities Research and Practice, 14*, 215–226.

McGee, L. M., & Richgels, D. J. (2003). *Designing early literacy programs: Strategies for at-risk preschool and kindergarten children*. New York: Guilford Press.

McGill-Franzen, A., & Goatley, V. (2001). Title I and special education: Support for children who struggle to learn to read. In S. B. Neuman & D. K. Dickinson (Eds.), *Handbook of early literacy research* (pp. 471–483). New York: Guilford Press.

McKenna, M. C. (2002). Phonics software for a new millennium. *Reading and Writing Quarterly, 18*, 93–96.

McKenna, M. C., Labbo, L. D., & Reinking, D. (2003). Effective use of technology in literacy instruction. In L. M. Morrow, L. B. Gambrell, & M. Pressley (Eds.), *Best practices in literacy instruction* (2nd ed., pp. 307–331). New York: Guilford Press.

McKenna, M. C., Reinking, D., Labbo, L. D., & Kieffer, R. D. (Eds.). (in press). *Handbook of literacy and technology* (Vol. 2). Mahwah, NJ: Erlbaum.

McKenna, M. C., & Stahl, S. A. (2003). *Assessment for reading instruction*. New York: Guilford Press.

Moody, S. W., Schumm, J. S., Fischer, M., & Jean-Francois, B. (1999). Grouping suggestions for the classroom: What do our basal reading series tell us? *Reading Research and Instruction, 38*, 319–331.

Morris, D. (1981). Concept of word: A developmental phenomenon in the beginning reading and writing process. *Language Arts, 57*, 659–668.

Morris, D. (1999). *The Howard Street tutoring manual*. New York: Guilford Press.

Morris, D., Shaw, B., & Perney, J. (1990). Helping low reading in grades 2 and 3: An after-school volunteer tutoring program. *Elementary School Journal, 91*, 133–150.

Morris, D., & Slavin, R. E. (2003). *Every child reading*. Boston: Allyn & Bacon.

Morris, D., Tyner, B., & Perney, J. (2000). Early Steps: Replicating the effects of a first-grade reading intervention program. *Journal of Educational Psychology, 92*, 681–693.

Morrow, L. M. (1984). Effects of retelling on young children's comprehension and sense of story structure. In J. A. Niles & L. A. Harris (Eds.), *33rd yearbook of the National Reading Conference: Changing perspectives on research in reading/language processing and instruction* (pp. 95–100). Rochester, NY: National Reading Conference.

Morrow, L. M., Gambrell, L. B., & Pressley, M. (Eds.). (2003). *Best practices in literacy instruction* (2nd ed.). New York: Guilford Press.

Mosenthal, J., Lipson, M., Sortino, S., Russ, R., & Mekkelsen, J. (2002). Literacy in rural Vermont: Lessons from schools where children succeed. In B. M. Taylor & P. D. Pearson (Eds.), *Teaching reading: Effective schools, accomplished teachers* (pp. 115–140). Mahwah, NJ: Erlbaum.

National Reading Panel (NRP). (2000). *Teaching children to read: An evidence-based assessment of the scientific research literature on reading and its implications for reading instruction* (NIH Publication No. 00-4754). Washington, DC: U.S. Department of Health and Human Services.

Neuman, S. B., & Dickinson, D. K. (Eds.). (2001). *Handbook of early literacy research*. New York: Guilford Press.

Opitz, M. F., & Rasinski, T. V. (1998). *Good-bye round robin: Twenty-five effective oral reading strategies*. Portsmouth, NH: Heinemann.

Palinscar, A. S., & Brown, A. L. (1984). Reciprocal teaching of comprehension fostering and comprehension monitoring. *Cognition and Instruction, 1,* 117–175.

Patterson, W. A., Henry, J. J., O'Quin, K., Ceprano, M. A., & Blue, E. V. (2003). Investigating the effectiveness of an integrated learning system on early emergent readers. *Reading Research Quarterly, 38,* 172–207.

Pearson, P. D., Barr, R., Kamil, M. L., & Mosenthal, P. B. (Eds.). (1984). *Handbook of reading research* (Vol. 1). New York: Longman.

Peters, T., & Waterman, R. H. (1982). *In search of excellence: Lessons from America's best-run companies*. New York: Harper & Row.

Pinnell, G. S. (1989). Reading Recovery: Helping at-risk children learn to read. *Elementary School Journal, 90,* 161–183.

Pinnell, G. S., Lyons, C. A., DeFord, D. E., Bryk, A. S., & Seltzer, M. (1994). Comparing instructional models for the literacy education of high-risk first graders. *Reading Research Quarterly, 29,* 8–39.

Pittelman, S. D., Heimlich, J. E., Berglund, R. L., & French, M. P. (1991). *Semantic feature analysis: Classroom applications*. Newark, DE: International Reading Association.

Popham, W. J. (2001). *The truth about testing: An educator's call to action*. Alexandria, VA: Association for Supervision and Curriculum Development.

Pressley, M., & Block, C. C. (Eds.). (2001). *Comprehension instruction: Research-based best practices*. New York: Guilford Press.

Pressley, M., El-Dinary, P. B., Gaskins, I., Schuder, T., Bergman, J., Almasi, L., et al. (1992). Beyond direct explanation: Transactional instruction of reading comprehension strategies. *Elementary School Journal, 92,* 511–554.

Raphael, T. E. (1986). Teaching question–answer relationships, revisited. *The Reading Teacher, 39,* 516–522.

Rasinski, T. V., & Padak, N. D. (2001). *From phonics to fluency: Effective teaching of decoding and reading fluency in the elementary school*. New York: Longman.

Readence, J. E., Moore, D. W., & Rickelman, R. J. (2000). *Prereading activities for content area reading and learning* (3rd ed.). Newark, DE: International Reading Association.

Reese, J. L., Myers, C. L., Nofsinger, C. O., & Brown, R. D. (2000). Retention of academic skills over the summer months in alternative and traditional calendar schools. *Journal of Research and Development in Education, 33,* 165–174.

Reinking, D., McKenna, M. C., Labbo, L. D., & Kieffer, R. D. (Eds.). (1998). *Handbook of literacy and technology* (Vol. 1). Mahwah, NJ: Erlbaum.

Reutzel, D. R. (1999). Organizing literacy instruction: Effective grouping strategies and organizational plans. In L. B. Gambrell, L. M. Morrow, S. B. Neuman, & M. Pressley (Eds.), *Best practices in literacy instruction* (pp. 271–291). New York: Guilford Press.

Reutzel, D. R., Sudweeks, R., & Hollingsworth, P. M. (1994). Issues in reading instruction: The views and information sources of state-level textbook adoption committee members. *Reading Research and Instruction, 34,* 149–171.

Reynolds, A. J., & Temple, J. A. (1998). Extended early childhood intervention and school achievement: Age thirteen findings from the Chicago Longitudinal Study. *Child Development, 69,* 231–246.

Richardson, V. (1990). Significant and worthwhile change in teaching practice. *Educational Researcher, 19,* 10–18.

Richardson, V. (Ed.). (2001). *Handbook of research on teaching* (4th ed.). Washington, DC: American Educational Research Association.

Roser, N. L., Hoffman, J. V., & Carr, N. J. (2003). See it change: A primer on the basal reader. In L. M. Morrow, L. B. Gambrell, & M. Pressley (Eds.), *Best practices in literacy instruction* (2nd ed., pp. 269–286). New York: Guilford Press.

Ruddell, R. B., Ruddell, M. R., & Singer, H. (1994). *Theoretical models and processes of reading* (4th ed.). Newark, DE: International Reading Association.

Samuels, S. J. (1979). The method of repeated reading. *The Reading Teacher, 32,* 403–408.

Santa, C., & Hoien, T. (1999). An assessment of Early Steps: A program for early intervention of reading problems. *Reading Research Quarterly, 34,* 54–79.

Schmitt, M. C., & Hopkins, C. J. (1993). Metacognitive theory applied: Strategic reading instruction in the current generation of basal readers. *Reading Research and Instruction, 32,* 13–24.

Shanahan, T. (1998). On the effectiveness and limitations of tutoring in reading. *Review of Research in Education, 23,* 217–245.

Shanahan, T., & Barr, R. (1995). Reading Recovery: An independent evaluation of the effects of an early instructional intervention for at-risk learners. *Reading Research Quarterly, 30,* 958–996.

Shannon, P. (1989). The struggle for control over literacy lessons. *Language Arts, 66,* 625–634.

Shannon, P. (1994). People who live in glass houses. In C. B. Smith (Ed.), *Whole language: The debate.* Bloomington, IN: ERIC.

Showers, B., & Joyce, B. (1996, March). The evolution of peer coaching. *Educational Leadership,* pp. 12–16.

Shulman, L. S. (1998). Theory, practice, and the evolution of professionals. *Elementary School Journal, 98,* 511–526.

Simmons, D. C., Kuykehdall, K., King, K., Cornachione, C., & Kame'enui, E. J. (2000). Implementation of a schoolwide reading improvement model: "No one ever told us it would be this hard!" *Learning Disabilities Research and Practice, 15*(2), 92–100.

Singer, H., & Ruddell, R. B. (1976). *Theoretical models and processes of reading* (2nd ed.). Newark, DE: International Reading Association.

Singer, H., & Ruddell, R. B. (1985). *Theoretical models and processes of reading* (3rd ed.). Newark, DE: International Reading Association.

Slavin, R. E. (1987). Ability grouping and student achievement in elementary schools: A best evidence synthesis. *Review of Educational Research, 57,* 293–336.

Slavin, R. E. (1990). IBM's Writing to Read: Is it right for reading? *Phi Delta Kappan, 72,* 214–216.

Slavin, R. E., Madden, N. A., Dolan, L. J., & Wasik, B. A. (1996). *Every child, every school: Success for All.* Thousand Oaks, CA: Sage.

Slavin, R. E., Madden, N. A., Karweit, N., Dolan, L. J., & Wasik, B. A. (1991). Research directions: Success for All: Ending reading failure from the beginning. *Language Arts, 68,* 404–409.

Slobodkina, E. (1940). *Caps for sale.* Reading, MA: Addison-Wesley.

Smith, N. B. (2002). *American reading instruction* (special ed.). Newark, DE: International Reading Association.

Smith, S. B., Simmons, D. C., Gleason, M. M., Kame'enui, E. J., Baker, S. K., Sprick, M., et al. (2001). An analysis of phonological awareness instruction in four kindergarten basal reading programs. *Reading and Writing Quarterly, 17,* 25–51.

Smolkin, L. B., & Donovan, C. A. (2001). The contexts of comprehension instruction: The information book read aloud, comprehension acquisition, and comprehension instruction in a first-grade classroom. *Elementary School Journal, 102,* 97–122.

Smylie, M. A. (1996). From bureaucratic control to building human capital: The importance of teacher learning in education reform. *Educational Researcher, 25,* 9–11.

Snow, C. E. (2002). *Reading for understanding: Toward an R&D program in reading comprehension.* Santa Monica, CA: Rand.

Snow, C. E., Burns, S. M., & Griffin, P. (Eds.). (1998). *Preventing reading difficulties in young children.* Washington, DC: National Academy Press.

Sparks, D., & Loucks-Horsley, S. (1990). Models of staff development. In R. Houston (Ed.), *Handbook of research on teacher education* (3rd ed., pp. 234–250). New York: Macmillan.

Spear-Swerling, L., & Sternberg, R. J. (1996). *Off track: When poor readers become "learning disabled."* Boulder, CO: Westview Press.

Stahl, S. A. (1999). *Vocabulary development: From research to practice* (Vol. 2). Cambridge, MA: Brookline Books.

Stahl, S. A., Duffy-Hester, A. M., & Stahl, K. A. D. (1998). Everything you wanted to know about phonics (but were afraid to ask). *Reading Research Quarterly, 33,* 338–355.

Stahl, S. A., & Kapinus, B. (2001). *Word power: What every educator needs to know about teaching vocabulary.* Washington, DC: National Education Association.

Stanovich, K. E. (1986). Matthew effects in reading: Some consequences of individual differences in the acquisition of reading. *Reading Research Quarterly, 21,* 360–406.

Stein, M., Stuen, C., Carnine, D., & Long, R. M. (2001). Textbook evaluation and adoption
practices. *Reading and Writing Quarterly, 17,* 5–23.

Strickland, D. S. (1998). *Teaching phonics today: A primer for educators.* Newark, DE: International Reading Association.

Sweeney, D. (2003). *Learning along the way: Professional development by and for teachers.*
Portland, ME: Stenhouse.

Taylor, B. M., Pearson, P. D., Clark, K. M., & Walpole, S. (2000). Effective schools and accomplished teachers: Lessons about primary-grade reading instruction in low-income schools.
Elementary School Journal, 101, 121–165.

Taylor, B. M., Pressley, M., & Pearson, P. D. (2002). Research-supported characteristics of
teachers and schools that promote reading achievement. In B. M. Taylor & P. D. Pearson
(Eds.), *Teaching reading: Effective schools, accomplished teachers* (pp. 361–374). Mahwah, NJ: Erlbaum.

Tucker, P. (2001). Helping struggling teachers. *Educational Leadership, 58*(5), 52–55.

U.S. Department of Education. (1999). *Start early, finish strong: How to help every child become a reader.* Washington, DC: Author. [Full text available at http://www.ed.gov/pubs/
edpubs.html]

U.S. Department of Education, Office of the Under Secretary. (1999, December). *Designing effective professional development: Lessons from the Eisenhower programs, executive summary.* Washington, DC: U.S. Department of Education.

Vacca, J. L. (1989). Staff development. In S. B. Wepner, J. T. Feeley, & D. S. Strickland (Eds.),
The administration and supervision of reading programs (pp. 147–161). New York:
Teachers College Press.

Vacca, J. L., & Padak, N. D. (1990). Reading consultants as classroom collaborators: An emerging role. *Journal of Educational and Psychological Consultation, 1,* 99–107.

Vellutino, F. R., & Scanlon, D. M. (2001). Emergent literacy skills, early instruction, and individual differences as determinants of difficulties in learning to read: The case for early intervention. In S. B. Neuman & D. K. Dickinson (Eds.), *Handbook of early literacy research*
(pp. 295–321). New York: Guilford Press.

Vellutino, F. R., & Scanlon, D. M. (2002). The Interactive Strategies approach to reading intervention. *Contemporary Educational Psychology, 27,* 573–635.

Verhoeven, L., & Snow, C. E. (Eds.). (2001). *Literacy and motivation: Developing cross-cultural
perspectives.* Mahwah, NJ: Erlbaum.

Walmsley, S. A., & Allington, R. L. (1995). Redefining and reforming instructional support programs for at-risk students. In R. L. Allington & S. A. Walmsley (Eds.), *No quick fix: Rethinking literacy programs in America's elementary schools.* New York: Teachers College
Press.

Wasik, B. A. (1998). Volunteer tutoring programs in reading: A review. *Reading Research Quarterly, 33,* 266–292.

Wasik, B. A., Dobbins, D. R., & Herrmann, S. (2001). Intergenerational family literacy: Concepts, research, and practice. In S. B. Neuman & D. K. Dickinson (Eds.), *Handbook of
early literacy research* (pp. 444–458). New York: Guilford Press.

Wasik, B. A., & Slavin, R. E. (1993). Preventing early reading failure with one-to-one tutoring:
A review of five programs. *Reading Research Quarterly, 28,* 179–200.

Wolf, M., & Segal, D. (1999). Retrieval Rate, Accuracy, and Vocabulary Elaboration (RAVE) in
reading-impaired children: A pilot intervention program. *Dyslexia, 5,* 1–27.

Index

"f" following a page number indicates a figure; "t" following a page number indicates a table